the writings of Isabel Allende... Kassabova seems to have survived her grim start in Sofia remarkably unscathed, despite admitting that her portrait of Bulgaria is "always personal and almost never flattering". It is these two qualities, of course, which ensure that *Street Without a Name* makes for such a highly enjoyable read.' *Scotland on Sunday*

'Part memoir, part travelogue, this intriguing book sheds new light on both Bulgaria's past and present... Kassabova gives a personal, unflinching and funny account of the country's communist past and idiosyncratic current atmosphere' *Big Issue*

'Not many books on the travel shelves have the force of revelation, but this one does. Kapka Kassabova knows her native Bulgaria, the art of writing and the challenges of memory inside out, and she leads us into a country most of us have hardly read about with an elegant assurance, an acid wit and a heart-rending precision that can make you see the world quite differently. This book is a treasure.' Pico Iyer, author of *Global Soul*

'Kapka Kassabova's poignant evocation of a childhood spent under one-party rule is complemented by her sharply observed and devastating account of her return to post-communist Bulgaria. Her skilful blend of memoir and travelogue offers a highly readable introduction to a rarely described corner of Europe.' Vesna Goldsworthy, author of *Chernobyl Strawberries*

'[A] finely written, emotionally rich book that reveals how connected we are to the land in which we are born.' *Sunday Herald*

'Bulgaria remains a country in flux, coming to terms with capitalism and freedom, and Kassabova's excellent memoir contrasts her experiences growing up during the Cold War with the turmoil of today. Unflinching and unsentimental.' *The List*

'Kassabova is an astute and charismatic guide through her former Bulgaria. She is at once central to the story yet unobtrusive – a neat trick indeed. Realised in her lively and endlessly creative prose, *Street Without a Name* is a rare treat, striking just the right balance between bitter and sweet. Delightful.' *New Zealand Herald*

'There are no faults in the writing: it's enjoyable, precise, lucid and compelling. Added to her poet's eye and ear is a cool frankness and humour. Her writing is brisk and revealing... her language is constantly rich, fresh and enchanting. I doubt if you could have a more loyal or sympathetic observer of the tectonic shift [in Bulgaria's status] than Kassabova. Her first name, Kapka, means "a drop of water" – and this book is as refreshing and clear as that.' *The Press* (New Zealand)

'Within the first few pages I was hooked. In the West we have only a vague idea of what it was like for those that lived collectively behind the Iron Curtain and their subsequent struggles. The portrait that Kassabova paints is one that is not only darkly humorous, but very entertaining.' *Satellite* (New Zealand)

'*Street Without a Name* is Kassabova's humoured, measured answer to the question inevitably addressed to even the most cosmopolitan soul: where are you from? This book is a riveting tale of a journey from childhood to adulthood, through a country in the business of reinventing itself yet again. The writing, which bears the endearing trace of an accent, is lovely. Provocative and epigrammatic, it is also improbably funny, despite the gloomy material. If prose could shrug, that's what this book would do. Upon finishing it, I wanted to read it again, just to marvel at how jauntily Kassabova sketches history's great, tragic heft.' *New Zealand Listener*

'A profound meditation on the depth of change triggered by the events of 1989 throughout eastern Europe and the Soviet Union. It is also poignant, unbearably so at times, as she tries, but often fails, to defy the fatalism that she marks as a particular Bulgarian characteristic... She has an ability to describe in one or two sentences changes that some of us have spent entire books analysing... This is a very fine piece of writing.' Misha Glenny, *Guardian*

'[A] bitterly funny, brilliantly clever journey... The raw memoir is the first great achievement of this multifaceted book. The second is her meditation on nationality. Today we all live with the consequences of the tumbling economic, political and cultural walls. In a globalised world, Kassabova suggests, we are all Bulgarians now.' *Sunday Times*

Street Without a Name

Childhood and Other Misadventures in Bulgaria

Kapka Kassabova

Portobello
BOOKS

First published by Portobello Books Ltd 2008
This paperback edition published 2009

Portobello Books Ltd
Twelve Addison Avenue
Holland Park
London
W11 4QR

A CIP catalogue record is available from the British Library

9 8 7 6 5 4 3

ISBN 978 1 84627 124 3

www.portobellobooks.com

Text designed by Richard Marston
Map designed by Emily Faccini

Typeset in Fournier by Avon DataSet Ltd,
Bidford on Avon, Warwickshire

Printed in Great Britain

To my parents and my sister
who did their best in the worst of times

DISCLAIMER

This is a work of non-fiction. Nothing here is invented, in the sense that everything I describe happened. But the way I have described it is highly personal, and in that sense, not highly reliable. Those looking for a travel guide could use my slightly more reliable *Globetrotter's Guide to Bulgaria*. Those looking for a history book could go to the history section in their local library, where they will find one very reliable recent history of Bulgaria.

All names save those of public figures have been changed to protect people's privacy, with the exception of the author's family who aren't so lucky, and a few people who are no longer among the living – and I hope if they are looking down from heaven, they wouldn't mind.

CONTENTS

Prologue   1
'*I went into the woods...*'

1   Peach Street   5
    The émigré returns

CHILDHOOD

2   In the Students' Town   19
    Flawed beginnings

3   Youth 3   30
    A world of mud and music

4   East and West   60
    The poor cousin syndrome

5   Chernobyl Summer   82
    Life and death in the provinces of Socialism

6   Winds of Change   98
    Perestroika in the air

7   And Heaven Knows I'm Miserable Now   122
    Emigration

OTHER MISADVENTURES

8 She Grows but Never Ages   141
  Getting reacquainted

9 Freedom, Perfection or Death   169
  Macedonian misadventures

10 Balkan Blues   199
   Survival in the Balkán

11 The Curse of Orpheus   229
   A Rodopean story

12 Into the Memory Hole   253
   Bulgaria, Turkey, and the Death Strip

13 In the Enchanted Garden   278
   On the Black Sea

14 Danube Terminus   297
   Just a tourist

   Epilogue   327

   Acknowledgements   336

'I went into the woods…'

As children growing up in Communist Bulgaria, we played a pantomime game called 'I went into the woods'. It goes like this: I went into the woods, I shuffled the leaves, I found a picture of… Then you mime the thing that you found, and the others have to name it. Simple yet devilishly hard. Because anything could lurk under the leaves, from a mushroom to a dead body, and usually, it did.

Totalitarian regimes are not interested in personal stories, they are interested in the Party, the People, and the Bright Future. Nor are post-totalitarian democracies. They are too busy staying alive.

Equally, in the West there hangs about a vague idea of collective life behind the Iron Curtain, and life after it, but there are surprisingly few personal stories to go with the idea. There ought to be more. After all, half of Europe lived on 'the other side' for half a century. And perhaps half of that half (by my own rough estimate) still feels as if it's living on the other side of something in the shape of a wall. The ghost of the Wall won't go away until it is laid to rest. This book is, among other things, my own act of exorcism.

In 1990, after the fall of the Berlin Wall, I left Sofia for Britain, New Zealand, and again Britain, occasionally stopping in France and Germany for a year or so. In the process, I acquired lots of visas, one passport, some half-wasted lives, and an impressive collection of delusions.

My chief delusion was that by becoming deeply absorbed by every other country on the planet except Bulgaria (which I carefully tiptoed around as if it was a ticking bomb in the shape of a country ready to detonate at the slightest touch of memory) I could get rid of two things. One, my Bulgarian past, which was not of the miserable variety but bothered me nevertheless, like an infirm relative calling out from a darkened room at the back of the house. Two, the need to answer directly the question nice people ask when they meet you: so, where are you from?

Bulgaria. Capital: Bucharest. Uncle Bulgaria. A yogurt bacillus called *bulgaricus*. A republic of the former Soviet Union. The Bulgarian umbrella murder. Wrestlers – or was it weightlifters. Men – and women – with moustaches. And, lately, the place from where swarthy folk will come beating down the doors of the European Union with their plumbers' tools. A cheap place-in-the-sun property paradise – or was it skiing – about which we know that… well, it's cheap.

In the Western mind Bulgaria is a country without a face. It appears in English language literature as a chapter – the shortest one – which begins with an edifying sentence about the unjust obscurity of Bulgaria in the Western mind. Or as an appendix, a kind of afterthought.

In the last century, several clever travellers had a go at Bulgaria, but the country proved only partially penetrable for them. It remained the shortest chapter in their books. The last person who truly wrote and drew Bulgaria into existence was the Austro-Hungarian ethnographer Felix Kanitz. That was in 1860.

So it's probably time for a modern take. I know that Bulgaria has many faces – I have seen them – so I decided to write my own Bulgaria into being, as a preventative antidote to future appendixes. Have I got it dead right? I'm sure I have got it dead wrong, in places. But what I really wanted to do was write an interesting story about the drama of the place and its people. That's the most any travel writer or memoirist can wish for.

And the only authentic way to do this was to tell the story of growing up and coming of age in the not altogether sane last decade and a half of the Cold War, about scurrying to the coveted West in the chipped shadow of the Berlin Wall, and about returning sixteen years later, a changed person to a changed country.

The portrait I sketch of modern Bulgaria, then and now, is almost always personal and almost never flattering. It had to be this way if I wanted to be truthful to the times in which I was growing up, and the times in which Bulgaria is growing up today. And I wanted to be. Beauty might be more important to the ego of countries, but truth is more important to me.

Travelling around the country where you grew up, lost some of your virginity and a few of your illusions, acquired some lasting neuroses, and then left in a hateful mood, is a slightly schizoid experience. You are at once an outsider to the present and an insider of the past. Or perhaps the other way round.

Which is a way of saying that I grew up, went back into the woods, shuffled the leaves with my walking stick, and here are the pictures I found.

I Peach Street

The émigré returns

Where do nations begin? In airport lounges, of course. You see them arriving, soul by soul, in pre-activation mode. They step into no man's land, with only their passports to hold onto, and follow the signs to the departure gate. There, among the impersonal plastic chairs and despite themselves, they coalesce into the murky Rorschach stain of nationhood.

At Gate 58 of Frankfurt Airport, the Sofia flight is delayed, and then delayed again. The passengers sit in plastic chairs, patiently squashed by the intimacy of their fellow travellers. I sit next to a hunched boulder of a man with builder's hands and the cigarette-ash stubble of defeat. I look for the word *gastarbeiter* tattooed across his forehead.

I'm trying to dial a Bulgarian number on a borrowed mobile, and failing. I turn to him for help.

'Do you dial the zero?' I ask, cringing at the sound of my expat's voice. Expat voices are always slightly off-key, like an instrument that hasn't been tuned for years.

He smiles shyly with a mouth like a bombed-out village, and shrugs his great sad shoulders: 'I don't know about Bulgarian GSMs either, I haven't lived there since 1991.'

And he returns to his timid wait, like everyone else in the lounge. Nobody is complaining. They are used to waiting: in state hospitals, shop queues, immigration offices, visa departments…

Three Germans are standing in a small cluster, complaining loudly about the delay and glancing conspicuously at their gold-plated watches. They are instantly marked out by ruddy faces and expensive leather shoes, but also by their self-confidence. Investors on the Black Sea coast?

The Bulgarians sit in silence, their wide, lived-in faces and rounded shoulders matched by their battered luggage. The women have slapdash manicures and their hair is dyed either blonde or jet-black, with the odd root showing here and there.

The Germans are now laughing, slapping each other's backs with blond hands. At any other boarding gate I wouldn't mind them or even notice them, why would I? But here, at Gate 58, among these cowering fellow expats, I resent them. Here at Gate 58, and despite myself, I'm part of the Rorschach stain.

Are they sneering at us, the last passengers at the EU gates? Are they in fact laughing with perfect teeth as we run along the speeding bullet-train and wave our tattered bundles desperately, smiling to show that we mean well? Wait, we cry over the whistle of the train as the sausages in our bundles begin to fall out. Wait, don't leave us behind. We too are Europe!

But this is a borrowed 'we'. I left Bulgaria when I was a seventeen-year-old East European, and I am now, by all appearances, a 32-year-old 'global soul'. But everybody needs a borrowed 'us' from time to time, even a global soul. And after half a lifetime and several other countries, the Bulgarian 'us' is still the only honest one I have. And despite my apparently confident country-hopping lifestyle, this semi-genuine 'us' instantly makes the likes of the three well-fed Germans a 'them'.

Finally, we're gliding over the folding ranges of Vitosha Mountain, crisp with fresh snow. The young woman in the next seat – a nurse in Frankfurt – gazes out of the window and wipes tear after tear from her cheeks. Her face is otherwise impassive. The *gastarbeiter* in the next aisle peers down at the native landscape with some dim stirring of emotion on his face, his rough hands inert on his thighs. The plane touches ground smoothly and the passengers applaud, an old custom at Sofia airport. Bulgarians know not to take anything for granted. The Germans exchange looks of disdainful hilarity. Smooth landings are their birthright.

And now our Rorschach blur spills into the building of the world's worst-named airport, Vrajdebna. It means 'hostile'.

Inside Airport Hostile, we are collectively gripped by the confused emigrant syndrome. Hung over with culture jet lag, we queue up in the 'Non EU' line at Customs and study the try-hard advertisement posters:

Use Bulphone!

The Bulgarian word for goodbye is *ciao*

The Bulgarian word for thank you is *merci*

'Such optimists,' says one man to his friend. 'Already sounding European.'

'Why not? Watch this, I'm already one foot in the EU.'

And his mate steps into the EU queue, brandishing his Bulgarian passport and grinning sheepishly. Everyone smiles and looks away, embarrassed. After all, it's mid-2006 and the final green light for the EU hasn't come yet from the sphinx-like HQ in Brussels. What if it doesn't? What if we're not good enough?

There are only five people in the EU queue: the three Germans, and a sun-baked, middle-aged Austrian couple who clutch their designer cabin luggage with pinched mouths. The woman looks like powdered Habsburgian royalty touring the servant quarters.

At passport control, the attractive thirty-something officer with the face of a philosophy graduate who couldn't find another job looks at my photo, then at me.

'Where are you returning from?'

Returning? I hesitate for a second, then I go along with him.

'Scotland,' I lie. He flicks through the virgin pages of my Bulgarian passport.

And I suddenly want to be returning, to be welcomed home by his depressive, familiar face. I don't want to be just visiting. I want my name to be easily pronounced by clerks and written down correctly in a flash without having to spell it ten times. I want to stop explaining where I come from to the well- and not-so-well meaning. (Bucharest is the capital of Romania. Well, Bulgaria hasn't been communist for seventeen years. My English is good? Thank you, that's very kind.) But I know this is only a moment of inattention, a lapse, like the mechanical, quickly suppressed tears of the Frankfurt nurse.

'Where's your UK visa?' He breaks the spell. 'There's nothing here.' So I produce the other passport, the real one.

My luggage has been missing every single time I've landed in Sofia, and this time is no exception. Planes take you to places fast, but some parts of your travelling ensemble take longer to arrive.

There are two desks in the Lost Luggage office, and one is occupied by a ravaged-faced man who's arrived from 'Amerika'. He has an American girth and his gouty feet are bursting out of delicate white-leather moccasins. He can't decide what language to speak. His American has a heavy Bulgarian accent, and his Bulgarian comes out in small, involuntary spasms of village dialect.

'Forty five years I live there.' He points his thumb in the direction of Amerika. 'Now first time I come back. First time!' The impeccably groomed young woman across the desk smiles like a *Vogue* cover and hands him a form to fill out in duplicate.

My sun-tanned, middle-aged Lost Luggage officer startles me with a dazzling smile. 'Welcome home for the Easter holidays!' And he hands me the same form in duplicate. 'The skiing has been spectacular this year.'

I thank him for the tip, and for tracking down my missing luggage, which is for some reason stuck in Paris. Easter and skiing are the last two things on my mind as I step out of the booth and collide with the sweaty émigré from Amerika. He's having another crisis.

'Oh my gawd, I forgot about the levs.' He smacks his forehead with a hand like a red steak. 'Bulgaria don't have euros! Oh my gawd. I brought a pile of euros! What I'm gonna do now?'

But nobody's paying attention to him. He reels towards the 'nothing to declare' exit, empty handed. In the arrivals hall, he's greeted by a small bevy of beefy relatives who clasp him weepily to their bosoms. No such luck for me: between flight delays and lost luggage I am three hours late, and the friend who was meant to wait for me has given up. I feel slightly bereft in the taxi by myself, away from the huddling community of Gate 58.

'Next week Bulgaria will gift Europe one Bulgarian word,' announces a manically cheerful radio host. 'Suggestions from listeners are welcome, especially from children.'

I can't tell if this is some kind of bad joke, and I don't dare ask the young taxi-driver for fear of betraying myself as a clueless expat and getting ripped off at the end of the ride.

'How about "membership"?' I suggest to test him. He sniggers.

'Sounds ugly. There are so many beautiful Bulgarian words we could gift them. Gypsy words even. All of them short and to the point.' He examines me in the rear-view mirror while I stare at the peeling period buildings along the potholed Tsarigradsko Road, exactly the way you don't stare at things when you're a local.

'It's all good, it's all good,' he goes on with a magnanimous hand-wave. 'Because we *are* Europe, we've always been Europe, and now finally they remembered that.'

At that point, a black Mercedes with tinted windows overtakes us. The neckless driver, who has the body shape of a toad, sticks out a hairy arm with an extended middle finger. Digging into his thick wrist is a *martenitsa*, the little thin red-and-white woollen thread with which the Bulgars have always marked the coming of spring. Come March and April, the entire nation wears them, but on this gangsterish wrist it's an odd sight. Like seeing the Godfather with a string of garlic around his neck.

'I saw the bastard,' the driver mutters, 'I kept an eye on him, he's been tailgating me for a while. But my colleagues and I have made a decision, 80 kilometres on the open road, maximum 90. We're still in the city, for Christ's sake. See this corner? There was an accident here last night. A car sped into a truck at 160 kilometres per hour. The truck was stationary. The car driver died instantly and the man in the passenger seat was beheaded.'

I try to resist wishing the toad in the black Mercedes the same fate. We listen to talk-back radio. The condemned Bulgarian nurses in Libya come up. 'I know they're homesick', the radio host concludes cheerfully, 'and here's a song for them.'

Deposited in Peach Street and sweating in my Scottish layers, I pick my way between muddy holes.

I'm walking on the street because the pavements are occupied by parked cars. Between a convertible BMW and a Hyundai four-by-four, rubbish containers overflow. A building site has spewed mud and debris onto the pavement. A huge tangle of undeveloped film snakes in the mud, and the faces of holidaying strangers smile up at me in negative.

An old village house with a crumbling brick roof sits squeezed among the ambitious additions of the late twentieth century. On its rusty garden door hangs crookedly a hand-written sign – KNIFE SHARPENER – and behind it I see a small rose garden. The red and pink roses are budding.

Peach Street is in a posh central neighbourhood. At the far end of Peach Street, I see the blue bulk of Vitosha Mountain, crisp in the spring air like a giant poster photograph.

But more importantly, our family's new apartment is somewhere here, but I can't find it. The numbers on the entrance-ways of Peach Street are sporadic, and I start trying all the locks with the unfamiliar bunch of keys. Some workmen glance at me but don't ask questions. Eventually, the key works. I climb up the three floors. Again no numbers, so I try every lock until the key turns. The family's new apartment has an industrial-sized, bomb-proof double door fit for the Pentagon. Expat apartments are particularly attractive to burglars. The neighbours, who aren't even expats, have a similar Pentagon door. They've been burgled twice. But then they have, or at least had, priceless paintings and antiques. Somehow, we have landed among the new rich.

We have also landed among drug-traffickers of select Balkan nationalities. Just the other day, there was a shooting in the courtyard of our building. Masked men shot and wounded four people, including a baby.

I let myself in and walk over the tiled floor of the family apartment. In the bedroom, I discover that the floor has risen into a large bump, as if a family of busy moles is living inside the cement. I lift the carpet. The tiles are broken from the pressure and underneath, I can see cement. A bomb? A gunshot? I don't know who lives downstairs, and after the recent events, do I dare find out? I don't. I drop the carpet quickly, and with a nervous whistle I step outside on the unswept balcony overlooking the courtyard. A fleet of four-wheel drives with tinted windows is parked in the courtyard, ready for the next drug safari.

I cross the flat and go out on the other balcony, overlooking the street. I instantly make eye contact with a swarthy worker from the construction site next door. He's hanging in a harness at the level of our balcony, having a smoke. 'Good afternoon,' he says. 'How're you doing?'

'OK,' I say, 'I think.' And under his amused gaze I go back inside.

I examine the dusty interior. Our family apartment's riches consist of several hundred books printed before, during, and after Communism, and a half-broken Phillips TV from 1984 which brings back the first wave of memories. After six months of thrift and self-starvation at a Dutch university campus, my father's research visit culminated in the triumphant purchase of this TV. When we left Bulgaria, the TV went to my grandfather Alexander's apartment, on the edge of Sofia, where he sat in a rocking-chair by his window, looking out on the looming blue bulk of Vitosha Mountain. He used to peel apples, then offer the thinly sliced rounds to us on the tip of a blunt knife. We were his only family. When we left for New Zealand, he continued to peel apples, the TV turned up to maximum. On each of our birthdays, he bought a good book and inscribed it in his pedantic accountant's handwriting, to mark the occasion. He couldn't afford to send it or call us long distance. On my thirtieth birthday, he marked the occasion differently: by jumping out of a seventh-floor window to his death. The window was in the bedroom where he had slept with my grandmother Anastassia. My mother sold his apartment where, unsurprisingly, none of us wanted to go again, and this new flat in Peach Street replaced it.

The eyes of my Macedonian grandmother Anastassia, aged twenty-something, follow me around the room from a spookily lifelike oil painting. She died in the year of Chernobyl, when I was twelve, but she seems to recognize me now, and she seems to be saying something important from behind layers of oils, in a language incomprehensible to the living. It's all a bit too much.

I don't want to be left alone with her in this unfamiliar room, and since I don't have any luggage to unpack, I turn on the TV. Here's an ad. A manicured female hand holds a credit card to the sound of some breezy classical music. A treacly male voice says: 'What is the difference between a good man and a perfect man? Five centimetres.' The TV is so decrepit it only broadcasts two channels. Next, *Big Brother*, the local version. It features a *chalga*, or folk-pop sensation with silicone lips and breasts and the obligatory bleached hair, a footballer with blond highlights, a pop-singer and a general celebrity about town with a tiny forehead and even more modest talents. Their conversations go like this: wow man, no babe, yeah babe, wicked shit, check it out, no way! I can feel my brain cells dying by the millions.

I turn the TV off, and turn the radio on. It's talk-back and the subject is orgasm. A thick-accented man of few words is calling from an unnamed town and treating us to his liberal opinion on how he doesn't mind when his girlfriend does it with other men. What's your profession? the talk hostess asks. I'm a pimp, he says matter-of-factly. I've seen her do it with many others. I don't really care. Girlfriends come and go, but the main thing is that I'm free to live wherever I want because I'm financially independent.

I turn off the radio and turn to the bookshelves for therapy. I start picking up books at random. There are three generations of books here, with all sorts of forgotten inscriptions. My grandfather Alexander's hand: '1990, the first truly democratic Bulgarian elections this century.' A book for my father, inscribed on pencil lines by the diligent hand of some young Party commissar: 'for outstanding contributions to the Comsomol'. A book for my mother from my father before I was even a squeak in the bed springs: 'with love on her 21st birthday'. A book for grandmother Anastassia from an opera singer friend who always signed off in French: '*Voilà, ma chère*'. A book to me from some long-forgotten classmate in 1981, with the official Socialist child's birthday wish: 'Happy Birthday dear Kapka, I wish you health, joy, and high grades in school.'

And suddenly, without warning, I turn into the gouty airport émigré from Amerika. Stupid tears burn my eyes, I can't form thoughts or even feelings, and the fat of elapsed decades begins to suffocate me. In a fit of Proustian apoplexy, I grab handfuls of books from the shelves, open them at random, sniff them, search inside for signs and clues. Something, anything to tell me what went on in those distant, blurry years that I have so carefully forgotten.

I pile them up on tables and chairs, on the floor. I dig deeper into the cupboards, knocking over old knick-knacks, photographs pressed under glass, and more books.

And sure enough, every book causes a vague stirring. Dry Ordinary Biscuits and rosehip marmalade, a whiff of Nivea sun lotion on a German beach towel sniffed from a distance, the bracing tune of 'We were born of the red flag', the snowdrops of March, the ski-lift between the legs, the wail of alarms during Civil Defence school trips, roast peppers in the neighbourhood: a ghostly tidal wave of yearnings, fears, and adolescent sorrows submerges me and leaves me choking.

Dusk spills inside the Peach Street apartment, the chill of the Balkan night stabs at my Scottish boots and New Zealand scarf, and the cherry-black eyes of the painting are fixed on me.

I suddenly see that I have sleepwalked through my life between then and now. Between the hazy eighties and these grown-up days, there is a void. And in this void I see a familiar figure running frantically between continents, not knowing what it's running from. Just contemplating the tiny wretch tires me.

Since leaving Bulgaria, I have gone backwards and forwards across the world several times, propelled by a slightly manic energy. I managed to convince myself that I'd left Bulgaria behind for good. I chose to see emigration and globe-trotting as an escape, not as a loss. Nowhere to call home? No problem, the world is my oyster. Where are you from? they ask. Does it matter? I answer.

But it does. Because how can you truly know yourself, and how can you know other places and people, if you don't even know where you come from?

PART ONE

Childhood

We are three sisters.
The eldest is Struggle.
The middle one is Victory.
The youngest is Faith.
All born under Socialism.
And it really really shows.

Borba Brumbashka, from 'I Lived
Socialism', Sofia 2006

2 In the Students' Town

Flawed beginnings

I come from Sofia. I was initially happy, then with the onset of consciousness unhappy, then with the advent of adolescence wretchedly miserable, and finally, in the last throes of my domestic incarceration, convinced I was born in the wrong place and had to escape at all costs. In other words, an ordinary childhood followed by an ordinary adolescence, followed by an ordinary emigration – more or less.

But Sofia was not an ordinary place. Drab and unlovely – yes, like the regime that had planted its lardy apparatchik's behind in its centre. In many ways, Sofia was a fitting capital of the Socialist Camp, or Soc Camp, as we called it. Oddly, the grimly accurate overtones of the word 'camp' were ignored by its very inmates.

Like all self-respecting Cold War cities, Sofia had two official faces. The brave new world of its concrete 'residential complexes' on the outskirts was built to house those from the Province, the Workers, and Young Families (us). The old Sofia with turn-of-the-century buildings and leafy parks was for old Sofia families, the Privileged and the Connected (them).

There was a strict State quota on everything, from apartments and cars, to female sanitary pads and sunflower margarine. You couldn't just go and buy what you felt like, whenever you felt like it – that was capitalism. No, the State provided everything, and by the time you got it, you had waited so long that it felt like a small miracle – and you felt relief mixed with gratitude.

My twenty-something parents waited their turn for an apartment for years, meanwhile renting a minuscule studio flat on the eleventh floor of a high-rise in the Students' Town. My mother quickly learned to keep the windows shut, after she caught me in the nick of time, on the point of crawling out of the window to explore the world below. We shared a bathroom and a kitchen with a whole floor of young 'student' families. Children's birthdays were celebrated in the common room, which was always semi-dark and smelt sterile and vaguely official, like a dentist's waiting-room. On the long Politburo-style table we blew out our birthday candles and smeared our carefully ironed clothes with the small sandwiches carefully made by our mothers. Our crayon masterpieces decorated the grim walls. My hopeful depictions of springtime as a series of unlikely princesses with flowers sprouting from their heads were on display even in winter.

My mother had recently ceased to be a student and was now gainfully employed in a giant Central Institute for Computational Technology full of machines that spewed out tons of coloured perforated cards with tiny numbers on them. The institute buildings looked like the HQ of a nuclear power station. The floors, corridors and open-plan offices inside them were so immense that I couldn't understand how my mother didn't get lost every time she opened a door.

Going home on the overcrowded bus, my mother would look up at the lit-up windows of proper apartment buildings and think, Why, why can't there be a lit-up window for us too? From time to time, she would also have a sudden attack of nerves, and run down the eleven floors to get away from the claustrophobic little family stuffed inside the single room. Meanwhile, inside the room, my father typed up his mathematics PhD thesis on a noisy typewriter. When the last page landed on the neat pile, ending three years of hard work and paving the way to his compulsory military service, his first critic was already there: a one-year-old sitting on the table, peeing over his manuscript.

Thanks to the army, my father missed the second and third years of my life. He was sent to a place called Vratsa in the north, where the brand-new doctor of maths crawled in the mud towards the Western capitalist decadent enemy, and wrote rhyming couplets about a toddler running barefoot in summer grass somewhere far away. My mother became a single parent with no income and a sickly child that would regularly wake in the middle of the night and threaten to die from asthma attacks. The sickly child didn't die, but my mother nearly did, from insomnia and nervous exhaustion.

From time to time, she went to Vratsa to wait at the winter gates of the barracks for my shorn, emaciated father to appear, like the political prisoner that he really was, then waited some more at the railway station for the unheated train ride back to Sofia. When my father eventually returned home, I didn't recognize him, and resented having this shaven-headed, hungry stranger insinuate himself into our lives as if he belonged there. To prevent this, I insinuated myself between my parents as soon as they were within a metre of each other.

Then came the ordeal of kindergarten, where I discovered that Hell is indeed other people. And other people's cooking. Three things terrorized me at kindergarten: the food; compulsory afternoon naps; and the snotty-faced, rough-and-ready girl who had a vocabulary of sexual obscenities rich beyond her years, and took to singing a song about someone called Victor Jara, who played the guitar without hands in some stadium.

'That's not true!' I protested, holding back tears, already too impressionable at four. 'You can't play guitar without hands!'

'You can, like this!' She mimicked hand-stumps with her sleeves, grimacing all the time.

I asked the teacher about Victor Jara. My teacher looked like a Modigliani painting – tall, oblong-faced, doe-eyed and, on closer inspection, horse-toothed. Like my drawings, she was an unlikely princess, with her long glossy hair and her exotic Vietnamese husband who spoke a close approximation of Bulgarian.

'He was a musician from Chile,' she explained. 'Fascists in Chile killed him because he sang songs about the people.' I didn't dare enquire about the hands. The raw horror of the handless guitarist lives on in my mind thirty years later, next to the photograph of a young Chilean woman whose fire-melted face looked out of a magazine of the Bulgarian Telegraph Agency. Chile was clearly a place where for some reason it was OK to set people's faces on fire and cut off their hands. To be precise, the reason was the existence of countries like Bulgaria, where the Reds had taken over, and what could possibly be worse than that? In turn, all those grisly goings-on in distant South America were the Communist government's dream, and in this case the anti-Fascist propagandists didn't even have to make it up.

Every afternoon, in keeping with the old Bulgarian peasant myth that what healthy children need is lobotomizing amounts of food and sleep, we were put to our bunk-style beds and told not to make any noise, or else. Of course, most kids never slept. But some did sleep, and this was a first inkling of the inherent strangeness of other people. I lay in the enforced silence, listening to the breathing and sleep-talk of others, and counting the interminable minutes until it was time to be taken away from all this.

Oh, the food. Did anybody enjoy institutional food in the 1970s? The chief offenders were a spectral white soup where the corpses of carrots floated, a wobbling, menacing jelly dessert, and a certain rice pudding which was delicious when your mother made it, but tasted evil in the kindergarten canteen. The only edible thing was the 'Teddy' toothpaste which was pink and tasted of gummy strawberries, and which we secretly snacked on in the toilets, preparing our immune systems for Chernobyl.

It was 1979, the year my sister was born. An annoying, noisy cot was placed next to my bed, instantly dislodging me from my personal space and from my mother's exclusive affections. My mother now seemed permanently strung out, not surprising considering she'd had a horrific delivery after a difficult pregnancy, which had coincided with my father's hospitalisation with hepatitis, and featured doctor consultations which went like this: 'It might be born without a few fingers. If you're lucky', 'It might die in the womb', 'Why don't you abort it? You don't want an idiot child.' Abortions were illegal, and those resorting to hurried back-street jobs were often unintentionally sterilized.

Nineteen seventy-nine was also the year after the assassination by State Security of the dissident writer Georgi Markov in London with a poison-tipped umbrella – Bulgaria's main claim to fame in the last century, if we don't count weightlifters with hairy backs. But that year I was preoccupied by a far more momentous event: the kindergarten summer camp.

The summer camp was like one interminable day at kindergarten, with the accompanying trembling jelly desserts, afternoon naps and group activities on the beach. The toilets were communal and abominable, the sheets and blankets had holes in them, and there was the added degradation of being forced to strip naked on the beach as if we didn't know boy from girl. Only the teacher's son was allowed to keep his trunks on, immediately putting him in a position of authority over the timid nudists, and giving me a useful insight into the meaning of nepotism.

I sat with my legs firmly overlapping, hid under my straw hat, and made desolate sculptures from sand. Fortunately, my best friend was there too, and two bare bottoms are more comforting than one. And mercifully, for the happy group photo in the water, we were allowed to put our swimsuits back on. Then a storm broke out and there were no beach activities for a couple of days. We were forbidden from going anywhere near the shore. But, somehow, I sneaked out, and found a demonic grey sea, broken beach-steps and a dead dog washed up on the wet sand – an image that has made itself at home in my adult nightmares.

And just then, like guardian angels materializing in a cloud of dust, my glamorous grandparents Alexander and Anastassia turned up in their glamorous blue Skoda. They argued with the teachers to be allowed to take me away on a private seaside holiday while I waited outside, ready to burst into tears. Permission was granted, and the other kids watched my triumphant departure, like royalty whisked off in a limousine to some private seaside chateau. And, as it happens, I really did have my very own palace.

Balchik was a small ancient town on the Black Sea coast near the Romanian border. Its white limestone hills were slipping into the sea and people said that the houses wouldn't survive another twenty years. I walked over the hot dark cracks in the tar-sealed promenade, flowering like cracked chocolate cake in the oven of summer. I thought about the twenty years. It was clearly an adult trick, a way of saying that something was so far away it would never happen.

The slate-roofed houses with big verandas where we always stayed were safely away from the sea, up on a hillside. This was my grandfather's holiday bonus from the smelly leather factory in Dobrich where he worked as an accountant, ensuring that we had the best leather shoes and my grandmother the best leather coats. Every afternoon my grandparents had a nap while I stayed jubilantly awake. I was given a 50 stotinki coin, which I ran down the hill to deposit with the friendly ice cream man who knew how to construct a perfect two-scoop cup (fancy cones came much later). The choice was vanilla.

Then the exploration of my private premises, the Queen's Palace, began. Because everybody was napping or at the beach at high noon,

I had the place to myself, just like the Romanian Queen Marie for whom it had been built. She had lived a long time ago, perhaps as inconceivably long as twenty years ago; actually, she had died more than forty years ago. In any case, it was a vast maze of waterworks, alleys and giant cacti. Curious objects beckoned: giant stone thrones; carved stone crosses; and what looked like gravestones. Into the clay amphorae full of invisible slimy things, I tossed echoey greetings like 'Hello', 'Who's there?', and 'Bye-bye, I'll be back'. Then there was the algae-thick sea, which ended at the foot of the gardens' algae-encrusted walls.

I didn't know it, but along with the cacti and the hidden alleyways, I was discovering two things that went into my eventual personhood: the pleasure of solitude, and the pull of the exotic. That stone throne was from Bessarabia, the amphorae from Morocco, and the tombstones Ottoman. By a stroke of luck, Queen Marie had created a five-year-old's dream labyrinth. Only the fairies were missing. Better still: there was an enigmatic concrete penguin on the jetty, one wing amputated by the algae-thick waves.

Up the cracked road there was an open-air cinema with white walls and huge projector lights. One film that I choked on there, along with a paper cone of salted sunflower seeds, was *A Factory for Old Iron* from New Zealand. The anger and the bad hairstyles of the people made a deep impression on me. New Zealand stuck in my mind as a place where men with three-day stubble and bloodshot eyes brooded among car wrecks and women had their jeans forcibly pulled off.

Watching TV thirteen years later in New Zealand, I caught a glimpse of an unshaven, bloodshot-eyed Bruno Lawrence brooding in his car yard in *Smash Palace*, and was incongruously transported back to Balchik, and those long summers of sunflower seeds, algae, and vanilla ice cream.

Back in Sofia, my mother's bold dream finally came true. In 1979, we moved into an extravagantly spacious two-room flat in an eight-floor concrete building surrounded by thousands of identical concrete buildings, purposeful and sturdy like nuclear plants in freshly bulldozed fields of mud. This was Youth 3, and here I spent my youth.

Youth 3 was preceded by Youth 1 and Youth 2, followed by Youth 4, and its neighbours were Friendship 1 and Friendship 2. How many more Youths and Friendships were meant to spring forth was a State secret, but my parents' friends said that Youth 15 might have sea views. They laughed at this, but it struck me as an excellent idea, especially if Youth 15 could be somewhere near Balchik.

We lived in block number 328, which took up half the length of our street. Our street might have had a name, but nobody knew what it was. You got off at your bus stop, and that was that. When you received mail, your address looked like this: Sofia, Mladost 3, block 328, entrance E, floor 4, apt. 79. Your name came last, if there was room for it.

When I was given school homework – write an essay about your street and your house – I panicked. I knew the name of only one street between the Youths and the city proper: boulevard Salvador Allende. There was a bust of him, from which I could tell that he was a nice man with glasses. He was somehow related to the handless guitarist. But he couldn't solve my homework problem.

'Well,' my mother suggested, 'why don't you write about the kind of street and the kind of house you'd like to live in?'

So I did. In my story, we lived in a house with a red roof and a chimney near the sea. My grandparents lived in a similar house nearby. Our street was called Strawberry. The vanilla ice cream man came every afternoon and you could buy a two-scoop cup for 50 stotinki.

When she returned our homework, the teacher's red pen had scribbled in the margins, 'Very good, but a fantasy. Next time concentrate on reality.' I have no idea how the other kids handled the cruel homework of reality. After all, we were all living in the Youths. Nobody had a street or a house.

To escape this universe of mud, my mother took us – baby in pram and me running along – to the Park of Freedom, only half an hour away by bus. Renamed in 1945 from its original monarcho-fascist name Boris's Garden, after Tsar Boris III, it really was a park of freedom for us. It had century-old trees, benches and playgrounds, mossy ponds whose bottoms were covered with 'lucky' coins, and alleys over which the crowns of spring trees arched like green-lit tunnels.

The centrepiece was a giant statue of the Red Army, with ropey arms propelled forwards and upwards from revolutionary unisex bosoms into futuristic, proletarian fists. But you didn't really notice these statues: they were everywhere, they were identical, and somehow you sensed that they were fake, like stage props.

At around that point, I began to suspect that something was wrong with us, or with where we lived. It was the mud. I watched my mother wash the pram from top to bottom every time we returned from an outing, because the mud managed to get even onto the pram's roof. But Balchik didn't have any mud and in another part of Sofia my grandparents' neighbourhood, named Emil Markov after a Communist who'd been shot there by the police in 1944, had children's playgrounds and even grass.

I summed things up with a cruel question one day, surveying from our balcony the concrete mudscape: 'Mum, why is everything so ugly?'

To which my mother couldn't find an honest answer, except to hide her tears.

3 Youth 3

A world of mud and music

When an outsider comes to a new place, Walter Benjamin wrote, he sees the picturesque and the freakish, whereas the local sees through layers of emotion and memory. In other words, they see completely different things. So while a newcomer would have looked at Youth 3 and seen an uninhabitable dystopia of concrete and mud, I learnt to see it for what it really was: my home.

Block 328, for example, looked friendlier than the rest: it had our balcony, with our fridge on it, and our bedroom curtains. The local bus stop, where you boarded bus 305, had a unique atmosphere about it too, its shelter plastered with *necrologs* or public announcements of recent deaths in the neighbourhood, which always made for interesting reading while you waited; for example:

Zdravka Pencheva, 74 yrs (photo)

You will always be in our hearts. We miss you dearly. Your devoted son

Pesho, grandchildren Hristo and Vladko, daughter-in-law Veneta.

There was also the butcher, the baker, the kindergarten, the grocery store, the Universal Store, the bottle store. So what if they were all housed on the ground floors of blocks, or in small, bunker-like concrete buildings we called trafoposts because they were built to house the suburb's electricity transformers? So what if the butcher only had mixed mince and bloody legs that she wrapped up in coarse brown paper? Or the baker had only two types of bread, white and wholemeal, and the Universal Store was universally empty except for, say, a just-arrived pull-out sofa-bed? Or the bottle store only sold lemonade and beer? You liked lemonade, and you liked meatballs, and you already had a pull-out sofa-bed anyway. It's not as if you lacked for anything. It's not as if there was anything more you wanted. After all, you didn't *know* there was anything more to want.

Furthermore, I came to realize with a pang of pride, Youth 3 was superior to the undeveloped Youth 4 which petered out into desolate fields. But it was inferior to Youth 2 with all its shops, cinema and gym, while the older, well-developed Youth 1 was practically the garden of the Youths. Central Sofia with its pretty yellow tiles, grand old buildings and leafy streets was for special occasions only, such as visiting relatives in the heart of Sofia, like Auntie Lenche and her daughter Pavlina.

They lived in a spacious ground-floor apartment with their husbands – although for some reason Auntie Lenche had divorced hers. I suspected they lived together because he had nowhere else to go, and because Pavlina was disabled by a nasty illness. She was confined to a couch in the living-room, from where she drew complicated plans for architectural projects. Every time I visited them, we ate marble cake and drank Turkish coffee in small cups which were then turned upside down so Auntie Lenche could gaze at their smeared insides and profess wondrous things about our futures. I would travel a long way this summer (to the seaside). Pavlina's health would improve (it wouldn't). Money would come to all of us (it didn't). Then we'd go for an excruciating walk along the fashionable Vitosha Boulevard, where Pavlina's severe limp drew looks and jeers from passers-by. 'Ignore them, darling,' her mother whispered. 'They are ignorant souls.' But I could see that Auntie Lenche's heart broke, and I hated the ignorant souls. Pavlina, however, was always upbeat, as if the limp, the excruciating walks, and the drugs that made her swell up were irrelevant details. I concluded that living in an old apartment, with a leafy courtyard full of cats and blossoms, probably compensated for everything else.

Meanwhile, back in the Youth 'panels', as my parents' friends called the hastily built concrete blocks, things were grim. Within a few years of being erected, bits of the panels' walls were falling off. Seen from a distance, their hide was peeling and they wept grey tears, like mutant monsters squatting in their own waste.

Giant, glistening black cockroaches with hard carapaces and long feelers travelled up and down the water pipes, and frequently dropped in for a visit. They liked walls and the insides of slippers, and occasionally they fell on top of you while you slept. You fought them with poisonous sprays that gave you respiratory problems, but the cockroaches just shook off the spray and continued on their travels. My parents' friends said that the cockroaches were the rightful residents of the panels, and that when the panels eventually fell on top of us, they'd be the only survivors.

This explained why the Youths and the Friendships were separated from the Students' Town by a suburb called the Bug. My parents' friends also said that the cockroaches were Party agents and had listening devices embedded in them. This explained why people said that the walls had ears.

Our statistically perfect family – two adults, two children – lived in a two-room apartment. My sister and I shared a room and a fold-out sofa-bed. Our parents' bedroom, complete with another fold-out sofa-bed, doubled up as the living-room. My father's study-corner doubled up as my mother's dressing table. The two balconies, encased in glass panels against the winter cold, doubled up as additional small rooms.

It's hard to understand how a family's entire life could fit into two rooms, but then it wasn't a big life. Some books, some clothes, some toys, a typewriter, an imported washing-machine gifted by my grandparents and kept inside a wardrobe, a Russian black-and-white TV branded Yunost or Youth, and later updated to a Dutch Phillips TV and stereo… what more could we need?

A hundred thousand statistically perfect families like us lived in exactly the same apartment, with the same glass-panelled balconies housing the family barrel of pickled cabbage for winter salads. The same fold-out sofa-beds. The same view of panels, trafoposts and buses puffing with black smoke. The same Skoda, Moskvic, Warburg, Trabant or – for the more glamorous – Lada, underneath which fathers spent half the weekend fixing a leak. The same naked concrete bathroom which fathers spent the other half of the weekend covering with tiles in a desperate attempt to beautify it.

It was late twentieth-century tenement living. Balconies bristled with washing on lines, the 'peasants' chucked food waste out of windows, as they'd do in the countryside to feed the pigs, and you heard the people upstairs flush their toilet, argue and, in the case of our hefty neighbours, even walk.

In the attempted communal spaces between blocks, on the dry, patchy grass, we played hopscotch (*dama*), elastics (*lastik*), cat's cradle ('cat's eye'), and cops and robbers ('cops and vagabonds'). Our keys were secured around our necks with elastic, a contraption which had the added function of being pulled by your playmates then released in your face from a maximum distance, the pain surprising you to tears each time.

At night, the streets emptied and the thousands of tiny windows lit up like TV screens. The nation was gripped by the trials of *The Slave Isaura*, a 1976 Brazilian soap opera. Isaura is a beautiful slave on a plantation whose master falls in love with her and frees her. But it takes months, years, my entire childhood, before Isaura is free of her capitalist-imperialist chains.

During the Olympics or other international sports events, we watched breathlessly as our gymnasts, athletes, and weightlifters battled with the West for medals. It was a serious matter, and whenever gold or silver was won for Bulgaria and the national anthem was played, the whole nation shed a tear together with the long-suffering, steroid-fed medallist on the podium. It was collective therapy: in those few minutes, before we were plunged behind the Iron Curtain again, back in the drab anonymity of the Soc Bloc, the world knew that we existed, and that we were good at something, and that was balm for a nameless wound.

But the top TV hit of the 1970s and '80s was the Bulgarian series *We Are at Every Kilometre*. This was the story of a group of partisans risking their lives fighting the Fascists-imperialists in the Bulgarian mountains during the Second World War. There was a handsome, brave partisan literally at every kilometre, waiting to spill the blood of the enemy and his/her own blood in the name of Freedom and the Party. The bracing soundtrack of the series, to which I always sang along, in joyful anticipation of the heart-throb of Bulgarian cinema Stefan Danailov scowling behind his Kalashnikov, went like this:

> We were born of the red flag,
> We are not afraid of dying.
> We are at every kilometre.
> And so until the end of time.

> A comrade falls in deadly battle.
> For you, he falls, freedom.
> He falls and rises to become
> A small red star.

It was propaganda at its sexiest. Of course, nobody told me that the partisans were so few in number that they were only at every kilometre within a hundred square kilometre area of the country, and then only in the last two years of the war. The series also skirted around the fact that most of them, rather than martyr themselves to the vicious fascist police, waited until the tide turned, then heroically took the bigger towns from frightened government clerks and officers.

And nobody told me that one of the series' scriptwriters had defected to London and was murdered by the Bulgarian secret police with a poison-tipped umbrella; and that Bulgaria was better known in England for this 'umbrella murder' than for our partisans and athletes.

Every now and then – usually now – the power cut out without warning. The Youths were plunged into darkness, and the evening was cancelled, together with the central heating. My mother's casseroles half-cooked, our school homework half-done, my father's lectures half-prepared, the partisans caught in mid-shootout with the Fascist-imperialists, we wrapped up in blankets and played dominoes by candlelight.

In winter, with the first snow, we grabbed our sledges and ran to the nearest inclined surface, which was just a mound of earth left from a building site. At the end of summer, the smoky smell of roast peppers floated above the Youths as every family prepared 'jars' for the winter on their balcony, with the help of a contraption called a pepper-roaster.

'We're late with our jars, have you done yours?' the chemist (my best friend's Russian mother) asked the engineer (my mother), leaning over from the neighbouring balcony. 'The Lada's gone to hell, how's the Skoda?' the nuclear physicist from the Academy of Sciences (my best friend's father) said to the engineer (my father) on the outside pull-up bar, which was also used for beating dust out of carpets and skinning the occasional lamb.

The chemist, the nuclear physicist and the engineers knew that their everyday life, when put into words, sounded like a joke without a punchline. Not unlike the Russian deficit joke they laughed at: 'A man in the deli section of a supermarket says to the butcher behind the counter, "Can you slice up some salami for me?" The butcher replies, "Sure. Just bring the salami."'

But they also knew that life without the jars was no joke. Produce was seasonal, so in the winter you had no fruit, and the veg were of the grim root variety. You had to be organized, though if you were lucky enough to have relatives in the Province that you were on speaking terms with, they would send you jars too, in cardboard boxes tied up with string, in the back of somebody's sputtering Trabant.

Block 328 was a perfect human cross-section of the imaginary Socialist cake. On the ground floor, next to the elevator, lived a Gypsy family of unknown dimensions. It contained three generations of pregnant women and girls, men who dwelled in a vague alcoholic mist, and countless kids. Once, through their open front door, I got a fascinating glimpse into their apartment. They had stripped the carpet and were living on bare concrete, without furniture.

Occasionally, one of the older girls knocked on a door – always our door because all others were slammed in her face – and shyly asked for a cup of flour, a bit of sugar, and my mother always obliged. Once, a *nekrolog* appeared on their door: a boy of seven had died. The neighbours whispered that he was probably murdered in some vendetta or beaten to death, just as a man had died in a knife-fight a few months before.

Once, on St George's Day, a religious festival in May which survived the clampdown on all things religious thanks to its heavy focus on eating lamb and drinking red wine, the Gypsies brought a live lamb. To the children's delight, they tethered it on their ground-floor balcony. It bleated and trembled piteously for days, then they hung it up on the pull-up bar, cut its throat into a plastic bucket, skinned it, and dismembered it. Rivers of blood flowed along the pavement.

The neighbours watched from their balconies, and buses stopped to see the gory spectacle. Our street experienced its first traffic jam.

Some people shook their heads in disgust, others laughed, appreciating a properly surreal sight in their already surreal lives. My father, the only man in the block who spoke to the Gypsies, went down to represent the neighbourhood. They washed the blood away, and come next St George's Day, they bought lamb from the butcher's.

And so the Gypsies camped among us, unloved and unwelcome, forcefully urbanized, living their parallel life of parties, violence, reproduction and animal-slaughter. But despite the blood and the animal guts, they weren't the scariest of our neighbours.

On floor two, in darkened rooms, lived an old woman and her disabled son. She always wore black, either mourning her husband's death or, I thought, preparing for her son's. She scared me, as if her grief was contagious. Sure enough, her son's *necrolog* appeared on their door one day, and I never saw her again.

Next to her lived my parents' friends: a bald vet and an engineer with the soft accent of my father's town in northern Bulgaria. They had two daughters who wore ugly cardigans knitted by country grandmothers, and always smelt musty because their apartment was never aired out, from fear of catching cold. Every day, the vet travelled two hours on buses to get to work. The engineer worked in my mother's Central Institute for Computational Technology.

On floor three, beneath us, dwelled a psychopath who wore braces and a stained wife-beater singlet, although he was a bachelor. When a large white Czech piano, purchased with my parents' entire savings, was put in our bedroom and I started playing scales, he launched a violent, sustained protest. He bashed his ceiling with what could only be a very large hammer whenever I played. Sometimes, he bashed away in the middle of the night. My father duly braced himself to protect his brood, and went down to 'sort him out', but only got screamed at every time. 'I'm gonna kill you, I'm gonna gut you like a pig!' he yelled, while my sister and I cried upstairs. When my parents called the local militia (the police was a term associated with the pre-1945 monarcho-fascist government), two lethargic militiamen came, talked to him, issued a warning, and left us exactly where we were before: a floor above the psycho. After all, he was retired militia himself.

On floor six lived my friend Hope who was shy, sweet, and thin as a stick-insect. Hope didn't have a father. She lived with her mother and her grandmother: soft-bodied, slow-moving women who floated in and out of my world like bundles of laundry.

On floor five, right above us, were the Mechevs, comprising a crane-driver, a worker in the nearby Kremikovtsi Factory, and their two offspring. The name Mechev meant something like 'bear clan'. Whenever I ran into mother-bear, she slapped my cheek and said, 'You need to put on some weight, luv, your glasses are falling off.' The elder Mechev son, who felt sorry for me, Hope and everyone smaller than him, which was most kids, personally offered us his bodyguard protection against potential aggressors in the neighbourhood: 'Just show us who's bothering you, and I'll rearrange his face, no problem.'

The Mechevs lived in a one-room apartment, known as a 'garçonniere', even smaller than ours. Father-bear would pop in uninvited some evenings, to watch TV or simply enjoy sitting in a larger room. 'Come on, bring out the meze,' he'd say as he plonked on the table a bottle of village home-made rakia that might have killed off an entire colony of cockroaches. My father preferred reading his computer manuals or helping us with maths homework, and my mother didn't have many common topics of conversation with Comrade Mechev. Besides which, he filled out the living-room, effectively ejecting the rest of us. But you didn't want to appear snobbish. It was already bad enough to be an 'intellectual'. It was better just to put up with it once in a while. After all, the proletariat were the ruling class, weren't they.

Yes, but who were the proletariat? Not the Mechevs. They were proletariat only under duress. In truth, they came from generations of land-owning peasants. Had it not been for the destruction of agriculture and the birth of the Youths and Friendships, and monster factories like Kremikovtsi which bellowed perpetual black clouds over us, the Mechevs would be enjoying the self-sustained lifestyle of pig-farming and potato-growing. They were really just commuting to the outskirts of Sofia. Every weekend they squeezed into their clapped-out Moskvič, which seemed to be held together by twine, and off they went, back to the village.

The tiny apartments in the residential complexes tried to make 'citizens' out of the peasants and the Gypsies. Citizen, how proud this sounds, to paraphrase Gorky. But what they actually made was dispossessed peasants and displaced Gypsies. And in a double whammy, the native citizens, like my mother who was born and raised in central Sofia, were turned into 'workers' with no access to the pleasures of city life. Youth was not a city. It was citizen storage.

The typical day of the young citizen began at 6.30 in the morning, a bleak and inhuman hour that seemed manufactured by the State in order to crush all intelligent thought. My mother woke me up for school, and we had breakfast in the kitchen. The radio was always on, purely to keep us awake, since listening to the news was pointless. We already knew it by heart:

> The Head of State and Chief Secretary of the Central Committee of the Bulgarian Communist Party Comrade Todor Jivkov yesterday received Comrade Erick Honecker, Leader of the German Democratic Republic, on an official State visit. At Sofia airport, Comrade Honecker was cordially greeted by the comrades...

'Listening' to the news was like 'reading' the paper *The Worker's Deed*, which was the only national paper, and seemed to simply rearrange the same content on its pages from day to day, year to year.

On a normal day, the young citizen drank her hot chocolate and chewed her slice of honeyed bread at 7.15 to the heavy-hearted tune of a folk song about Tsar Ivan Shishman's heroic army facing the Ottoman Turks in 1393. Shishman was defeated and Bulgaria fell into Ottoman hands for the next five centuries – but the song ends before disaster strikes. As the music faded out, the daily documentary feature began: 'Bulgaria: Deeds and Documents'. It traced, in carefully staged episodes, Bulgaria's modern history, which began by means of a giant leap of about four centuries from Tsar Ivan Shishman to the National Revival in the 1800s. Narrated by a velvety male voice, it seemed specifically designed to send you back to sleep. And it went on for years. How could there be so many deeds and documents within just a century and a half?

Later in the day, when I returned from school, the radio treated us to bitter-sweet Italian pop tunes, and I tried to sing along, parroting the strange sounds: Toto Cutugno (*'Lasciatemi cantare con la gitarra in mano, lasciate mi cantare, una canzione piano piano'*), Adriano Celentano (*'Susanna, Susanna, Susanna Susanna mon amour...'*) and Al Bano and Romina Power (*'Felicita, felicita...'*). Now *that* was cool.

Otherwise, foreign radio stations like Radio Free Europe, the Voice of America and Deutsche Welle were deliberately fuzzed with the help of electro-magnetic contraptions in the countryside, especially installed to interfere with radio signals. We passed them on our way to the seaside. They looked like something out of *War of the Worlds*.

This was how the world sounded: pop music and static noise pierced by distant, distorted voices. The very keen managed to tune in with the help of special equipment. But for the vast majority, including my parents, it just wasn't worth the trouble. It's not as if it would change anything.

In between 'Deeds and Documents' and the Italian radio songs, the young citizen attended school. My school, the Unitary Secondary Polytechnic School 81, was ambitiously named Victor Hugo. It was across the road from us, a smaller, squatter version of the residential blocks. It was a primary and secondary school in one, but the secondary grades were only really for kids who weren't bright enough, ambitious enough, or well-connected enough at age thirteen to get into the specialized colleges.

Does anybody ever manage to purge their system of their school? I envy them. The black iron-and-glass-panelled entrance doors, wide staircases, semi-dark corridors, vast courtyard where we formed neat rows every morning for organized gymnastics, and rooms haunted by the spectre of Comrade Gesheva, are with me to this day.

Like Block 328, our Class E was a social experiment. If Block 328 was a microcosm of the Socialist worker's world, Class E was a dress rehearsal for that world. Class E consisted of thirty-two kids who were alphabetically numbered, and I was Number Sixteen.

Here were kids with 'intellectual' parents like mine. Kids like smug Penka, whose father was a director of a factory and clearly a big-shot (my parents: Careful what you say in front of Penka). Kids like overfed, aggressive Kiril, who lived with his grandparents and was cut out to be a factory director one day. Kids like mathematical wunderkind Sergei, whose mother was a Russian 'intellectual'. Kids like my brainy best friend Esther, whose unusual name suited her appearance of an androgynous visitor from outer space. Her physicist parents lived in a bare apartment and never hosted birthday parties; stranger still, her father had a beard, the sure sign of the dissident. Kids like overachieving Dima, whose ambitious parents had drilled her to come top in every subject and avoid anybody with low grades.

Compared to Dima's parents, my own were apathetic slobs. However, on the one occasion that I got a four in a maths test, instead of the usual five or top six as befits the child of 'engineers', my mother impressed upon me, with the help of tears and broken plates, that if I continued in the same vein I would end up washing dishes in some dismal kitchen, married to a truck-driver who would beat me. I was nine.

Now, if my mother's reaction seems neurotic, it was appropriately neurotic. Because what could an educated person hope for their child to be, except educated? To have special privileges, money and status, you had to be a big-shot factory director like Penka's father, and that was a rather vulgar, social climbing thing to be in the eyes of my parents and their friends. Besides, you had to be already connected. We weren't.

So all you were left with was education. It gave you an inner world and the company of other educated people. It gave you an inhabitable space in the uninhabitable Youths. It gave you the possibility to emigrate 'internally'. It gave you the chance to subvert the Marxist motto which proclaimed that the Exemplary Socialist Citizen's existence determined his conscience. The trick then was to make your conscience determine your existence, because it was the only act of freedom left to the Citizen. Otherwise you were stuck with the mud, the psychopath downstairs, and the bear clan above.

Until that traumatic four, maths had left me cold, but the threat of that truck-driver husband propelled me to sudden mathematical heights. Within a year, my father had revived my interest in maths with home-made problems to solve. This beat the textbook maths problems (Sample: 'A record-breaking truck-driver transported fifteen tons of grain in one year. If his productivity increased two-fold every year, how many tons of grain would he transport in five years?') Soon I was ahead of Dima and duly attending maths and physics Olympiads along with the more obvious literature Olympiads.

The Olympiads were academic marathons separated from exams only by their seemingly voluntary nature. You *could* decline to participate in an Olympiad, but that would mark you out as suspiciously unambitious. So you went voluntarily. At the Olympiads you, the bespectacled pride of ambitious parents, sat for half a day with an exam paper, and composed essays or solved advanced mathematical problems. The idea was to identify the most gifted kids in each subject, starting with your school, then your district, and ending with city-wide, national and international Olympiads. Why? For the same reason that the State generously sponsored athletes who then went on to demonstrate to the world the explosive muscular power of Socialism.

So here was a regime where the head of state and his cronies were, in my mother's whispered phrase, 'idiots in brown suits'. A regime where intellectual, bourgeois, elite, and individualistic were dirty words. But where, at the same time, academic, sporting and musical achievements were state-encouraged, state-sponsored, and even state-imposed.

People were too preoccupied by the chore of daily survival to notice this brisk irony. And if they did, like my parents they kept their insights to themselves. You never knew who might be listening.

If you came top at the Olympiads, you could even end up travelling abroad or winning a medal. I made it only to the Sofia Literature Olympiad, where I wrote an essay on the topic of 'Sofia: she grows but never ages'. The fatal crunch came when I wrote, in inspired prose, about the heroic mid-flight stance of the horse of the Russian Tsar Liberator statue outside the Assembly Hall, as he charges towards the Ottomans to liberate Bulgaria. Coming out of the Olympiad, I looked at the statue, and saw with a sinking heart that far from charging, the horse had all its hooves planted on the ground. I'll never know whether this small glitch separated me from a medal but, as I said, in the general scheme of ambitious Sofia parents and child-geniuses, we were very low key.

By age ten, I had learned several vital lessons.

One (Literature): streets in the West crawl with drug addicts, criminals, and capitalists. Nobody protects you there. This was confirmed by my reading of a magnificently illustrated *David Copperfield*, where the evil Uriah Heep had red hair and a crooked nose, and every woman wore a different-coloured fabulous dress. The editor's postscript to the book read: 'Every morning thousands of children in England and the entire capitalist world disappeared into dark mines and factories. This is the dreadful legacy of capitalism.' You couldn't argue with that.

Whereas we luckily had the Mother-Party:

She watches over us each day
like a mother tender and dear.
At school, at work, at play,
She gives us strength and cheer.

Two (History): in the history of humankind there are several progressive stages of socio-political order – Primitivism, Slavery, Feudalism, Fascism, Capitalism, Socialism, and Communism. Capitalism is only slightly better than Fascism. After Communism, there is nothing except the blinding light of the Bright Future, and this is what we aspire for. We're not quite there yet, but we are pretty close.

Three (general knowledge): the nuclear family is the smallest structural unit in the Mature Socialist Society. Children from broken homes become delinquents and anti-social elements. They go to Corrective Labour Schools where they are corrected through labour.

Four (an unsettling gut feeling): at School 81 you have roughly three options – excel and be noticed at your peril, blend in and be safe, or rebel and be broken. I wasn't sure which option I should take. But before I had time to figure it out, I experienced a further clarification: I had little choice in the matter. I was to excel and be noticed at my peril.

My first experience of the dilemmas of School 81 came at age eight, which was when we started learning Russian. I had already decided not to bother with Russian. I just couldn't see the point. It was a compulsory subject, and therefore one of life's tedious musts, like algebra and chemistry, and it sounded too similar to Bulgarian to be of any obvious use. All the Russians I knew – my parents' friends – were married to Bulgarians and already spoke perfect Bulgarian. For some reason, though, the Russian teacher decided from day one that I was going to excel in her subject, whether or not I wanted it.

'Number Sixteen,' the teacher snapped, breaking her ruler on the desk after I made a mess of the genitive case at the blackboard yet again, 'you have no respect. You should be ashamed of yourself.' And I was. Because I could see that deep down the Russian teacher was a nice woman, and it wasn't her fault that she had to teach a language nobody wanted to learn. But soon I began to see some practical advantages to linguistic excellence.

In November 1981, the Soviet leader Leonid Brezhnev died and our school had a morning of mourning. We stood in the yard in neat, frozen units, listening to giant speakers thunder out recorded Soviet Army songs like '*Vstavai strana ogromnaya*' ('Rise, oh Mighty Country'), a motivational anti-Fascist war song from the 1940s.

The school director Comrade Geshev, a dour apparatchik in a brown suit, gave The Speech. All his speeches were identical and all we heard was a continuous drone. The Russian teacher stood on the platform next to him, in place of honour, weeping into her fringed shawl. She was dressed in black, like the grieving woman on the second floor of our apartment block. It was, she told us through a microphone, a sad day for everyone in our two brotherly countries. I wondered how you could be sad for someone you didn't actually know, but I knew there were questions you didn't ask. When we were finally released and allowed inside, I saw that Brezhnev's bushy-eyebrowed portrait was guarded outside the director's office by star pupils who stood erect and proud. Had I tried harder at Russian, I too might have had that honour, I reflected, and been discharged from Russian classes. At last, a reason for genuine sadness.

A reason for geniune interest in Russian came in the form of a pop song, 'A Million Scarlet Roses'. It was performed by none other than the rising star of Soviet pop music Alla Pugacheva, who sang it with glossy lipstick, white furs, soulful eye-shadow, and enormous hair. The only bit of the song I could understand was the refrain ('millions, millions, millions of scarlet roses') and one evening, when the glittery Alla was on TV, I asked my mother to translate the song for me.

And here was the story – a true story, my mother said – of a poor painter who loved an actress so much that he sold all his paintings to buy her a sea of roses. When she woke up and opened her window, she thought she was dreaming: the street was all awash with roses. She wondered who this fabulously rich admirer was. And down in the street – my mother stifled a sob – stood the ruined painter. It was romance on a grand scale, and it was like nothing else we had in our lives. It was also proof that Russian songs could be more personal than the military choir of 'Rise, oh Mighty Country'.

Around that time, I also became infatuated with Pushkin's novel in verse, *Evgenii Onegin*. The story of the noble Tatiana and the tormented Evgenii in nineteenth-century Russia was worlds away from grammatical cases at the blackboard. Here were deadly duels, impossible love, philosophical musings about happiness, and amazing clothes. And it was all in couplets. I suddenly saw the point of learning the genitive case. The Russian teacher started smiling at me, and calling me Kapka instead of Number Sixteen.

A good young citizen excels not only in the classroom, of course, but also outside, and our extra-curricular activities were just as important as lessons. On Civil Defence days, we were taken into the city centre and down into a stuffy, claustrophobic underground bunker. There, we saw horrific photographs of devastated places called Hiroshima and Nagasaki, and of people wearing gas-masks. The masks themselves were there too, and we all had to put one on, to get used to it, for the day when the Fascist-imperialist enemy attacked our Fatherland with a nuclear bomb. The scenario was deadly serious, but practising in masks with elephant-like trunks at the front was hilarious – until you couldn't breathe any more and the mask had to be removed by a teacher.

Then there were the visits to the mausoleum of our Great Leader Georgi Dimitriov. In the arctic chill and silence of the marble tomb, I stood in line behind my comrades for a peek at the great man. I wondered if the two young guards who stood, stiff and unblinking, on each side of the display cabinet were in fact frozen solid. The Great Leader had a slightly more relaxed air, but only because he was horizontal. He lay in a glass box, dressed in a suit, and looked like he was made of plastic.

The good citizen must also be a good Pioneer. The Pioneers' uniform was white shirts, navy-blue pleated skirts or trousers, and red polyester tie-scarves soaked in the blood of dead partisans. The Pioneers took over from the youngest comrades, the blue-scarfed Chavdars, who had to recite the following programmatic lines:

> The little Chavdar works hard.
>
> At home and in school
>
> the little Chavdar is number one.
>
> He knows: he'll be a Pioneer soon.

After the Pioneers came the Comsomol at high school, culminating in full-blown Communist Party membership, which was optional. Being a Pioneer wasn't. It was indistinguishable from going to school. To be thrown out of the Chavdars/Pioneers/Comosomol was a rare but complete social disgrace, and could end with a Corrective Labour School.

Each class was a Unit, and each Unit had its Pioneer committee: the Unit Leader was responsible for the overall excellence of the Unit, followed by a Unit Secretary who handled the funds, a Cultural Officer responsible for events, and the lesser posts of Physical Education Officer and Recycled Paper Officer, who was only activated on Recycled Paper Day when each Unit competed for the top quota in accumulated used paper. The bulk of used paper was supplied by *The Worker's Deed* to which some parents subscribed. Mine didn't, so my quota of used paper usually consisted of my parents' old maths manuals. Turning up empty-handed was a disgrace for your Unit.

My default career as a Pioneer started with the post of Cultural Officer, which I did resentfully. I didn't want to be organizing the Unit's cultural events, I wanted to be organizing my own culture. But the Unit had to be present at key cultural moments, such as the 'Flag of Peace' Assembly on the outskirts of the Youths. There, we posed for class photographs in a concrete, open-air complex called The Bells. The Bells featured the national bell of every country in the world, and after the photos and the speeches we were allowed to toll the bells and have a picnic on the grass.

The idea of the Bells and the Assembly came from the Minister of Culture, Lyudmila Jivkova, daughter of Comrade Jivkov. She was an enigmatic woman who wore an eccentric Eastern turban. The intention was to unite all the children of the world – white, black, yellow, red – in an assembly of peace and comradeship. Surrounded by 120 national bells, in my red Pioneer scarf, I wondered when the colourful children of the world would finally arrive.

They never did, and Lyudmila died suddenly and mysteriously, aged thirty-nine. Her death, like her life, was a State secret. Now we know that the autopsy report was signed by eminent professors who were not there. Speculation abounded and still abounds today: illness; accident; suicide; KGB-inspired murder. After all, the Soviets had issued several warnings about her internationalist projects, her interest in mystic teachings and unorthodox faiths, and her promotion of modern and ancient cultures. She created hundreds of art museums, opera houses, concert halls, and Sofia's most prestigious humanities college for classical studies. She was a follower of Agni-Yoga teaching and made regular trips to India. In short, she was straying from the ideological struggle of Mature Socialism in its most advanced stage. After her death, an official cult of her person was loudly proclaimed, but her progressive cultural initiatives were quietly strangled.

Around that time, I was relieved of the Cultural Officer post, and suddenly promoted to the terrifying heights of a Unit Leader. Whenever Class E was called out by the school officials, I would step forward, sick with stage fright, with my right arm lifted across my face in the Pioneer salute, a salute separated from its Nazi cousin only by a fold in the elbow, to report to the more senior Brigade Leader.

Brigade Leader: 'Unit ready?'

Unit Leader (me): 'Always ready!'

It wasn't clear to me what exactly we were ready for, but I was certainly always ready to step back into the ranks of my unit and fade away from the spotlight.

In the classroom, though, it was less easy to say your lines and disappear, especially with the arrival of our new Class Supervisor, Comrade Gesheva. She was short and neckless, with bulldog jowls. For a while we thought she was Comrade Geshev's wife, a match made in comrades' heaven, but they only shared a surname and an ideology.

Unfortunately, Comrade Gesheva was a teacher of literature, my favourite subject. She wore a worker's buttoned mantle over her civilian clothes, as if she was in a factory. And as far as she was concerned, she was: School 81 was a factory for education. There were two ways with Comrade Gesheva: public praise or public humiliation.

She couldn't stand 'hooligans' and 'retards', which meant anyone who was late for class or slightly dim. Her favourite method of discipline was to attack the top of your head with the blunt end of a key that she always carried in her mantle pocket, or to pinch your ear lobe with her sharply manicured nails. If you weren't on the receiving end of her corporal punishment, she tried to make you complicit in inflicting them on others.

By Gesheva's decree, one of my tasks as the Unit Leader, and the tallest girl in the class, was to intercede in hooligan fights, a manicured index finger helpfully directing me towards the fray. I was also expected to report on my comrades, to her and to their parents. Who was exhibiting signs of being a hooligan or a retard, who had said what about whom, who had behaved badly? It was a daunting task, made more complicated by the fact that one of the two chief hooligans was my friend Toni. Toni, the son of our balcony neighbours with the Lada, had been my best friend since we were seven. He ran a bit wild at school as a result of having a father with great ambitions for his kids, and even greater anger management problems, which resulted in beatings for Toni. My first task as a Unit Leader was to go to Toni's parents and report his bad behaviour. After several days of anxious procrastination, I finally confessed to my mother, who promptly gave me my first lesson in ethics. It's not your job to report to anybody, she said. You are his friend.

Comrade Gesheva's response to my failure revealed that she followed a different ethical code. It came in the form of a brief but devastating speech in front of the class: 'The fish starts rotting from the head' (me), and 'The class must know that its Unit Leader is a zero. Kapka, you are a complete zero. You must reflect on this very carefully.'

Meanwhile, other girls were throwing Gesheva morsels of information about well-known hooligans like Nikifor. Nikifor had no full-time father, and his mother was an alcoholic. In other words, they were official degenerates, which in a strange way proved useful for Nikifor: he had nothing to lose. He was beyond Gesheva's terror tactics. He sneered at her and her key, driving her into a frothing rage.

But after a traumatic accident in which the son of a teacher was pushed out of the top-floor window and shattered on the pavement below in a mess of glass, Nikifor disappeared. An awed whisper went around: he had been sent to a Corrective Labour School. It would be years before any of us saw Nikifor again and I imagined his life there, guarded by growling, whip-wielding Cerberuses exactly like Gesheva.

My own fear of Gesheva manifested itself in two ways: in increasingly regular attacks of gastritis and in increasingly escapist books. I was joined in my psychological truancy by Esther, who was congenitally incapable of toeing the official line. We tried to write science-fiction stories which closely resembled the translated books we devoured – *2001: A Space Odyssey*, Isaac Asimov's *I, Robot*, and Ray Bradbury's *I Sing the Body Electric!* and *Dandelion Wine*. Our characters had suitably foreign names like Peter and Jack. Esther was a better sci-fi writer than me, which I put down to her otherworldly physicist parents.

We followed fanatically the TV series *Blake's Seven*, and we played teleporting games where you left behind the mud of the Youths and suddenly found yourself in an invented world, whose small but select populations spoke like characters from *The Hitchhiker's Guide to the Galaxy* and said things like 'Don't let me depress you' or 'You're turning into a penguin, stop it immediately!' Around the same time, we were gripped with *Star Wars* mania. Life was only worth living if you could see *The Empire Strikes Back* and *Return of the Jedi* for the third time. The trade in Turbo chewing-gum wrappers reached a frenzy, and my bookmarks now consisted of wrappers with Luke Skywalker, Han Solo and Princess Lea gazing across distant galaxies. If my schooling under Gesheva was a long ideological battle, it was my decadent Western fantasies that triumphed in the end.

The year was 1986 and our primary school class now dissolved into the big bad world of secondary education. As some stayed behind and others went to specialist schools, all of my classroom friendships, except Esther, ended with School 81 and the onset of pubescence (Toni, lying: I'm screwing girls. Me, jealous: I bet they have syphilis). But my non-school friends, the kids of my parents' friends, were there to stay. After all, our parents shared the same world: a world where political jokes and birthday parties were the norm, and you were united by a distrust of the idiots in the brown suits.

Thanks to my mother's unfulfilled childhood dream to learn the piano, I was also about to discover the existence, right there in the Youths, of a parallel world of the muses and music, a world away from the stiff ranks of the Pioneers, and the utilitarian ways of Comrade Gesheva.

My piano teacher Keti Marchinkova was exotic in every conceivable way – foreign name, blonde face, husbandless, and childless. Her grandmother had been German. She lived with her mother in a central city apartment. It was an enchanted place: cats in the communal courtyard; giant plants inside the darkened, carpeted rooms smelling of cigarette ash, perfume, and closeted bourgeoisie. Keti's red lipstick left sensuous traces on the edge of glasses. The scent of exotic flowers enveloped the piano while her sturdy fingers worked miracles in C minor.

I was officially enrolled in the children's music school Flag of Peace, which meant that I initially had my lessons with Keti in one of the Youths' Cultural Centre premises. The space allocated to us was a squat, concrete trafopost which consisted of two rooms: a tiny room with a piano, and a larger room for cultural activities like concerts by the Centre's pupils. The heating inevitably broke down in winter, and Keti wore her coat and shawl, her throat constantly tickled by a bohemian smoker's cough. The massive electricity transformer was right next to us, humming its industrial radio-magnetic noises, driving my teacher mad with tinnitus, and chipping away at our immune systems.

Keti seemed to have stumbled into the Youth world of panels, overcrowded buses and nervy working families by mistake. She belonged to another era or another country, and yet here she was, sitting with me and the electricity transformer, patiently nurturing my musical efforts from scales all the way to Beethoven.

'*Moderato!* Slow down, are you late for an appointment or something?'

'Well, if he could hear this, uncle Mendelssohn would turn in his grave.'

Over time, my parents befriended her, and she would join other family friends at our birthday parties, the only arty person in a crowd of 'poor engineers', mathematicians and physicists. One night, she drifted away from the adults who were talking and chain-smoking in the living-room, into the kitchen where we kids were playing. 'This is a great party,' she said. 'It's wonderful to feel part of the family.' Her eyes were bloodshot, she was a bit drunk, and a pang of sadness went through me, for her or for me, I didn't quite know. I wanted her to be part of the family, but I knew that we were far too ordinary for her, and at the end of the evening, she would always walk off into the blackness and the late-night buses alone.

Some afternoons, I went to see her play at the plush café of the National Palace of Culture, the epicentre of all things luxurious. In the café, bigwigs and State-approved artistes sipped cocktails and nibbled complicated cakes. Official guests were brought here to admire the dramatic view of Vitosha Mountain. Jaws clenched, fingers steady, Keti accompanied a violinist. Afterwards, proud and nervous, and introduced to everyone as her star pupil, I sat with the musicians who smoked, drank heavily, and laughed at cryptic jokes. She spoilt me with cakes, but ate nothing herself. The tension in the smoky café was palpable, and I always felt on edge. I put it down to feeling an outsider among the artistes. But with my childish antennae, I also sensed that Keti was grappling with something in the shadows that only she could see.

Gradually, as we got to know each other well, she started sharing with me scraps of horror which jarred with her glamorous persona.

'If I sound a bit funny today, it's because I had a tooth extracted yesterday. The dentist was a charming man, didn't give me anaesthetic. Fortunately I fainted, so I don't remember much.'

'A sewage pipe burst in our building last week. I had to wade ankle-deep in excremental matter trying to fix it. Eventually the plumber came. A day later. Ah, what an interesting life we have! OK, Hungarian Dance number five. Let's hear it.'

I hummed Mozart sonatas to myself, trying to block out these black visions, which she had dragged out of some garbage dump. I attempted to push them back, desperate that they wouldn't engulf Keti and her piano. Because if she succumbed to the forces of darkness, what hope was there for the rest of us?

Keti's hopes for my musical career ended when my parents decided that I should apply for a language college. A State education in music or any of the performing arts – or anything else prestigious – involved either genius or heavy connections, and I had neither. My parents were humble technocrats, and although we managed to dig up a distant relative who was a famous composer, it just wasn't enough. It didn't help that I suffered from crippling stage fright, and the sight of any audience bigger than my parents and Keti made me forget my own name along with Dvořák's Hungarian Dance number five. But Keti continued to give me lessons, now privately, in her central city apartment, where I drugged myself on the heady scents of perfume, cats, and old velvet upholstery, while she treated me to hot chocolate and petits-fours.

Keti and I were forced apart the year after Chernobyl, when I went into hospital with a rare auto-immune disease. She brought me rich home-made desserts which I was too sick to eat. I was grateful that she still wanted to see me despite my abject failure not only as her star pupil but as a pianist altogether. When I finally came out of hospital, Keti treated me to a celebratory dinner at a swanky restaurant in town. It wasn't actually swanky, and it was more akin to a canteen than a restaurant, but I was impressed. There were only a few restaurants in Sofia, and I'd only been out to dinner once before, to The Hungarian Restaurant where my father had come to blows with a rude waiter in a greasy waistcoat over some meatballs.

Now it was just me and Keti, and for the first time she invited me to call her simply Keti instead of Comrade Marchinkova. The pork chops and mashed potato was the *plat du jour* and the only *plat*, and I was puffed up with the adult luxury of it all. But as I sipped my yellow lemonade, I sensed that something had shifted in her diva universe. Or was it that the hospital ordeal had relieved me of my childish illusions and now I saw her through different eyes? Either way, Keti was no longer the princess of Bohemia. She had put on a lot of weight, and her fair complexion had gone grey, with dark rings around her green eyes. She chain-smoked and didn't touch her pork chops. She talked nervously, racked by that deep smoker's cough that no longer sounded romantic.

'Life doesn't always turn out the way we want,' she said, blowing rings of smoke away from the table. 'I never thought I'd be a piano teacher, for example. I was already started on a piano concert career at the Conservatory. Then I broke my wrist, and thanks to our wonderful doctors, it never healed properly. So that put me out of circulation as a pianist, and I had to fall back on the flute as my second-best instrument. But I didn't love the flute. I didn't love it.

'Sometimes life just happens to you. Don't let it happen to you, Kapka. And don't let other people dictate their terms to you. When I got pregnant, my husband asked me to abort. Then he left me to run away to the West, but that's another story. The abortion was botched up, illegal doctors and... Anyway, you're too young to know such things. I couldn't have children after that. But it was my mistake, I was young and stupid. I could have had two girls like you and your sister, someone to love...'

I couldn't think of any grown-up response to this, so I said, 'Aren't you hungry?' She wasn't. She was fed up with pork chops and with life. She gave me her dinner and I ate it with a heavy heart, so I wouldn't have to speak.

Somewhere along the way, I had lost Keti. I had lost her to that unnamed darkness that slowly drains luminous people first of their dreams, then of their beauty, and finally of their lifeblood. Keti was too refined for our lumpen world of humming trafoposts, burst sewage pipes, and dentists who pulled out teeth without anaesthetic. Between the garbage dump and her piano, the battle was cruelly unequal. I went home on the bus that evening, sick with pork chops and with the awful knowledge that something was very wrong.

Not just with us, as I had thought until now, but with our world. And somehow, it was worse this way, much worse. It meant that to survive and thrive, you had to be more like Comrade Gesheva and less like Keti. And I wanted to be like Keti.

This was the last time I saw her. Several years later, when we emigrated to New Zealand, she wrote, saying how happy she was that we were in paradise, asking if I could still play Dvořák's Hungarian Dances. I wrote back, lying, awkward, finding little to say.

In 1997, news reached us that she had died of lung cancer. She was fifty. I didn't even know she'd been ill. In the excitement and trauma of immigration, I'd almost forgotten her. And to my lasting regret, I had never found a way to thank her for lighting up my ugly Youth with the sparkling gifts of music, beauty, courage and laughter.

4 East and West

The poor cousin syndrome

When my father was eighteen, his school band unwittingly revolutionized the provincial town of Pavlikeni by playing a Beatles song at a school festival. Someone, somehow, had got hold of the music sheets and the lyrics. The four teenagers, including my father on accordion and my uncle on the guitar, accompanied the singer who shyly mouthed the lyrics to 'And I Love Her', without understanding a word, because the approved foreign languages at school were German and French. So they strummed their guitars, and avoided making eye contact with the local Party functionaries in the audience. The reason why such brazen display of Western decadence didn't lead to any punishment was that nobody, including the local Party functionaries, knew what The Beatles actually sounded like. After all, they were banned.

However, everybody knew what the dissident cult Russian song-writer Vladimir Vysotsky sounded like, although he too was officially banned. It was from him that my father took his cue on the guitar. Vysotsky died of alcoholism and exhaustion in 1980, but I didn't realize this because my father, together with the entire Soviet Union and a large part of the Russian-speaking Soc Camp, went on listening to his records well into the nineties. It wasn't just the minor-key chords that touched a chord in my father's guitar. It was the fact that Vysotsky's bilious, ironic lyrics told the story of the ordinary Socialist citizen.

One of my parents' favourites was 'Moscow–Odessa', where the singer is stuck at Moscow airport as his flight to Odessa is cancelled. All other routes are open – Leningrad, Tbilisi, Paris, London, Delhi – places where the sun shines and tea grows – but no, he must go to Odessa where heavy snowfall is expected for the next three days. Finally, in despair, he decides to hell with it, he's getting on the next plane, no matter where it's going.

To me, all his songs sounded the same: an angry guy shouting musically in Russian. But for my parents, the song was rife with metaphors of frustrated escape in general, and escape from Moscow in particular.

Both my parents went on occasional work trips to Moscow. My mother and her colleagues visited some sort of sister Central Institute for Computational Technology where Bulgarian-made computers were tested and sold.

To the vast wasteland of Soviet Russia, little Bulgaria was a sunny, friendly back garden of agricultural plenty and shops semi-full of goods. So some of the institute's more enterprising employees snapped into action and took along bagfuls of Bulgarian-made trainers and proto-jeans. In the parks of Moscow, they sold them surreptitiously to passers-by, at top rouble. With the proceeds, they bought Yunost TVs and whatever else was for sale that week in Moscow.

In my mind, there was a black hole to the east of Bulgaria, an antiplace where things and people got lost. That was Moscow, and Moscow appeared to be in the centre of an even bigger black hole, the Soviet Union. The Soviet Union was officially referred to as 'the big Soviet land', 'our big brother', and 'the Brotherly Soviet Country', appellations that for some reason sounded funny in the mouths of my parents and their friends.

From my parents' accounts of their work trips, the Brotherly Soviet Country sounded to me like a very cold Bulgaria on a massive scale, but without the watermelons and tomatoes, the skiing, the sea, the people I knew, and with the addition of six grammatical cases. Moscow was a place with shops even emptier than ours. A place where women wore heavy-duty fur hats in winter, and didn't remove them indoors all day long, so as not to show their ruined hairdos. A place which contained Siberia and Stalin. A place where people queued up for kilometres without knowing what they were buying because anything was good — if they already had it, they could trade it for something else later. It was a place where people didn't live in their own apartment, but rented, because ownership was a capitalist crime. A place where people ate desperate things like black bread and black caviar, and drank vodka, and froze to death in the icy streets. A place from which all my parents' nice Russian friends had obviously escaped. A place from which my parents were always grateful to return.

One night, I woke up to the sound of my parents talking. My father was back from Moscow. We crawled out of bed to see him. 'I'm home, I'm home,' he kept saying. He looked slightly unhinged, his hair dishevelled, his horn-rimmed glasses misted over. He smelt of foreign winter. 'Now calm down,' my mother was saying, but she wasn't that calm either. She looked upset, as if he almost hadn't made it.

Which was exactly right. That night, his return flight from Moscow had been cancelled due to an engineering fault. He was facing a night on a park bench: no hotel would take him in after his official visitor's permit had expired. Officially, he'd be an over-stayer and could even be arrested. The other Bulgarians on the flight were in the same plight. They remonstrated with the staff of Balkan Airlines until the harassed Bulgarian pilot came out and explained the situation. One of our two engines is faulty, he said, that's why the flight is cancelled. We could still fly, but with one engine it'll be at your own risk. Do you still want to fly tonight? The vote was unanimous and jubilant: a quick death was better than another night in Moscow.

So much for the East. The West, however, was the stuff of exotic rumour and fantastic legend. Occasionally, it reached us in the shape of glossy objects. My mother's cousin, for example, lived in friendly Libya for many years, where he built dams in the desert. His family lived back in Sofia, and they had a magnificent VCR with a remote control. My atlas confirmed that Libya was technically in Africa, which was in the south, but judging from the lavish things the cousin brought us, it was also somehow in the West.

He showered us with gifts like oval Lux soap bars with women smiling on the packets, colourful panties for the girls in packs of threes, chocolate bars in shiny foil wrappers which I smoothed out and kept between the pages of books, roll-on Nivea deodorants the likes of which I'd never seen. These objects were like messages in a bottle from the other side of the divide, but I couldn't tell whether they were friendly or not. They seemed coded, sealed inside their smug luxury.

Occasionally, the West assumed a human face and upset the order of things. On the Black Sea coast where we went for our summer holidays, the West became flesh and blood – and occasionally bare breasts, the prerogative of their decadent society. But you knew better than to stare at their bodies, clothes, towels, and bright Nivea bottles. You pretended you weren't impressed by them and just spied on them from the corner of your eye, fascinated, while reading your school-prescribed summer titles, and hoped that one of the blond boys would notice you.

One summer, one of them did, and we spent two weeks sending surreptitious, unspoken messages of lust and longing across the beach, while our parents dozed in the sun, dull and oblivious. One day, he stood behind me in the ice-cream queue, causing me to seize up with excitement and nearly faint. That's as close as we got. I never found out where he was from, I didn't care, and it didn't matter: he was out of reach, they would soon fold up their beach umbrella and leave my world. Pretending to sleep, I drenched my pillow with bitter tears every night in the darkness of our single rented room. One night, my parents had had enough and told me off, and bawling my eyes out under the full moon, I started walking towards the hotel where I knew the object of my desire was. My father ran after me and brought me back to our room, but I resented him even in his kindness. I resented them both for sharing the prison of our single concrete room without privacy, for having no choice, no foreign friends, and no Nivea bottles.

But we did have foreign friends of sorts. My father's Technical Institute 'Vladimir Ilich Lenin' had regular visitors from abroad, mainly France and Japan. And because my father couldn't afford to invite them to a restaurant, he invited them home. My mother would rush from work with bags of shopping, while my father turned up at the last moment, escorting the guest. After all, a foreigner would never find Block 328, or even Youth 3, unaided.

The foreigners were always extremely friendly in their lightly textured foreign clothes and shoes. They laughed with my parents, and expressed their appreciation of the food and wine, and especially of Rila Monastery where my parents would always take them, because that's where you took foreign visitors to show off our heritage. And after they left, the foreigners sent us exquisite cards from the other side. For a moment, you could even think we were equal.

But we knew, and they knew, that we weren't equal. Behind the laughter and the wine, I sensed my parents' permanent nervous cringe. They knew the foreign guests saw the ugly panels, the cramped apartments, the mud, the overflowing rubbish bins, the stray dogs, the empty shops, the crappy cars, the idiots in the brown suits, and they were ashamed.

Some of my parents' friends learnt to overcome the cringe by rationalizing it.

'Ashamed? I have nothing to be ashamed of,' my mother's cousin said. She was a medical journalist, and had a big, sensuous mouth that laughed a lot. 'On the contrary, I'm proud. Yes, we live in a shitty one-bedroom flat with a cat and an occasional grandmother, and I know exactly when my neighbour has diarrhoea. Even so, I have a medical degree, a journalism degree, a PhD, and three languages. My children are well brought-up and well-dressed despite the empty shops, and I can make a birthday cake without flour, sugar, baking powder, or milk. If anyone should be ashamed, it's *them*, not us!'

This struck me as a clever argument. But it didn't help my mother. In fact, it made it worse. It confirmed that we were living in a banana republic, but minus the bananas. It confirmed that the more languages you spoke, the more cakes without ingredients you made, the more political jokes you told, the more wretched you were.

My first real encounter with the outside world occurred at age nine, in Macedonia across the border. The prosperous veneer of people and things there stunned me. They spoke almost the same language as us, and looked the same as us, but ate chocolates with hazelnuts and peaches without down. And bananas. I had never seen bananas before. They sat in a bowl on my uncle's table. I didn't dare touch them. 'Are they plastic?' I whispered to my mother. They were real. My cousins overheard us and laughed. I was mortified. Everybody gave me chocolates and patted me on the head. It was obvious that we were the poor cousins.

The reason why we went to Macedonia – which was also inside Yugoslavia – was that my grandmother Anastassia (she of the seaside holidays) came from a small lake town called Ohrid. From there, we could see the hazy Albanian mountains. They looked no different from our mountains, but apparently they were.

My uncle, a fat, jolly professor of physics, had been to Albania's Tirana University many times, and he told us how the shops in Tirana had nothing except loaves of bread piled up on the floor. He told us how the border guards each time unlocked the eagle-embossed gates at the border, let my uncle and his driver in, and then locked them again. He told us that the people of Albania weren't allowed to go anywhere, not even to the Brotherly Soviet Country. It sounded like a terrible place. So despite the humiliation, it was better to be the poor cousin and enjoy the perks than to have poor cousins yourself.

Two years later, we went to East Berlin, invited by one of my father's colleagues, a university professor called Wolf. The city looked bright and glitzy, a kind of dress rehearsal for a Western city. The large avenues and buildings, the blond people and *wurst* stalls, the foreign language, it all appeared festive and exotic to my eyes. Even the Wall, when we glimpsed it, was exciting, because on the other side was the West. We could almost hear the other side, almost see it. It was a mind-blowing concept, being so close, and I held my breath.

My parents and Wolf stood by the Brandenburg Gate barricades, their backs to the Wall and its armed guards. They didn't say much, they just stood there, as if paying their respects in a graveyard. Wolf's parents were on the other side, and I wondered why, but I knew this was one of those questions you didn't ask.

My sister and I ate sandwiches with salami and gherkins. It was like picnicking on the outer edge of our world. We'd gone as far as we could safely go.

That's right, we were safe on our side – safe from the stresses of alien worlds. Perhaps, thanks to the Wall, I would never leave the Soc Camp – and perhaps it was better that way.

After the picnic, we walked back along Unter den Linden, in the deep shadow of the Soviet Embassy, which was the size of a football stadium. I was happy. Like most people on our side, I had internalized oppression. The Wall was already inside me, the bricks and mortar of my eleven-year-old self. The Wall wasn't a place or even a symbol any more. It was a collective state of mind, and there is something cosy, something reassuring in all things collective. Even a prison.

Alexanderplatz, the favourite meeting place in East Berlin, was vast and it had the World Time Clock. I couldn't take my eyes off it, mesmerized by the wild possibilities it suggested: that the places shown on it – Rome, Paris, London – also had a local time, just like us. They had a local time and a local life, so clearly, in some way, they were like us. This was strangely disturbing.

It was much safer to know the world in an abstract way. That way, you didn't have too many doubts. And it's not as if we were ignorant, no. One of my father's educational games on the nine-hour drives to the seaside was 'capitals of the world'. He would say an obscure country, and my sister and I would come up with its capital. Mongolia: Ulan Bator. Angola: Luanda. Chile: Santiago. Uzbekistan: Tashkent – or was it Yerevan? No, Yerevan is Armenia. My father prided himself on knowing every single capital city in the world. My favourites were capitals that sounded the same as their countries: Mexico-Mexico, Panama-Panama, Algeria-Algiers. Those were the most honest never-never-lands.

The world was a geography lesson to us. Clusters of sounds. Coloured patches in the atlas. Radio static. But the order of things was permanently upset in 1984, when my father was granted permission to spend six months as a research fellow at the University of Delft in far-away Holland. It was his first trip west of the Berlin Wall. It was the longest we had been separated as a family since his two-year military service. My mother pined for him, and because he couldn't afford to call us and we couldn't call abroad, we sent him a voice-letter on a cassette, via an acquaintance who was also Holland-bound. My mother recorded her messages late at night, and although she stoically didn't cry, her voice sounds strangely broken on that tape.

He sent back photographs of futuristic-looking buildings, and brick houses along grey canals, and bikes, forests of bikes. He sent photos of friendly-looking people of different races — the other visiting fellows — whose curious names he wrote on the backs of photos. He was cheerfully waving at the camera, looking very thin in his big horn-rimmed glasses.

Here he was, my own dad, blending in with these Westerners, these people who had stepped off the pages of my atlas and somehow ended up in Delft, to become his friends. Just like that. I was at once proud and troubled. Proud that we were no less than them. Troubled by the thought that if it was so easy, so natural, if the people on the other side were so friendly, then what exactly was the Wall protecting us from?

It was protecting us from ourselves, as it turned out. That summer, amazingly, my mother was granted permission to visit my father in Holland. It was her first time West of the Berlin Wall, if we don't count a few visits to Yugoslavia — which, according to the atlas, was east of the Berlin Wall, but for some reason more to the west than East Berlin. It was complicated.

After months of nerve-fraying bureaucratic delay, my mother's travel visa finally arrived and my sister and I were packed off to spend the summer with our paternal grandparents, Kiril and Kapka, in the provincial town of Pavlikeni.

As far as I was concerned, Pavlikeni had nothing going for it. It had no mountain, no sea, no historic houses, just a factory on the outskirts which made spare parts for trains. It also had a park where the blossoming trees gave me hay fever, and a zoo with scabby animals. The most interesting fact I knew about Pavlikeni was that one of the zoo bears had chewed the fingers of a little boy who had fallen into its cage. The boy had survived, and so he joined the handless Chilean guitarist in my imagination.

Nothing ever happened in Pavlikeni's huge, empty square, purpose-built for official parades where dignitaries and citizens gathered on days like 9 September, the anniversary of the day in 1944 when the Soviet Army had liberated us from ourselves. The town had one shop, the half-empty Central Universal Store, which sold desolate things like extra-large cotton underpants, brown pantyhose for women with vein problems, and industrial proletarian bras made not so much for women as for female units. My grandmother bought these things, and I felt both ashamed and sorry for her.

From Pavlikeni, Holland seemed like another planet. My parents may as well have gone into space. What if we never saw them again? It didn't even occur to me to wonder why we, the kids, couldn't go with them. Everybody knew that you couldn't very well come and go as you pleased. After all, once an entire family was in the West, they might like it too much. They might want to stay. And everybody knew this was something defectors did. We weren't defectors, God no! We didn't even know any defectors.

Meanwhile, in Delft, my father had lost half his body weight saving from his meagre university allowance in order to buy luxury goods for the family. In his little campus flat, he'd been living on fried eggs and filter coffee for six months. A contributing factor to this diet was that fried eggs and coffee were the only things he could actually make. But for my mother's arrival, he'd prepared a feast: pork chops and salad, and even a bottle of cheap wine.

As a fellow computer specialist, my mother visited the university. And it was here, in the university toilets, that she broke down. It wasn't the supernaturally clean streets, the tidy bike lanes, the smiley people, but the university toilets that tipped her over from stunned awe into howling despair.

Now, there is something I must explain about Bulgarian public toilets. First, they were generally a hole in the floor, Turkish-style. Secondly, and more importantly, they were the ante-chambers of Hell. Wherever you were, however desperate your bladder and bowel situation, you held it in. You didn't eat, you didn't drink, you didn't go, until such time as a home toilet became available. At school, at university, at work, in hospital, and especially at railway stations, toilets were for dire emergencies only. And it showed.

If public toilets could be considered barometers of national self-esteem, then it was safe to say that the nation had none. But if they could be considered yet another tool of the State apparatus, it is safe to say that the State didn't like its citizens enough to clean the citizens' public toilets. It wanted its citizens to be publicly smeared with private shame. It wanted to break you with sheer excremental brutishness.

My mother had experienced the toilets of hospitals after giving birth, during kidney surgery, during her mother's hospitalization with cancer. She had endured the toilets at the Central Institute of Computational Technology, and the toilets at freezing railway stations. And now there she stood, in the sparkling, perfumed, pink-toilet-papered, flower-arranged, mirrored, white marble toilet of Delft University, clean as a surgery theatre, gilded as an opera hall, bigger than our apartment in Youth 3, and she cried.

My father's Dutch colleague, who was waiting for her in his office, became worried after a while and knocked on the door. 'Are you OK?' She wasn't. But even with enough English, she couldn't have explained her particular affliction to the well-meaning Dutchman in corduroy trousers.

Her next nervous collapse occurred in a department store, where she and my father had gone to buy things for us, the kinds of things that in Sofia were only available in Korekom, special dollar shops frequented by foreigners, Party officials, and those with connections. My sister and I only ever enjoyed one thing from Korekom: a small chocolate egg each on the occasion of having our tonsils removed.

A note about Bulgarian shops in the seventies and eighties: they weren't actually shops, not in the conventional sense of the word. They were unheated ground-floor rooms with shelves on which something may – or may not, depending on the day – be displayed, and perhaps even sold, if you could bear to queue up, fight with other citizens, and emerge battered but triumphant, clutching a pair of shoes, a kilogram of Cuban oranges, or a tub of margarine. This is why my mother became, early on, an expert tailor. She made most of our clothes, and her own. She couldn't bear to dress us in what she described as 'orphanage clothes'. But some things she couldn't make – shoes, for example, or knitwear.

Shopping, like most unpleasant things except fixing leaky cars and tiling bathrooms, was a woman's job. As a result, my father couldn't understand why I sometimes wore ugly black shoes with laces, fit for a senior Party functionary, instead of something more girly and cheerful; why my sister wore a coat a size too big one winter; why my mother gave him, just before Holland, a fuzzy red jumper the colour of a road accident. It's not as if she didn't have taste. It's not as if they didn't have money.

No, it was the shops that had neither taste nor money, just like the State that owned them and kept them half-empty. That way, the citizens were grateful when something – anything – was released. The operational phrase was 'let out on the market'. They have let out Cuban oranges this week! They have let out men's jumpers! They have let out red children's boots in the Central Universal Store!

I want new boots, my five-year-old sister declared, sick of wearing my old clothes and shoes, so off we went, to buy boots for Assia. The Central Universal Store was not universal, but it was central, and it was, occasionally, a store. It stood in a massive, multi-storeyed stone building, next door to the Communist Party HQ. The avuncular portraits of Lenin and Georgi Dimitriov looked down disapprovingly on the materialistic mothers of Sofia who flocked here desperately whenever something was let out. The State only let out a limited number of each item, and you had to fight for it.

That day, half of Sofia's mothers fought for red boots while a handful of distressed-looking militiamen tried to hold the crowds back from the shoe counter, to prevent small children being crushed to death. By the time we arrived, children were already crying, scared for their dishevelled mothers and sensing disappointment on the boot front. My mother took one look at this scene, and quietly told Assia that she might have to do without new boots that winter. But luck was on our side: a woman had grabbed two different sizes for her child, just in case, and gave my mother the spare one, just the right size. My sister – who still remembers those boots twenty years later – walked out in her red boots, along with several hundred other children. Together, they formed a rag-tag army of little red-booted soldiers marching across the empty parade square between the Central Universal Store and the Party HQ.

Which is why, when my mother stood in the children's section of the departmental store in Delft, and saw shelf upon shelf of children's boots, all different colours and shapes, sizes for everybody, and not a single harassed woman or sobbing child in sight, she suddenly felt unwell.

And when she stood in the men's clothes section, where jumpers of every colour under the sun were folded and stroked by the pale hands of shop assistants, and she remembered her triumph with that fuzzy-red jumper wrenched from the clutches of some greedy woman buying in bulk, and then the quiet distaste of my father with his ugly present, she suddenly felt like throwing up.

My father, also overcome by this orgy of abundance, and sweating in his fuzzy-red jumper, helped her down the escalators and out of the store, and they stepped into the tidy street where people on bicycles breezed past them, and they held each other for a while.

My parents returned home triumphant and laden with presents. It looked like they'd smuggled back the entire contents of Holland's department stores. Our apartment in Youth 3 was transformed into a Dutch doll's house: canvas blinds in our bedroom, printed with little pig-tailed girls. Pink pens and pencils on our desks. In the living-room, an enormous silver Phillips TV with a remote control and a matching silver Phillips stereo with a double cassette-player. What's this? My five-year-old sister picked up the remote control. My father showed her the plus and minus volume buttons, and said 'this one is for fat, and this one is for thin'. My sister kept pressing on the plus button. It doesn't work, she declared, it's not making me fat.

They brought records of Western pop music you couldn't buy in Bulgaria, like Barry Manilow and a two-record album *The Best of The Beatles* — finally, twenty years late, my father could listen to his favourite band. A pair of tiny wooden clogs, a gift from my father's Dutch colleague, which took pride of place in our living-room. A tin of salted, peeled peanuts. We had peanuts, of course, but they were unprocessed and sold on street stalls. Someone in Holland had shelled, peeled and salted these peanuts especially for us. A giant packet of raisins. There were no raisins in Bulgaria, only grapes. Next, an electric blue T-shirt for me with a girl doing aerobics printed on it, and orange trousers with multiple pockets, in which I felt ultra-cool. In fact, wearing these clothes made me feel so obviously Western that I imagined the envious eyes of all Sofia were on me.

My parents had bought nothing for themselves except the records, but they looked happy to be back – at least my father did, even if he was very thin. My mother seemed a bit sad, a bit subdued, which I assumed was my father's fault, as usual. 'So what is it like there?' I asked them.

'It's another world,' my mother said.

'But it's not that much better,' my father added cheerfully. 'They're just normal people. OK, they have more material things than us, but otherwise their lives are not that different.'

'Of course they are,' my mother insisted. 'Whether we like it or not, they *are* different. They think differently. They take so many things for granted. They have rights, they demand things... They live in another world.'

I realized that it wasn't my father's fault; it was Holland that had made my mother sad, despite all the beautiful things they had bought there.

It was almost as if my parents had traded something in, as if they had crossed some Styx to reach a mythical land, and brought back otherworldly gifts. But in return they had left behind their shadows. And even if my father pretended otherwise, I knew there was something wrong with this exchange. But what was it?

I found the terrible answer to this question the following year, when my father's well-meaning Dutch colleague in corduroy trousers brought his family to visit us. They wanted to see the Bulgarian mountains, they declared on the phone, they wanted to go camping with us.

Feverish preparations began. My parents took time off work. My mother bought provisions. My father lay under the Skoda for an entire weekend, fixing a leak. They started asking around for a tent. A colleague of my father's offered them his. It's small and not very pretty, he said apologetically. It's actually a Russian military tent. Black. Oh it'll be fine, my parents said, it will do the trick. After all, the Dutch will be in a tent too.

But they weren't. They arrived in an enormous, brand-new white campervan. The neighbourhood kids surrounded it, not daring to touch it, their mouths agape. Their fathers came out from beneath their Trabants to gaze sorrowfully at this bird of automobile paradise. A UFO had landed in Youth 3.

The Dutch emerged from their vessel. They were bright, happy people in pastel colours, bouncing in squeaky new Adidas trainers. My father's colleague Hans was enormously tall and white-blond from his eyebrows down to the hairs on his hands. His wife Hannah was plump and practical-looking, like a milkmaid with a crew cut. Their daughter Elke was tall and spindly, with tooth-braces – like my sister – and long blonde hair, unlike anybody I knew. She played with pink and blue rubber horses that had long blond hair too. She gave my sister a rubber monkey, again with blond hair. In return, we gave her the most prized specimens from our paper napkin and stamp collections. There was nothing else we could give her without losing face.

Their son Jurg was a friendly giant. Taller than his father, plumper than his mother, his face erupting with adolescence, he banged his head on the doorframe and spilled into our apartment which suddenly felt like a real doll's house. A race of aliens had invaded our home.

I knew no English and, to my relief, neither did Jurg, who specialized in silent friendliness. I instantly liked him. Hans and Hannah told my parents about their traumatic experience at a campsite on the outskirts of Sofia called the Black Cat. The toilets were unusable, they said, and there was rubbish and dogs everywhere. It was a dump, not a campsite. And they charged them double. My mother disappeared apologetically into the kitchen to prepare lunch, and my father laughed, embarrassed.

In the kitchen, Hans produced a bloody parcel.

'I'm sorry,' he said to my mother, unwrapping the meat, 'we buy it from the shop, and they did not package well.'

My mother looked stressed already. But it wasn't the meat – of course she was used to the bloody meat – it was the Russian tent situation.

'I think we can safely forget about the military tent,' she whispered to my father. He chuckled mirthlessly and surrendered. We would rent a room instead.

The next day, we departed in a slow convoy: the little orange Skoda followed by the giant white campervan. I was proud to be seen by the whole neighbourhood. We didn't just have shiny Dutch objects at home, now we had shiny Dutch people too. For some of the journey my sister and I travelled with them in the campervan.

Everything glittered inside, everything was in different colours: their clothes, their toys, their food. They ate constantly. They ate chocolate-coated biscuits out of a large, elaborate tin that looked fit for a museum display. They ate gelatinous bear-shaped sweets out of another tin. They drank juices from cartons through little straws. They chewed gum, and then they ate again. I had never seen chocolate-coated biscuits, jelly bears, or carton juice. Everything in Bulgaria came out of green bottles or drab plastic wrapping that fell apart the moment you opened it, and sometimes even before. My sister and I sat very still on the padded seats and chewed the jelly bears in awed silence.

Our mountain adventure was fraught with crises. The Dutch parked themselves in a mountain campsite some way above the town of Bansko, and we rented a room in Bansko in the house of a local family. In retrospect, perhaps the alpine ranges of Pirin, the highest in the Balkans, weren't the best introduction to mountainous scenery for people who had never actually seen a mountain. Holland was completely flat, my parents explained, like a plate.

On the first day, we went up in gondola cabins and halfway up the electricity stopped. Elke became hysterical in Dutch, and her mother soon joined her in broken English. It's true that we were hanging above a vertical cliff face, but that's just the way mountains are, and besides, the electricity often stopped on these lifts.

Now I realize that it wasn't simply a fear of heights, but a fear of things breaking down in Bulgaria. If meat came wrapped in brown paper, the campsites were rubbish dumps, and everybody was driving a Trabant, then what was to stop the gondola cabins from plummeting? They didn't want to die on a godforsaken Bulgarian mountain whose name they couldn't even pronounce.

On the second night, the Dutch decided to have a barbecue at the campsite. We have the meat, they said, you just bring some potatoes from the village. My parents went looking frantically for potatoes in Bansko. There was only one shop in town, and all it sold was cigarettes and a few jars containing mystery pickles. In despair, my parents turned to our hosts. They laughed.

'Of course you won't find potatoes in the shop. Or anything else. This is the province, not Sofia. But don't worry, we've got potatoes to feed all of Holland.'

They gave us two kilograms of potatoes from their own garden, which my parents triumphantly delivered to the campsite. Hannah was delighted.

'People in the West say that the East is poor,' she chattered happily as we sat around the fire, munching. 'That is not true. There is everything. Yes, OK, the choice is little, but why do we need all these things in Holland? Ten varieties of potato? And this potato is so delicious.'

My parents exchanged looks and said nothing. It was too complicated to explain about the potatoes.

'We went to the furniture store in Youth 3, near your apartment,' Hannah continued. 'It is not empty. There are some nice bookshelves, and beds on display.'

My parents exchanged looks again. The furniture on display was just that – on display. Those shelves and beds were samples. If you actually wanted to buy something, you signed up at the shop and joined a waiting list. Then a few weeks or months later, you snuck out to the store in the dead of night, to queue up as they unloaded furniture from trucks, and fought tooth and nail for your precious bookshelves. Just because your name was on a list, it didn't guarantee anything. But again, it was too complicated to explain.

Hannah had been for many years a housewife, a profession I'd never heard of before. But now the kids were older, and she was working again. She ran a small kindergarten in their house outside Delft.

'I buy this campervan with money I earn from the kindergarten,' she said.

'I'm very proud with her.' Hans patted her chubby thigh affectionately.

'Yes, it's very beautiful campervan.' My father nodded blankly, looking preoccupied.

'Very beautiful, yes,' my mother repeated, and stared at the fire with a polite smile.

I knew that smile. Each time it said something different, and each time it made my heart sink. This time, it said: I have studied and worked my whole life. I didn't take enough time off work to look after my kids because that's the way it is. We don't have housewives here, but I have effectively been a housewife all my life, while also having a full-time career. My husband never says that he's proud of me. Hannah is a woman without university education and without a career. She is happy with her campervan and her husband is happy with her. This campervan is worth about twenty years of my income. We are twenty years behind them. No, forty.

'I want to lose weight,' Hannah chirped on. 'But not here, I cannot lose weight here. This food is too delicious.'

By now I was madly in love with Jurg, but I sensed that something was definitely wrong that summer night around the crackling fire, under the mountain stars. An invisible army of shadows was tugging at us, at everything.

On the last day, we went off-track and got lost. After many hours of scrambling down a sea of boulders, underneath which gurgled glacial rivers, we made it back to the campsite, sunburnt, dehydrated, and delirious.

The Dutch finally left in their not so shiny campervan. We waved from the pull-up bar outside Block 328, and sighed a collective sigh of relief. And no doubt they did too.

But I also felt bereft. They were going back to where we couldn't follow. They had packed up the world and taken it with them. They had given us a chocolate biscuit from that tin, and then put the lid on.

In my eleven-year-old bones, I now understood why after Holland my father was so thin and my mother so sad. I understood the exchange of ignorance for Western goods. And that understanding hurt like hell.

5 Chernobyl Summer

Life and death in the provinces of Socialism

Three things happened in the year of Chernobyl: my grandfather died of heart failure, my grandmother died of breast cancer, and I grew up.

In the spring of 1986, a rumour circulated that there had been a nuclear incident somewhere in the Soviet Union, in a grim-sounding place that translated meant something like 'Black Place'. Later, much later, the State issued a statement that there was no cause for alarm. To be alarmed was to give in to Western propaganda against the Brotherly Soviet Country.

But Toni's father next door was a physicist at the Academy of Sciences. His job was to measure radiation levels and he was alarmed, very alarmed. He told my parents to stay away from fresh food that year. My parents' life took on fresh new meaning: to source rare foods like powdered milk and tinned feta cheese.

Four days after Chernobyl, on 1 May, Day of Socialist Labour, a festive radioactive rain fell on Sofia. The nation came out for the May Day parade to rejoice and wave carnations and little red flags at the row of Politburo comrades who stood under black umbrellas. My parents went too – the rejoicing was compulsory. But they didn't take us with them this time. My mother had a bad feeling about the rain.

Many people said 'What radioactivity? I can't see anything.' Many people also became suddenly ill and died that year, and in the years to come. One of them was my paternal grandfather Kiril, who died suddenly a month later. The word the family used to describe him was 'short-tempered', shorthand for a one-man terror regime. He and my grandmother, Kapka, were the ones who lived in Pavlikeni, an Exemplary Socialist Town, where my grandfather worked as a vet.

A nameless brown river ran outside my grandparents' 'cooperation', as small apartment blocks were called. They lived in a dark, two-bedroom ground-floor apartment with creaky furniture from the sixties and ambiguous wallpaper. I liked the apartment because it was big and old-fashioned, and I liked grandmother Kapka, although she smelt of Valium and was a little erratic. I could see why: forty years of co-existence with my grandfather Kiril had destroyed her personality. I pitied her so much that often pity became affection.

Grandma Kapka didn't have time for things like cleaning. She was too busy lying in bed trying to meditate back to some semblance of mental health. Despite the filth, the operational phrase in that household was 'sterile cleanliness' – a term that fitted with the ideal of Exemplary Socialist Homes. My grandparents flung 'sterile cleanliness' at you with such conviction that it left you stunned and, they hoped, blind to the truth.

Grandfather Kiril kept everybody within shouting range in a constant state of alert. When he ran out of insults for his wife, her family, my mother, and my mother's family, he moved onto the neighbours and, when necessary, to passers-by. From the mosquito-netted ground-floor window where he stood like a bulldog at the kennel's door, he greeted them with a sour smile, then as they moved out of earshot, he held forth on their suspect spouses and scrofulous children, and the illnesses which they deserved.

It was simple: everyone who wasn't of his blood was an enemy, and women were doubly so. Women were the fertilizer from which sons grew in order to continue the bloodline. His own mother, also married to a 'short-tempered' man, had tried to drown herself in the nearest river no less than three times, and each time she'd been dragged back – after all, who would cook and clean for the men?

The only person Kiril seemed to like was my younger cousin. The reason was that my younger cousin was male, and carried my grandfather's name. He was clearly destined for great things. My sister, my elder cousin and I were girls, but we were also of grandfather Kiril's blood, which presented him with a dilemma. He tried to be nice to us. He once took us along on one of his veterinary calls. It was an educational visit – get the city kids familiar with the animal world. After years in Youth 3, I couldn't tell a lamb from a dog. But I could tell a pig when I saw one, and that one was huge. He injected the beast with some drug, and it squealed and kicked so violently that I ran, in the grips of my first phobia. After that, the fear of the pig and the fear of my grandfather Kiril somehow became confused. The very word 'veterinary' still carries, irrationally, the piggish weight of his contempt for the world of humans.

Grandmother Kapka took me and my sister on therapeutic walks. We went mulberry-picking in the park, to see the scabby animals in the zoo, and to the pine forest above town. Grandmother Kapka often seemed absent, as if she existed somewhere on the periphery of her own life. As if, like her mother-in-law, she could drift off into the nearest river any day. Sometimes, in these soul-mending moments, she picked up the pieces of her tattered self. We played card games on benches, ate the greasy pastries and meatballs she had made at home, and gossiped about the town people – who'd married, who'd died – while she knitted endless, shapeless doilies for our dowries.

We often took along my best and only Pavlikeni friend, the blonde and downy Malina. She was from the same 'cooperation' and I had a crush on her brother Ivo. Malina's father, the director of a local factory, had just died of cancer. Malina and I hung out in the communal vegetable garden, and in between the tomato vines we spied the young army recruits lodging in a warehouse building next door. I was sometimes allowed to visit Malina's apartment, which was an oasis of calm voices. We sipped Coke, listened to cool Western music, ate cake, and, once, Ivo and I danced in our socks to 'Nights in White Satin'. He held me delicately and my heart was in my throat. He was a staggering four years older than me.

That summer of Chernobyl, Grandfather Kiril died of a heart attack, no doubt in the middle of a shouting fit. At the wake in the Pavlikeni flat, the stuffy living-room was full of half-rotten flowers and melting chocolates. He lay in an open coffin in a dark suit, his flesh risen like dough. Grandmother Kapka, her head covered in black lace, flung herself on top of him with tearless wails. Public grieving was expected of a dutiful wife, and she had always been dutiful.

But there was something stranger than my grandmother's wailing. It was the sorrow of the man who had been a chauffeur at the veterinary clinic. He stood at the back of the small congregation, raked by silent sobs, black mascara running down his cheeks. Nobody commented. That's the way grandfather Kiril would have liked it – a show of sterile cleanliness.

It took me many years to understand that he had been a deeply unhappy man. That he victimized those weaker than him not only because of his tyrannical character, inherited from his father's tyrannical character, but because he too, in his own unnamed way, had been a victim of something bigger than him. After all, there was no homosexuality under Socialism.

Another thing that didn't exist under Socialism was terminal illness. My other grandmother Anastassia had been wearing a wig for some years now, and I sensed that there was a breast missing somewhere, but the word cancer was never uttered. And because I loved her second best after my parents, I preferred to pretend that she would get well again. But I knew, from the way my mother waved from the bus to the two figures on the seventh-floor balcony, one of them half-blind, her wig slightly askew, and from the way my mother then wept inconsolably like a grown-up child, that she wouldn't get better.

When grandmother Anastassia had been diagnosed with advanced breast cancer four years before, she never heard the oncologist's diagnosis. Eventually, my grandparents must have grasped the truth, but it was never spoken.

Lies, big and small, nibbled at the fabric of our lives like moths. But the truth could be so cruel – remember the Dutch – that it wasn't clear which was worse. So when in doubt denial did the trick. If the Politburo comrades were heroes of the anti-Fascist resistance, if the labour camps were for enemies of the people, if after Chernobyl there was no cause for alarm, if grandfather Kiril's special friend was just his chauffeur, well, then perhaps cancer was just a lump that would go away.

It didn't go away. After Chernobyl, grandmother Anastassia took a sudden turn for the worse. We didn't visit her any more. My mother and her father became full-time nurses at home. Since terminal illness didn't exist, neither did hospital wards for the terminally ill, nor palliative care for the dying. A nurse came by once a week to bring morphine, and my mother slipped her some cash.

We hardly saw my mother these days. From work, she went straight to my grandparents' place. Or accompanied my grandmother to the hospital. Once, I picked up the phone and called grandfather Alexander at home. 'I'm alone,' I said. 'I'm alone too,' he said, and started to cry. I held the receiver against my face, and eventually hung up. I knew what this meant. Grandmother Anastassia would never return to us. We'd never go to the seaside with them again. And I didn't know who I felt most sorry for – my mother who was being worn down by exhaustion and grief, my grandmother who was dying horribly, or my grandfather who couldn't live without her.

My sister and I were evacuated to Suhindol for the summer. Suhindol, or Dry Vale, was half an hour's drive along a potholed road from our paternal grandparents' house in Pavlikeni. It was where my grandparents' competition lived: great-Uncle and Auntie.

My sister and I stood outside their peeling yellow house on the edge of the village, silently grateful for grandfather Kiril's death – it meant that now we got to stay here, and not there. True, the outdoor latrine in the courtyard stank and buzzed with fat flies, but it was an honest peasant latrine.

The creaky wooden gate opened to a vine-shaded courtyard where cheerful lettuces and radishes greeted us from a moist dark patch. Uncle rushed out of the house with alarmed cries – he was always alarmed, his nerves were weak – to greet us. Auntie sat in her cooking chair by the stove, regally fat in a printed cotton gown, stirring heavenly broths. 'Hungry? Auntie will feed you up.'

Uncle was grandfather Kiril's brother, but they might as well have never met. All they had in common was a handsome nose. Auntie, twice the man Uncle was, had the strength of a bull and the cheek-bones of a Tatar. She came from a line of sturdy, wealthy, educated peasants. She knew how to cook, toil in the field, run a big house, and make you feel loved. At high school, thanks to her busty, hippy measurements, Auntie had been named Exemplary Young Sports Woman. Fashions had changed since then, but she lived with the pride of those days and kept up her high-calorie diet. I wondered exactly what sports she had done – perhaps discus- or javelin-throwing.

But Auntie and Uncle were childless. All their lives, they had tried to make up for this terrible Socialist failure – statistic imperfection – by giving everything they had to my father and his twin brother, treating them and us as their own children. Auntie and Uncle had a field where the biggest, juiciest watermelons and tomatoes in Europe grew, and their house overflowed with great excesses of cooked and stored food, crates of soft drinks which Uncle called 'beverages' and drank instead of water, stacks of boxes of chocolates which Uncle 'disclosed' after every meal, and chickens that were slaughtered as soon as we arrived.

They never left their village except for short trips to Sofia. They lived the same life in the same house for half a century: she an accountant at the local council, he an accountant for the local wine cooperative, and in their spare time they toiled in their allotment.

That summer, our two cousins were there to keep us company. The matter of grandmother Anastassia's imminent death was never explicitly named, which allowed me to pretend that I was too young to understand what Auntie meant when she said, sorrowfully shaking her leonine head, 'the worst might happen'.

Activities for children in depressed downtown Suhindol were limited. At night, we watched *The Thornbirds* and fell in love with Richard Chamberlain. In the afternoon, we would drop into the only store for a few bottles of fizzy yellow 'beverages'. The store didn't sell much else, but it did sport a faded red banner which fluttered despondently in the wind while entreating us, 'Let us Construct Socialism with a Human Face!'

This was a motto we had seen elsewhere and even a twelve-year-old could spot the implications: a) Socialism with a Human Face did not occur naturally, it had to be constructed like so many blocks of flats; and b) there was also Socialism with an inhuman face. But such things were difficult to talk about, a bit like 'the worst' and the private chauffeurs of vets.

Another activity was visiting our other great uncle, Uncle Kolyo, who lived in one wing of a vine-shaded house that smelt of roses, yellowed newspapers, and old people's cardigans. Uncle Kolyo was a white-stubbled bachelor, and he specialized in two things: slapping you on the cheek affectionately with a shaky hand, and making fish soup with coriander and fish heads which he sucked on avidly, while we looked on, transfixed. Despite his feeble physique, he had been quite the lad in his youth, and there were even whispers about some tragic love that was nipped in the bud, just as he now nipped the bad buds in his rose garden. The reason for the romantic nipping was that the girl he fancied happened to be the sister of a boy who'd helped drown Uncle Kolyo's elder brother in the Danube. But that's another story.

In the other wing of Uncle Kolyo's house lived a quiet Turkish family. The blue-eyed woman Fatimé covered her head and padded softly in her sun-baked feet, as if stepping on rose petals. Her brother had died mysteriously while serving in the army – a 'tragic accident'. He had been accidentally beaten to death by fellow recruits, an ethnic Turk among ethnic Bulgarians, at the start of the State's campaign against the Turks.

Aside from these attractions, there was nothing to do but eat. In the vine-shaded coma of that white-hot summer of boredom, budding hormones, and waiting for the worst to happen, my first cousin and I spent the days wolfing down ovenfuls of Auntie's pastries, and reading instructive novels like *Wuthering Heights*, *Captain Blood*, and *Lorna Doone*. Breakfast: slices of warm white bread with thick layers of butter and honey from Auntie's own honeycomb. We swallowed watermelons the size of small planets, peaches big as heads, lettuces like forests. It was a fertile year, 1986. We competed, under Auntie's adoring supervision, to see who could eat more pieces of walnut cake in one sitting. Who would have thought that summer was the prelude to our distinguished careers in eating disorders. Only a few years later, we would compete to see who could go longer without food.

By the end of the summer, my cousin and I were small, round versions of Auntie. The only thing that still fitted was our pyjamas. When my father came to pick us up, he didn't recognize me. But Auntie was overjoyed to have fed us so well.

Back in Sofia, in the doorway of our apartment, stood a spectral apparition in black. This was my mother, and she saw that overnight I had risen like dough. Now I suddenly awoke from my Suhindol coma, and I was ashamed. My adolescence had begun in disgrace. I had breasts now, but they were not female breasts, they were porcine pockets of fat. I was a pig who'd spent the summer in Auntie's kitchen-trough, while my mother had been transformed into a saint. I was so self-disgusted that I forbade myself from being sad about my grandmother Anastassia to whom, there was no denying it now, the worst had happened. Only thin people could have emotions, while porkies like me ate, slept, and wallowed in honey.

I didn't allow myself to remember all the seaside holidays and mountain holidays with my grandparents; all the gourmet meals cooked by Anastassia; all the evenings I had spent talking with her about life, French which she spoke, poetry which she wrote, and what I wanted to be when I grew up (a radio journalist, like her). I didn't think about that last summer holiday with them, when we drove in the blue Skoda and Joe Dassin came on the radio singing *'Et si tu n'existais pas'* ('If you didn't exist'), the way my grandfather Alexander cried while he drove, and my grandmother pretended not to notice because she loved life even as cancer chomped away at it. It was her favourite song, and for him the words were painfully close.

I started doing punishing hours of aerobics at home to the sound of 'Like a Virgin', 'Material Girl', and 'Flashdance'. These records were licensed and locally released by the Balkanton studios in crumbly rough covers with fuzzy photocopies of Madonna and Jennifer Beals in curls, headbands, and gaiters. This distracted me from having to deal with 'the worst'.

My father, who also found emotions hard work, was busy planning an academic visit to the German Democratic Republic. On the morning of my grandmother's funeral, he had an early flight to Berlin. My mother drove him in the orange Skoda. On the way, there was a crisis: he'd forgotten his passport. We went back for the passport, and my mother was late for the funeral. But there was nothing my mother couldn't cope with. Not even this. And what choice did she have? After all, nervous breakdowns didn't exist under Socialism with a Human Face.

At the funeral, I saw my grandparents' neighbours. The neighbour from downstairs had run across the city in the forty-degree heat to get a death certificate when my grandmother died, and come back with all his shirt buttons missing, from the mêlée in the buses. Every single button, my mother said. Those missing buttons were a measure of his affection for Anastassia.

My grandmother's brothers from across the border in Macedonia were here too. My Uncle Slavcho, the physics professor who had laughed continuously that happy summer in Macedonia, now sobbed continuously, his big body shaking like jelly. I found some consolation in that: evidently, fat people could be sad too.

My mother spoke to the congregation. I suddenly became aware that she had lost the person who – after me, of course – loved her most. She stood there alone and wasted, and it seemed that we were not worthy of her: me, because of my corpulence; my father, because he wasn't even there; only my sister twitched impatiently, still uncontaminated, still ignorant of just how ugly we all were.

I escaped from all this in the usual manner: by watching fantasy films like *The Neverending Story* and *Return of the Jedi* and re-reading fantasy books like André Maurois's *Impossible Worlds*, carefully translated as *The Country of a Thousand Wishes*. In that country, the little girl called Michèle had dresses made out of the night sky. 'With or without cloud?' the heavenly seamstress asked. 'Without,' Michèle and I answered.

But as soon as I looked away from the book's pages, I noticed that bad things continued to happen. Someone had opened Pandora's box and emptied its contents over our family. Uncle Kolyo in Suhindol died suddenly, my parents' relationship was breaking down, and our flat became a building site. For months, while our bathroom was being renovated, as soon as you ventured out of your bed, you walked over rows of tiles and bags of cement from which a white dust rose and entered your mouth, where it turned to paste. Over the barricades, my sister and I dodged the crossfire of my parents' fights. They were now quarrelling incessantly – mostly about tiles and cement, it seemed – and each night my sister and I lay in bed in quiet depression as my father hurled abuse at my mother and she hurled back books with hard covers: Goethe's *The Sorrows of Young Werther*, Maxim Gorky's *Collected Works*, Montaigne's *Essays*. Classics and cement: that was the stuff of our lives.

One day, the cement was gone. My sister, aged seven, triumphantly went to test the shower in the new bathroom. The new ceiling came crashing down, all of it, missing her by a few seconds. That night, as a special concession, my parents called a temporary ceasefire.

In the summer of Chernobyl, I was desperately clinging to something slippery which was drifting away. In retrospect, it was childhood. Here was life with the thighs of an Exemplary Young Woman, with the black of mourning and nuclear fear, with the sound of my parents hurting each other through clouds of cement dust. Here was life without Richard Chamberlain (he'd recently died in *The Thornbirds*) and without my grandmother Antastassia, whose black and white face now smiled from an anonymous *necrolog*, like the ones we read at the bus stop. I started having nightmares in which she came back and laughed, her gold tooth flashing with mirth. She took off her wig, and there was her real hair. She'd never been dead at all. I'd wake in the middle of the night in the empty silence of the Youths and wonder which was worse – sleeping or waking, life or death.

But soon, these existential worries were put into fresh perspective when I was struck down with a bizarre auto-immune disease. It filled all my joints with fluid and slowly blew me up into something resembling a Michelin man. Rheumatic fever, the doctors said, and wheeled me off to the 2nd Regional Children's Hospital for Rheumatic Diseases, where I spent my second worst summer looking out from behind window bars at a squat, impersonal monolith called Russian Monument and, next to it, a faceless high-rise called Hotel Motherland.

At least there were no cakes to tempt me. In fact, there was no edible food at all at the hospital canteen. My mother and Keti brought me jars of mushed-up food to stop me from floating away, because by now I was entirely made up of joint fluid. The toilets were purgatory, so all the kids – four of us – suffered from constipation.

In the large, empty hospital, it seemed that the four of us had been forgotten. It was urgent to perform tests in order to diagnose and treat the Michelin man disease but everyone was on holiday. The only staff around were young nurse apprentices who practised freely on me. For some reason, they needed to take half a litre of blood every second day. After a week of blood-letting, I began to feel like one of Dr Moreau's experiments in H.G. Wells's *The Island of Doctor Moreau*, which I'd just read. They came to me, all sharp nails and blue eye-shadow, and I followed them to the blood-letting room, an obedient zombie. Five of them searched the blue-black surfaces of my skin for a healthy vein that hadn't already collapsed. Eventually, only one foot of useful veins was left, and when they broke the last vein there too, my slipper filled with blood. This annoyed them, because it was wasted blood, and they shouted at each other. Too dazed to protest, I apologized for being such a nuisance – my parents had taught me good manners.

My mother, however, lost her own good manners after the clinic's creepy head doctor (my Dr Moreau) informed her that my condition was untreatable. It wasn't rheumatic fever, it was worse. But they didn't know what it was. They could do nothing except monitor me, and my parents should expect 'the worst'. The medical folder was slammed shut like a slap on the face.

My mother used all available connections in the medical world to arrange private appointments with expensive specialists, those who weren't on holiday. Then she arranged more expensive private tests to rule out horrific degenerative diseases which the first set of expensive specialists had suggested I might have.

Meanwhile, life in the 2nd Regional Children's Hospital for Rheumatic Diseases wasn't all gloom and doom. There were good times too. I made three friends. Stocky Valentin, fifteen, had been training to be a weightlifter when he was diagnosed with juvenile arthritis, a misfortune which he bore with dignity. Marko was a spunky sixteen-year-old Gypsy with Elvis Presley hair and raging rheumatic fever. Kiki was an enterprising fourteen-year-old girl, who got into bed with Marko one night, leaving me with Valentin whom I didn't fancy. It didn't matter though, because we didn't do anything. We just lay next to each other in our pyjamas with the lights off, and talked about the great things we would do when we got out of hospital (become a wrestling champion and play the piano). But word of our escapades reached the hospital authorities and we were reprimanded for immoral behaviour, driving our already frantic parents that bit closer to the edge.

At night, while Kiki slept, I listened to the traffic, gazed at the grubby stars through the window bars, and composed rhyming couplets about eternity and my mother. I was terrified of somehow losing her in this labyrinth of hospital corridors, blood tests, and ominous whispers. And I read the highly strung poetry of Petya Dubarova, the girl prodigy from Burgas who had killed herself at seventeen in protest against the school authorities.

I listened on my portable cassette-player to *The Eagles*, which a friend of my mother's had managed to tape from an imported record. 'Hotel California' was my favourite. Although I didn't understand a word of it except 'Welcome to the Hotel California', I tried to sing along to 'such a lovely place, such a lovely place...'. I listened to it over and over, in a trance, trapped in this place I would never leave.

It was my parents' angry despair that saved me. After a month, they took me out of hospital on signature, which meant that Dr Moreau was no longer in charge. It happened so fast that I didn't have time to say goodbye to my cell-mates. Valentin's parents had connections, and he was taken to France to be treated. Marko didn't have connections, and stayed behind with Dr Moreau. Kiki was moved to a hospital for heart diseases.

Once out of hospital, I was in the private care of a famous old professor of immunology who came to our flat. Private practice was of course illegal, and both he and my parents risked getting into trouble if the other turned out to be an informer. He refused the extra cash my desperate parents kept offering him and took only the small, State-fixed rate.

The professor suggested that my disease might be related to that nuclear incident the previous year. By now, he said, many children were suffering from freak diseases, and the word Chernobyl was whispered in hospital corridors. I thought of the enormous lettuces and the watermelons at Auntie's house, the peaches and the honey. During my hospital confinement, I had become allergic to every food under the sun except, it seemed, rice.

My father drove me everywhere by car, to protect me from infections on the crowded buses. I observed this strange new world of healthy people from inside our orange Skoda, like a Party functionary gazing through the tinted windows of a limousine.

The Michelin man had deflated and come back to earth, and the earth looked a changed place. It was a place without my third favourite person in the world, without piano lessons, without the guarantee that bad things wouldn't happen again. Childhood was a distant memory.

6 Winds of Change

Perestroika in the air

When I turned thirteen, the time came to say goodbye to the Unitary Secondary Polytechnic School 81 and begin a new life at a specialized college. I decided I would be a scholar of archaeology and ancient cultures. There were rumours that senior students went on archaeological trips to Egypt, Italy and Greece. That in itself was sufficient incentive. I spent the summer swotting for the entrance exams at the prestigious College for Classical Studies and Antique Languages.

I liked to lose myself in the illustrated *Classic Greek Myths and Legends*, the further removed from the present, the better. I knew the extended family trees of all the gods and heroes, including disputed parentage. But it soon became obvious that all this wouldn't get me into the Classical College.

What would get me in was to demonstrate, in written and oral form, a thorough knowledge of Bulgarian history. That meant medieval history, history of the National Revival period, and last but by no means least the history of the International Communist Movement in general and the Bulgarian Communist Party in particular. So I gritted my teeth and picked up the badly misnamed *Brief History of Bulgaria* which was 500 pages long and written by the world's dullest historian. I struggled to overcome my confusion in the face of medieval history (who can remember the order of all the tsars and who blinded whom and for what reason?), my catatonic boredom with the National Revival period and its endless pantheon of moustachioed heroes who died young, and the sudden narcolepsy I experienced at the mention of such key figures from the Communist martyrs' roll-call as 'the five from the Revolutionary Youth Union (RMS)'. They were presumably known as 'the five' because no one could remember their names – no one except the examiners, that is.

Education, like medical care, was free. But only if you were happy to rot away at School 81, with Comrade Gesheva breathing down your neck. The words prestigious and elite were never mentioned, but if you – and your ambitious parents – had your sights on a prestigious and elite school, you had to take private lessons with privately paid school teachers and university professors who set you sample essay topics. I was already paired up with a literature teacher, who was pleasant enough, but more importantly happened to live in the same 'cooperation' as Bulgaria's top pop singer Vassil Naidenov, also known as Vasko 'the trainer'. Vasko was sexy, he wore trainers, he sang about 'telephone love', and I nearly fainted when I passed him once in the staircase. Nobody had told me he was gay, because of course there was no such thing.

As the exams got closer, my parents' historian friends found me a private history teacher too. He was in fact a teacher at the Classical College, and on the examination board – how handy! He wasn't going to teach me history, as such – that was my responsibility – no, he would just test-examine me, as it were, run me through things, give me an inkling of what the exam questions might be. In return for a hefty fee.

I recoiled from him the moment I saw him. He had a slimy smile and, worse, a slimy, drooling son who was also 'applying' to get in; and it didn't have to be spelt out to me that the son was already running ahead of me in the race. And he wasn't the only one. Many comrades' children and grandchildren were among the aspiring classic scholars at the gates. In fact, some Party Fighters in the Struggle against Fascism and Capitalism adopted their own grandchildren on just such occasions, because the right surname could open the heaviest doors.

My parents' and grandparents' names counted for nothing in the world of humanities, and even less in the world of Party Fighters. They were only 'poor engineers', and there wasn't a single Fighter in the Struggle against Fascism and Capitalism in the family.

I began to feel like a doomed gladiator in the arena, faced with twenty armoured chariots representing Rome, and a whole menagerie of wild animals thrown in for good measure. My parents, who also took an instant dislike to the history teacher and the necessary palm-greasing, pulled me out of the private lessons. I'd just have to go for it, trust my wits, and hope for the best.

I swotted twice as hard, but panic had already crept in. My written exam went well – it was on the Second Bulgarian Kingdom, and somehow I managed to get the order of tsars, religious conversions and blindings right. In the room, among the other kids, I spied the drooling son chewing his pen in bewilderment, and I gloated.

But when I entered the oral examination room, where the teachers were lined up like police commissars and the portraits of 'the five from RMS' gazed at me from the wall, I heard the clatter of those chariots and the roar of the lions. Then the fatal question came: in which year was the Fatherland Front established and what were its chief goals? I don't know if it was nerves or ignorance, but I went blank. I had swotted madly on the 'five from the RMS' and the history of the Bulgarian Communist Party, but the Fatherland Front remained a mystery. It was somehow related to the Workers' Party, which was somehow related to the Communist Party... But this was not an answer. In my despair, I looked up at the five from the RMS, but they gazed at me expressionlessly from the blur of their youthful heroism, and gave away nothing about the Fatherland Front. In silence, the commissars wrote something on their papers, and this concluded the oral examination. I dragged my wounded self outside, and who was waiting in the corridor but my drooling rival who already knew the questions, of course, and the answers.

The countdown to the results began, and my parents, sensing disaster, decided that I should also sit entrance exams to the Language College, just in case. This proved a smart move, because the list of the first lot of successful scholars, posted on the gates of the Classical College, included little Caligula's name, but not mine. By the time I finally saw my name, near the bottom of the list in the next round of admissions, I knew that a triumphant career in the blood-stained arena came at too high a price.

The only dignified choice was to walk away. So I stood outside the gates of Rome like a latter-day Spartacus, and I said goodbye to Jason and the Argonauts, goodbye to the Byzantine ruins on the Black Sea, goodbye to the archaeological trips abroad. I would never see the pyramids, the Colosseum, or the Acropolis. But I would be free.

I had been accepted into the French College – no history exam there, just good old neutral maths and literature. And instead of *Civis romanus sum*, I would learn to say the more humble *Je parle français*.

Et voilà: the yellow building of the French College was smack in the middle of Sofia, which meant that for the first time I had direct access to the buzz of inner-city life. But it also meant that every morning, at the stroke of seven, I boarded the first of two crammed city buses that forty-five minutes later would eject me, harassed and groped, near the school gates.

In the winter, the buses smelt of morning breath and garlic. In springtime, they smelt of morning breath and sweat. They were packed with school kids like me, poor engineers like my parents, and factory workers like the Mechevs. And there was always the panting, fat-fingered middle-aged groper of nubile girls who reached for any palpable breasts or bottoms. I was too well brought-up to make a spectacle of myself, which was exactly what the groper counted on. He groped, and I squirmed in private revulsion, and the people on the bus pretended not to see.

On the first day of the Lycée, before we knew what was happening, our class supervisor Madame Taleva said in Bulgarian, 'From now, I will only speak French.'

But we don't speak any, some brave soul piped. His name was Maxim.

'That's exactly why. The only way to learn French is to listen to French.'

It was too much for the girl sitting next to me. She started sobbing quietly, then a sudden explosion of unmistakable stench announced to her immediate neighbours that a catastrophe had occurred. Madame Taleva performed her first act of mercy and discreetly asked me to escort the girl to the toilets, which was where she stayed, sobbing, until her mother came to pick her up. I knew how she felt, and I was grateful for the control I had over my own bowels.

Another initiation ritual was entering the Comsomol, which was compulsory. Back at School 81, the Pioneers had seemed deadly serious, but here the Comsomol was a farce. The test was elementary, so much so that jokes about sample questions floated around (Question one: How many are the Five of the RMS? Question two: What's the name of Todor Jivkov?). Even so, with the ideological fiasco of the Classical College still fresh in my mind, my knees shook outside the teachers' office when my turn came. Somehow, I got the answers right this time (Five. Todor Jivkov. Or something to that effect.) and was issued with a brand new red Comsomol 'passport', which remained empty of activities and distinctions. I had been too clueless to escape a career with the Pioneers, but I knew better now and kept a low profile.

In the first year or '*année préparatoire*', our grade was known as 'little preps'. Little preps learnt between fifty and one hundred and twenty new words a day. Life was good. Here was a foreign language that wasn't Russian, and that promised ferry passage across the Styx that separated us from the West. As the poor cousin, you could perhaps reach the other shore by paying in language units. And so every day I went home and euphorically copied every new word twenty times and deposited it in the hungry piggy-bank of my mind.

Soon, under Madame Taleva's inspired baton, we were singing French songs like 'Ma Normandie', which seemed to be about a mythical place somewhere in France. We already loved la Normandie, even though we hadn't even seen a picture of it, and at the end of each stanza, we sang at full throttle:

> C'est le pays qui m'a donné le jour.
> (It is the country where I saw the light of day.)

This clearly didn't apply to us, but even so, we felt illuminated.

We also sang 'La Marseillaise': 'alons enfants de la patrie, le jour de gloire est arrive…'. We weren't sure when, and what, that day of glory was, but just to sing these words in French meant that we were, somehow, marching with the French children of the motherland, on our way to… well, somewhere.

To drive the point home, an enormous painting of *Liberty Leading the People* by Delacroix overlooked the central staircase of the Lycée. The bare-breasted Liberty was leading the citizens under a glorious French flag. Each day, we ascended and descended those steps under the banner of *liberté, égalité, fraternité*.

Alas, the dreary school canteen didn't offer a revolution in cuisine. In fact, its forlorn meatballs, floating like turds on the congealed surface of soup, was a déjà-vu of my kindergarten canteen. In any case, I was still allergic to practically everything under the sun and brought for lunch the only brand of biscuits on the market, honestly labelled Ordinary Biscuits, which I ate squished together with rosehip marmalade. This, along with my top grades in French and literature, established me early on as a weirdo as well as a nerd.

After all, once you got into the French Lycée, the general idea was not to get top grades, but to mix with Sofia's brightest brats, wear your navy-blue school mantle short at the bottom and unbuttoned at the top, smoke in the toilets, wear blue make-up, and sulk. Most of these things were prohibited, which is why it was essential to achieve them.

But I was obsessed with achieving a large French vocabulary. So, early on, I joined the ranks of the two other chief nerds. Short-sighted Tedy was a default top student in everything. She just couldn't help it. Chubby Gregory, or Grégoire as he became known, already spoke excellent French because he'd spent a few years in Libya where his parents had worked as dental surgeons. This confirmed Libya as a place where dams were built in the desert and people had their teeth extracted, with or without anaesthetic, Gregory couldn't say. Eunuch-bodied, diligent and bespectacled, Grégoire sang '*Ma Normandie*' in perfect, melodious inflections, like a chanting Gregorian monk.

We had two real, flesh-and-blood French teachers, Madame Mathieu and Monsieur Laroche. Madame Mathieu appeared on an evening TV language programme and gave well-articulated French lessons to the nation. Why a French person voluntarily chose to live in Bulgaria was a question to which I only found an answer much later: Madame Mathieu was an unreconstructed French Socialist who read *l'Humanité* and believed, despite the empty shops and neurotic citizens, that Socialism with a Human Face still had a chance.

Monsieur Laroche didn't seem quite so certain about anything. He had silver hair, the narrow face and hands of a sceptic, and the delayed reactions of a man recovering from a personal calamity. I sensed that

Bulgaria was either an exotic adventure for him, or a place to lie low for a while and regroup. Naturally, I had a crush on him. One day, I ran into him on the bus, and he told me he was going back to France. Write to me, he said and gave me his address. I proudly copied it in my address book: I now had a French name among my contacts.

But he might as well have gone to the moon. I never dared write to him; I lay in bed at night, and Monsieur Laroche's narrow face gazed mournfully at me from a retreating mythical land, and I clutched my French vocabulary like a money-belt, hoping that one day I might be able to afford the crossing. By the end of year one, the little preps spoke fluent French – which was the idea, since in the second year most subjects were taught in it.

In year two, the French president François Mitterrand graced us with a visit. The school went into paroxysms of preparation, not least of which was to find two presentable girls who spoke fluent French and who would greet him with flowers and generally hover about, demonstrating the school's excellence in producing perfect little Francophones.

And the Francophones had to be little, because the president himself was also little. At 1.67 metres tall, I was instantly disqualified. This was obviously upsetting for any aspiring presentable girl at the French Lycée, but I recalled the portrait of Comrade Brezhnev in School 81, and pulled myself together. Diminutive French presidents and dead Soviet leaders were not going to be the measure of my linguistic worth.

By the end of year two, I could discuss in French the phosphate resources of the Balkan region, molecules with triple valence, and the Bulgarian National Revival struggle for self-determination against the Ottoman yoke. I took perverse pleasure in speed dictation, full of tricky-to-spell words that no modern French person would dream of using – like *bruissements innouïs*, inaudible murmurs.

We also listened to French songs by people like hoarse, angry Renaud:

> *Putain qu'il est blême, mon HLM!*
> (How it sucks, my council block of flats!)

Or sexy Michel Sardou who wrote acerbic social lyrics, like '*J'accuse*'. Every song with a political message resonated with us. It didn't matter what the original meaning of the message was. We were so hungry, so alive, and so isolated that the mere bones of a human voice thrown from the outside fed us. And we grew stronger with the certainty that we lived behind a wall. A wall that didn't protect us from anything any more, except from the things we wanted.

We didn't realize that many of these songs came from the early eighties and even from the seventies. They may have come from Europe's recent past, but they played in our present. Nobody told us that singers like Renaud and Michael Sardou were permitted to circulate in the language school precisely because of their politics: they were Socialist rebels raging against the capitalist machine. But to our ears, there was only one machine to rage against, and that was Socialism with a Human Face.

So, in a sublime twist of irony, these angsty rebels' voices against the West sang especially for us, the angsty adolescents of totalitarianism's twilight years.

Alongside the political rock, there were hormonal passions. The two came together in the form of Maxim, the school's number one heart-throb. Maxim was ultra-cool, ultra-ironic, and in addition to attending the Lycée was studying at the English College as an external student. He also spoke Russian as a mother tongue, thanks to his Russian mother. Maxim mocked students and teachers alike in a mixture of four languages, and always got away with it. His polished good looks of a matinee idol helped. He cultivated anti-establishment stubble as soon as he physically could, played the guitar, and sang in a velvety voice at school concerts.

Maxim sat on the podium with his guitar, jeans tight around his crotch, and sang Michel Sardou's '*Je vais t'aimer*'. It described in poetic hyperbole and twelve erotic stanzas all the ways in which he was going to love some lucky girl. This blatantly decadent eroticism was tantamount to a political statement and, sure enough, Maxim got reprimanded afterwards by the school director. But Maxim had the last word, because while he sang, every budding woman in the Lycée was gripped by spasms of nameless longing, including, I suspected, some of the female teachers, who sat there flushed with disapproval and pleasure.

At camp that summer, Maxim did love a couple of girls, but only for a night or two. You knew from the way they looked miserable the following days and weeks: they were discarded tunes in Maxim's poetic repertoire. As for me, I knew I was too nerdy for Maxim, and even if I had been 'easy', he'd use me and discard me along with the rest. From time to time he pressed his erection against me, to let me know that he wasn't entirely indifferent. But it was an impossible love, and I suffered in stoic silence.

In the meantime, I took comfort in my friends Tedy and Grégoire. Tedy now had a boyfriend: a very polite boy called Bogdan who was just back from Algeria. His father was a diplomat. After years in Algiers, Bogdan spoke flawless French and even looked Arabic with his dark skin and fierce facial hair. I didn't fancy him, except for the fact that he'd lived abroad.

His extrovert, freckled, gum-chewing friend Kaloyan had also lived abroad and became my boyfriend by escorting me home on the bus one night, and sticking his tongue in my mouth. I didn't fancy him either, but I hadn't had any tongue offers before and having no one to kiss was surely worse than having to kiss Kaloyan. Kaloyan and I parted ways after it dawned on him that I wouldn't have sex with him at very short notice, and it dawned on me that he wasn't interested in music, books, me, or even French, which he already spoke. He was only interested in sex. So was I, but not with him. Even if he'd been to Algeria and wore French eau de cologne.

Otherwise, I had a steadfast admirer who was more sophisticated than Kaloyan and nicer than Maxim. Boris was interested in books, music, French, and me, and he was a gentleman who would hold out a hand when you stepped off the bus, and walk on the outside of pavements to protect you from traffic. He brought you flowers on International Woman's Day on 8 March, and let you stand in front of him in the canteen queue without pressing his erection against you. All this should have made him the ideal first boyfriend.

But something told me that there was an unwritten law of wretchedness in the world, according to which you never fancied the people who fancied you, and vice versa. Boris and I went out a few times, and he impressed me with tales of his evening job at the hospital morgue across the street. He worked there not because they paid him – they didn't – but because he wanted to study death close up. Death was honest, he said, unlike life. Bound together by this metaphysical insight, we held hands and kissed when he saw me home on the bus, but there was no chemistry – or perhaps there was the wrong chemistry. He was intellectual, sensitive and good looking, but he had the pallor and chill of the morgue about him. Soon, it was over. Boris snapped into action and threatened to commit suicide. Knowing his intimate relationship with death, I became worried. His father was worried too and met my mother to discuss these delicate matters. Although I was absolved of responsibility, the guilt of Boris's suicidal threats haunted me for a long time, especially when I looked out of the school's windows into the basement of the hospital across the road, where fresh corpses were laid out on slabs.

One day, on the way to the bus stop, Grégoire adjusted his glasses on his chubby face and said, 'If I asked you to be my girlfriend, would you agree?'

I squirmed with awkwardness. 'I don't know,' I said. 'But I think it's better if you don't ask me.'

'Good,' he said. 'That clarifies things.'

It didn't clarify anything for me, but he looked relieved, and this squirmy episode was never mentioned again. For my fifteenth birthday, Grégoire gave me a plush teddy bear and a card in which he'd written a quote from Saint Exupéry's *Little Prince: 'l'essentiel est invisible pour les yeux'*, the most important things are invisible to the eyes. I wondered if this was a covert love declaration, or a declaration of something else, or a coded warning. I didn't find out until ten years later.

In my third year at the Lycée, I started attending the new lunchtime philosophy classes which somehow managed to pitch camp on the periphery of the school curriculum. There were no exams, no grades, it was just for the interested. There was only a handful of the interested. The idea, as far as I could tell anyway, was to demonstrate how the philosophy of Hegel had led to Marxism and Communism, and how French existentialism was an extension of those. It was all very complicated, but Sartre's 'existence before essence' – or was it 'essence before existence'? – provided me with new questions to ponder. And a new object of impossible desire.

The thirty-something philosophy teacher had the absent look of someone who was either about to go or had just returned from somewhere dangerous. He also had the red-veined nose and trembling hands of the alcoholic. I gazed adoringly at him, transfixed by Sartre's Being and Nothingness, and lived for the moment when his eyes met mine. But he had other things on his mind, in particular the married geography teacher. She had a cloud of gorgeous red hair and one leg shorter than the other. She dutifully took us through the phosphate resources of the Balkan region, but from the way she often limped to the window and looked out, I could tell that she had other things on her mind too. I saw them smoking in the teachers' corridor, briefly locked in the unmistakable embrace of clandestine lovers. And then, one day, they disappeared. The rumour went that they had deserted to the West. Clearly, she knew her geography well. The philosophy classes were suddenly over. I felt abandoned, but like everybody else I was also silently cheering for the escaped lovers. They had made it, and that was a sign of something important.

And so was the autumn of 1988, when TV's most beautiful presenter, Tatiana Titianova, disappeared from the screen. The rumour was that some comrade in the upper echelons had censored her out once and for all because she had become inconvenient. She'd been too beautiful and too public for her own good. The official version was that she'd thrown herself from her block of flats. Nobody believed it. Disbelieving the worst was suddenly a luxury we couldn't afford any more. And so the body of the tragic Tatiana kept falling endlessly, in slow motion, from the top of that collective block of flats where we all huddled in fear. Nobody knew who might be suicided next.

But it soon became obvious. In an attempt to distract the nation from the winds of change blowing across the Big Soviet Country, the regime organized a mass campaign cheerfully called the Revival Process. It aimed to revive the true roots of citizens of other ethnicities, namely the Turks and the Gypsies. This involved them 'remembering' their Bulgarian names and denying the Muslim names and customs which they had accidentally or forcibly acquired in the Ottoman past. Identity forms were distributed throughout the country, to help revive citizens. Ahmed remembered that his Bulgarian name was Assen. Ayshe remembered that hers was Ana. People also had to remember their dead parents' and grandparents' Bulgarian names, as though they had lived in a state of amnesia their whole lives.

Around this time, a new historical film about Bulgaria's Ottoman past was released at the cinemas. It was called *Time of Violence*, and the violent timing was flawless. In the story, based on a historic novel, a janissary called Karaibrahim comes to a seventeenth-century village in the Rodopi mountains to convert the locals to Islam, or else torture and slaughter them. Over the space of two instalments and four horror-drenched hours, this is what happens – conversion, or torture and/or extermination, and all the characters you like die. Schoolchildren and students were encouraged to see it although there were scenes of mass rape, slaughter, beheadings, and impalement. My parents barred me from seeing part two. Too late: I was already traumatized out of my wits by part one, which was precisely the idea. Because the next thought you were supposed to have – which I did – was this: how could you compare mere name changes with mass rape and impalement? You couldn't. The Ottomans had brutalized Bulgarians for five centuries, so why not brutalize their distant descendants just a bit too? It was apparently that simple.

People like my parents suspected that terrible things were happening to the ethnic Turks, but it was all rumour. The State controlled the media, and the media controlled our ignorance. He who controls the present controls the past, went the official motto of the Revival Process. And, by extension, the future.

Nobody stood up for the Turks because only a handful of very brave souls stood up for anything under the low ceilings of Socialism with a Human Face, and most of them had already had a spell of breaking rocks in labour camps.

Spontaneous 'manifestations' were staged in Sofia by student activists and other upright citizens my mother described as 'idiots in brown suits and their idiot children'. They waved indignant placards with 'Bulgaria for Bulgarians, Turkey for the Turks'. They were few in number, but they were loud. Comrade Jivkov made a televized statement declaring that the border with Turkey was open and those citizens who really liked Turkey would be issued with international passports so they could visit it. They did: about half a million of them. The roads were clogged with endless caravans of carts and clapped-out cars hurriedly borrowed or bought from neighbours in exchange for entire houses.

The country was now full of empty homes where photographs, dowries, livestock, and family treasures accumulated over generations were left for the taking by the executives of the Revival Process. The citizens had departed voluntarily, just as they had changed their names and religion voluntarily.

The ethnic Turks were the tobacco-growers, the agricultural workers, the humble workforce that buzzed away in the background, propping up the diseased body of the State. There was no official acknowledgement that the Turkish exodus had dealt a deadly blow to the already decrepit economy, but it soon became obvious. The power-cuts and water shortages became so frequent that we now did our homework by candlelight and filled buckets with water every time they 'let it out' of the taps. The fields remained unharvested, the tobacco rotted away, entire villages were deserted, schools, hospitals and shops closed down. This was yet another act of provocation from our compatriots of Turkish origin. They had deliberately undermined the great five-year plan.

The Worker's Deed informed us that our compatriots had taken a holiday in Turkey. A long holiday. An irresponsibly long holiday. They were irresponsible citizens. They had always been suspect anyway, the fifth column of American imperialism whose nearest gateway was Turkey.

We were living inside George Orwell's *1984* but we didn't know it because it was on the list of banned books. Nobody had heard about the Ministry of Truth where lies are the only currency, the Ministry of Information which specializes in disinformation, the Ministry of Plenty whose only product is reports of ever-increasing productivity, and the Ministry of Love where people are tortured with their worst dream until they are broken. But although we had no names for them, these were the ministries from which our lives were made and, increasingly now, unmade.

We knew, even in the torpor of our ignorance, that the long holiday of our compatriots was no holiday. It was a purge. And there was nothing anybody could do except shake their head and whisper 'the worst, the worst is happening'.

Around that time, a strange little piece by a young writer appeared in the satirical paper *Wasp*. It started with the sentence 'I dream that I'm living in a stupid joke', went on to tell a black parable about a neurotic man who is building a fence to protect himself from his friendly Western neighbours, and ended with the sentence 'Why the hell do I live in such a stupid joke? Why am I not in control of my dream? No, I can't take this anymore. I go to sleep again.' This publication was either a momentary lapse on the part of censors or a signal that there was no turning back.

One night at the Opera, an old radio colleague of my grandmother Anastassia approached us. Would my mother like to join their group which met in private to discuss ecological matters? My mother wouldn't. She was too scared.

She was right to be scared. When the underground movement Eco-Glasnost emerged from their secret meeting places, they huddled together with their placards in the Artists' Garden near the Communist Party HQ. They were a crowd of artists, intellectuals, and men with beards, and they were dispersed, beaten by militiamen, and loaded onto army trucks. But by now it was obvious that the Human Face of Socialism was twitching with panic.

But all this happened on the periphery of my life. In the centre were the torments and thrills of adolescence. One such thrill was my membership of the literary journal for young people *Mother Tongue*, which was edited by a brooding, bearded poet with dark circles around his eyes and dark thoughts in his clever head. He dynamited my imagination with an epic poem about *Pygmalion* which I barely understood and which was full of coded imagery of art, obsession, and erotic love.

From my early light verse about summer crickets, the sea, and the moon, heavily influenced by the playful style of Bulgarian writer Valeri Petrov, I moved onto dead-serious poems about time, the universe, and the meaninglessness of life, heavily influenced by my reading of Italian inter-war poets like Umberto Saba, Giuseppe Ungaretti and especially Eugenio Montale ('This alone is what we can tell you today/that which we are not, that which we do not want'). That was us!

The magazine published my poems – the absolute pinnacle of my literary aspirations – and I started turning up for semi-clandestine evening discussions with playwrights and poets who seemed to be borderline dissidents. In any case, they had beards. My crush among the young poets was a bespectacled seventeen-year-old who wrote complicated metaphysical poems about cats. Cats were decadent and mysterious in the dead heat of the afternoon. Cats were the agents of time.

I wasn't entirely clear about the cats, but *Mother Tongue* was definitely the agent of change in my inner world. It showed me that it was possible to put inexpressible things into words, and then share the results with brooding, like-minded people. This offered me an escape from the social pressures of the French Lycée. At *Mother Tongue*, you didn't have to have a particular look, smoke, act deliberately dumb, or lose your virginity at short notice with a random person – you just had to write or say something interesting to be part of the crowd.

Then, one day, browsing in the school library, I found *The Outsider* by Albert Camus. Here was a book about how I felt: disconnected and numb, and yet full of unexpressed emotion. Here too was a new object of impossible love: Albert Camus. And being dead made him the ideal lover, because he couldn't run away to the West.

One day, while I was re-reading *L'Etranger* at the local bus stop in Youth 3, someone asked me in butter-smooth French, 'Do you like Camus?'

A stunning Arab with small round glasses was standing next to me.

He was quite old – perhaps thirty – but his *café-au-lait* skin, tight black curls and dazzling smile took my breath away, along with most of my brain. The remaining parts were trying to form a clever sentence in French. I had never actually spoken French to anyone other than Madame Mathieu and Monsieur Laroche.

'*L'Etranger* is set in Algeria,' the apparition continued. 'I come from Algeria.'

This stunned me. I had assumed that, like any French book, *L'Etranger* was set in France.

'I have a classmate who lived in Algeria,' I said, blushing the deepest hue of crimson.

'Ah, you must be from the French School.' He gifted me with a white-toothed smile. 'If you like, we can meet again and talk about Camus.'

By the end of our romantic Francophone bus ride, Fadhel had told me that I had beautiful eyes, and I had given him my phone number. That weekend, without telling my parents, I went on my first date.

He took me to a fancy café-bar in Vitosha Street, the epicentre of Sofia, where I had an enormous installation of ice cream and he an enormous cocktail. Fadhel was studying engineering in Sofia. He took off his glasses, folded them up in his pocket, and kissed me. I went straight to heaven and back. He held the door for me. Fadhel was clearly a gentleman.

For some reason, my parents didn't grasp this, and when Fadhel called again, inviting me to his place to watch videos, it was over my parents' dead bodies – both of them. He just wants to use you, my mother said, can't you see? What's he doing with schoolgirls anyway, my father frowned, he's obviously a pervert. He wants to lure you with his videos and then have sex with you, my mother said. That didn't strike me as such an unpleasant proposition; in fact, watching home videos and having sex with Fadhel was pretty much my idea of bliss. I didn't know anybody who had a VCR, except my mother's cousin, the one who built dams in Libya. But there was no way to put this into words without sounding to everyone I respected like an under-age slut ready to sell herself to the first Arab who came along waving a remote control.

It didn't help that my new school friend Rado teased me for using with Fadhel the word *engagée*, busy. It makes you sound like a prostitute who's booked up, he said gleefully. I desperately hoped that Fadhel would still find a way to see me, at least to have that conversation about Camus — I wanted to discuss *Le mythe de Sisyphe* in particular — but he never called again.

Rado was the biggest alpha male around. He was a year behind me, and he shook his big wild head to the nihilistic screams of AC/DC and Metallica. We became platonic friends. He lent me his prized Metallica cassette *Fade to Black*, which I hated, and I lent him Sartre's *Nausea*, which he hated. They were, of course, about the same thing: rejecting the ugly world we lived in.

We were ironic, we believed in nothing that was on offer to us, and we wanted everything that wasn't. We dressed in dark colours, and we had two main emotional states — sad or angry. I was mostly sad, and Rado was mostly angry. Why, we couldn't quite say.

While Rado roared darkly with Metallica, I frowned at the world, nauseated with Sartre, estranged with Camus, and lovesick for Fadhel. We delighted in small things, however, for example a flash-looking record of the Scorpions' he brought back from a trip to Belgrade, which featured a screaming man with bandaged head and talon-like forks digging into his eyes. He felt our pain.

The biggest hits at school were no longer the wishy-washy Michel Sardou and Renaud – no, that stuff was for little preps – but the more hard core Pink Floyd and the Scorpions. Someone had spray-painted 'THE WALL' over the wall of the school courtyard.

We had come of age.

Rado had occasional parties in his parents' apartment, where he played seminal progressive rock, such as the Scorpions' 'Still Loving You'. We sat on the floor by candlelight, smoking and heavily doused with our mothers' Libyan perfumes and our fathers' Russian eau de cologne, in dark clothes decorated with home-made badges of Pink Floyd and 'glasnost'. We drank vague, diluted alcohols which scrambled our already confused brains. We played kissing games, with tongues. And we listened to words we didn't understand very well (we were from the French school, after all). But we knew those words were important by virtue of being English and sad – or angry. They seemed to express the Zeitgeist of longing and disillusion of our life and times.

Then, on the way home in a taxi, driving through the semi-dark desert of the Youths, I would cry for nothing in particular. Because my mind had overgrown my body, or my body had overgrown my mind, I wasn't quite sure. Because I wanted a boyfriend but didn't have one. Because the philosophy teacher and the geography teacher had run away to the West. Because I too wanted to go places or at least *know* that I could, but couldn't. Because I was, we were, almost on the brink of something, but I didn't know what it was, and what was going to happen.

What happened was that the Berlin Wall fell. It was November 1989.

At first, like Chernobyl and the murder of the TV presenter, it was a rumour. But we knew that kind of rumour could only be the truth.

Not least because the next day, the TV news presenter announced that Comrade Todor Jivkov, Head of the Central Committee of the Bulgarian Communist Party, had resigned. In other words, there had been a bloodless coup inside the Party.

'I don't believe it,' my mother kept saying, staring at the screen of our Dutch TV. 'It can't be true. They're lying to us again. I don't believe it.'

'Maybe they're staging a coup,' my father said. 'To keep up with what's happening in Berlin.'

'Exactly, they're staging it,' my mother said. 'They stage everything. It's all a theatre of the absurd, with props and actors. It's not for real.'

But it was. The Communist Party would stay in power for another few months, but it was obvious that Socialism with a Human Face had permanent egg on it. And when you're sixteen, there's no going back.

Now it was normal to see people on buses and in waiting-rooms chuckling to themselves or grinning madly. Strangers talked feverishly in shop queues.

Now, at school, alongside our Pink Floyd and Scorpions badges, some of us wore blue badges with 'DEMOCRACY' and 'SDS' on them. The SDS were the Union of Democratic Forces, a rag-tag opposition party made up of those intellectuals and people with beards who had recently dared to demonstrate in the Artists' Garden. Eco-Glasnost had come of age and become a political party.

Someone had spray-painted 'DEMOCRACY' in blue over the wall of the school's back yard. Soon, we'd be listening to the Scorpions' mega-hit hit, 'The Winds of Change'. It seemed to be about what was happening to our world, even though I only understood four words: 'Gorky Park' and 'like brothers'.

The nation's new year present was the televized execution of Nicolae and Elena Ceauşescu by a three-man firing squad. It wasn't quite as good as having our own Todor Jivkov shot in the head, but it was better than nothing. As the Ceauşescus fell, bloodied, to the ground, Bulgaria cheered at the TV screens.

'Kids, don't look!' my mother warned us half-heartedly, but it was too late. Besides, I had long stopped being a kid.

'That's it!' my father kept repeating in front of the TV, dazed. 'That's it, that's it, it's over. It's over!'

That was it, then, that was the last act in the 45-year-long theatre of the absurd that had been our lives.

7 And Heaven Knows
I'm Miserable Now

Emigration

Before we knew what had hit us, my father found himself on a two-year university fellowship in a place called Colchester. Soon, my mother and my sister followed, while I stayed behind to finish my year at the French College. Grandmother Kapka came to live with me. She soon gave up any pretence of cooking, cleaning or exercising authority, and lay down with her Valerian drops, while I went out to parties and literary discussions veiled in cigarette smoke.

Colchester was in England, which was inconvenient, because my

French would be of no use. But England was where The Beatles were from, and I had *Best of The Beatles* to help me. I applied myself to deciphering, with a dictionary, the lyrics of 'And I Love Her', 'In My Life', and the more problematic 'Yesterday', which drove me to floods of tears every time. Yesterday, all my troubles were so far away. Now the Wall was down, my family were in England, I was sixteen and probably the last virgin at the French Lycée, and I had to learn a language that was full of phrasal verbs like 'turn up' and 'turn in' that made no sense.

When I arrived in Colchester in the summer of 1990, hyper-ventilating with excitement, I looked like an impersonation of Madonna in her 'Like a Virgin' video clip from 1984, which of course I hadn't seen. Clad in a leather mini-skirt made by my mother and a leather jacket sourced by my grandfather Alexander from his leather factory, I wore an enormous coiffure of gelled hair atop a blurry face exploding with lipstick and hormones. To my amazement, nobody in Colchester looked like this. This was confusing. Wasn't this the West? They could wear anything they wanted. Why didn't they?

My sister was already speaking English with the local Essex accent (ei' o' clo' for eight o'clock). This sounded very different from both The Beatles and the Scorpions. In fact, I understood almost nothing, except the endless thank you, please, and sorry that the polite people of Colchester specialized in.

My sister, eleven, was already writing mini-essays in English. Her latest homework was 'Write about your house'. She did. The teacher very nicely corrected her English. Your parents' bedroom can't be in the living-room, she said. A bedroom is where we sleep. We don't sleep in the living-room. But my parents do, my sister said. And when my grandmother comes to visit, she sleeps in the kitchen. It was like explaining about potatoes to the Dutch. Even in fluent English, some things about our lives were inexplicable.

Soon, I realized that the polite people of Colchester didn't know where or even what Bulgaria was. This was confirmed by a multi-choice quiz in a tabloid paper, where I found the following:

Bulgaria is a) a character in a children's story; b) a Soviet republic; c) a country in south-east Europe; d) a wild river in Mexico.

And then there was the shock of discovering that England was like a giant Korekom mall. There were nostalgia shops that specialized in teddy bears and antique dolls; music shops where all the records of the Scorpions and Bryan Adams could be purchased at once; and glossy chemists like Superdrug which dazzled with rows of roll-on deodorants just like the ones from Libya.

When the new school year started, I found myself at Colchester's Sixth Form College with rudimentary English. What subjects do you study in an English Sixth Form College when you want to hide your rudimentary English? French and Russian of course.

In the French class, I made my only two friends: Angelica, who had grown up in France, and Helen, who was black. I had never had a black friend before. The only other races in Sofia were construction workers from Vietnam, university students from friendly African countries, or Arabs like Fadhel. Diversity didn't exist in the glossary of our lives. Helen didn't seem to have many friends at the college, which in turn didn't seem to have any other black kids, and she took me under her wing, for which I was speechless – literally – with gratitude. At lunchtime we ate our sandwiches and packets of crisps. Helen talked at breakneck speed, while I desperately clutched at words, trying to work out what she was saying.

Meanwhile, my sister was befriended at her school by a little boy from Cameroon. They were the only foreign kids at an all-white, all-English school, which explained why nobody else wanted to befriend them. One day, the boy said to my sister, 'Assia, I really like you.' My sister, gripped with nameless feelings, spat back, 'And I hate you,' and ran away in tears. What she really meant to say but couldn't was that she was lonely, and that she didn't want to feel like a freak from a country that nobody could find on the map, just like him.

Helen invited me to her house for the weekend. It was a palace. Each kid had their own room, their parents slept in a proper bedroom, and no grandmothers camped in the kitchen. Helen's dressing-table was filled with the entire contents of Superdrug and Boots. I couldn't comprehend how it was possible to live in such opulence when her father was a self-employed electrician and her mother a secretary. It looked as if the revolution of the proletariat had failed in Bulgaria, but somehow succeeded in England. It was very odd.

Unfortunately, taking A-level languages meant that I also had to take a GCSE in English. It was terrifying. It didn't help that in the English class, the kids were ultra-cool and not interested in learning anything. The chief heart-throb, Jamie, was also the chief bully. He had wavy blond hair and a rugby-player's jaw, and presided over a court of lackeys who laughed at his jokes.

He didn't miss the opportunity to point out that I came from a country that wasn't a real country, but a character in a children's story called *The Wombles*. In Phys. Ed., Jamie mocked my cheap canvas sports shoes from the height of his bouncy Puma trainers, 'Are these made in Russia? They look like shit.' Jamie's lackeys sniggered. They all wore trainers like him.

'I'm not from Russia,' I said, 'I'm from Bulgaria.'

'Same thing.' Jamie said.

I remembered how chuffed I had been with these canvas shoes just a year before. Now I went home and threw them in the bin. I begged my parents to buy me Puma trainers, but they had no money for such whims. I dropped out of Phys. Ed.

In one of the first English classes, the teacher told us that he'd just seen a production of Beckett's *Waiting for Godot*. Had anyone heard of this play? Nobody had, or if they had, they weren't going to admit it. They chewed gum and didn't give a shit.

'It's a funny play, isn't it?' the teacher tried to involve them. I had just seen *Waiting for Godot* in a Sofia theatre, three times in a row. I knew the carrot dialogue by heart. In Bulgarian.

'It's not funny.' I ventured to speak for the first time. 'It's very sad.' All heads turned towards me. Jamie whistled. I wished the floor could open up.

'Ah.' The teacher smiled enigmatically with blue eyes. 'Thank you. But you see, in English, funny means two things: funny ha-ha, and strange. It's a funny language, English.'

In the Russian class I met my first proper boyfriend. Jimmy was tall and bespectacled, played the guitar, wore pointed boots like his hero the electric guitarist Joe Satriani, spoke crystal-clear English, and never laughed at the clothes I wore or the mistakes I made.

Jimmy lived with his mother in a semi-detached house which was almost as opulent as Helen's. His father worked in Birmingham as an engineer and was never home. He'd lost his job in Essex ten years ago, Jimmy explained, and was forced to take up work in the north, and all this had something to do with Margaret Thatcher. Now, as far as I knew, Margaret Thatcher was anti-Communist, so how come her policies resulted in Jimmy's father having the same crappy lifestyle as, say, the Mechevs above us in Youth 3? But Jimmy and I had better things to do than talk about politics.

For instance, Jimmy listened to a deathly pale singer called Morrissey, and a band called The Smiths who didn't exist any more. They specialized in a faux cheerful drone and their lyrics – often about accidents and Armageddon – seemed to be written in code. Jimmy was particularly enamoured of a song where each stanza ended with 'And heaven knows I'm miserable now', to which he sang along with an ironic expression; but somehow, I sensed that, deep in his bones, heaven knows he *was* miserable.

What was going on, why the misery? They had everything in Colchester. Jimmy had two guitars, hundreds of records, two pairs of pointed boots, and he could go anywhere he liked with his British passport. He didn't even have to learn Russian, he was doing it for fun. He didn't have to fear anything except the likes of Jamie.

But I was already beginning to suspect that material possessions and political freedom only brought you so much happiness. That, in fact, they could bring you unhappiness too.

When I went out with Jimmy and two friends, we sat in a pub and shouted over loud music all evening. They did something called rounds, which was a kind of drinking competition. At the end of the night, everybody won, and they vomited all the way home.

Another time, Jimmy took me to spend a weekend with a friend of his in one of the tidy nearby seaside towns, all of which ended with -on-Sea, as if you might miss that fact otherwise: Clacton-on-Sea, Frinton-on-Sea, Holland-on-Sea. His friend lived in an enormous Georgian mansion. We had a huge double room to ourselves and this was where we camped after it became clear that the rest of the night would be dedicated to something called tripping. This meant snorting cocaine. Jimmy wasn't into hard drugs, but his friend was. He could afford it, Jimmy said, they were filthy rich. But Jimmy was also worried that, despite being filthy rich, his friend might commit suicide one of these days. His friend seemed very unhappy. He spoke of that bitch his absent mother, of that bastard his absent father, and he said this Town-on-the-Sea was a miserable dump and he might as well shoot himself.

This threw me. I'd never heard anybody speak of their parents that way, not even Nikifor at School 81 whose parents hadn't done anything for him except land him in a Corrective Labour School.

Like Morrissey, Jimmy's friend evidently spoke a different language. Dump didn't mean there was rubbish lying around. As Grégoire had written in that birthday card, *'l'essentiel est invisible pour les yeux'*. Jimmy's friend lived in a castle but his future was a dump. I couldn't figure out how Jimmy and his filthy-rich friend had got to this point, but that's where they were, and I felt sorry for them.

Soon, I started feeling sorry for myself too. Even before I had proper answers to the complicated questions of happiness versus over-abundance, The Smiths had infiltrated me. I took to trawling the second-hand music stores of Colchester, trying to acquire every one of their albums. Even though the lyrics continued to mystify me, the more I listened, the more I became permeated with a damp, English despair.

After losing our virginity together – not pleasant, but a relief to have it over and done with – Jimmy and I became inseparable. If we ever parted, I knew I would cut my veins lying in a bath, to the soundtrack of Morrissey at his most miserable.

At the end of the school year disaster struck. Our visas to the UK expired. We had to go back and wait for new ones. At first, the separation from Jimmy seemed almost bearable, because like him I had already been accepted into Leeds University, my father had been offered a permanent job in a northern city called Hull, and anyway, there was no going back to our previous life now. You don't go from riches to rags.

So it was just a matter of weeks. Four weeks at the most, the Home Office said, and we packed up our two-bedroom house in Colchester, I said goodbye to Helen, Angelica, and Jimmy, and we went back to the cramped life of Youth 3.

Back in Sofia, things were grim, very grim. The euphoria of democracy and blue badges was gone, and what we had now was chaos, crime, and deficit. The only attempt at order was the coupon system. My mother had resigned her job at the Central Institute for Computational Technology, and her days now consisted entirely of queuing up with coupons to buy bread, sugar and petrol, sometimes for hours, sometimes for days. One day she joined a queue for petrol and vanished. She returned with a tank full of petrol a day and a night later. She'd waited for thirty-five hours.

It made no sense. Before, under Socialism with a Human Face, we had semi-empty shops. Now we had democracy and not much else. Even the last of the electricity was gone. Hot water – what's that? Toilet paper – what's wrong with newspapers? *The Worker's Deed* newspaper was a particular favourite in Sofia's toilets.

And there were rumours, conspiracy theories and sick jokes. One spring day we were at my uncle's flat in Youth 2. The satirical programme *Cou-Cou* was on TV. We were just tucking into roast chicken when, suddenly, the programme was interrupted by breaking news. An alarmed-looking presenter announced: 'There has been an industrial accident at the nuclear plant Kozloduy on the Danube. Citizens are advised not to leave their homes, and await further news. Radioactivity levels are being measured. We repeat: a serious accident has occurred at the nuclear plant Kozloduy. Citizens are advised...'

'Shut the windows!' everybody cried. Already there seemed to be a radioactive haze in the dead afternoon heat of the Youths. There was frantic discussion. Do we load up the cars now and drive across the border into Macedonia? Do we stay put? Do we stock up on tinned foods, like with Chernobyl? No, not another Chernobyl!

An hour and a collective mini-nervous breakdown later, the presenters of *Cou-Cou* gleefully informed us that the Kozloduy plant news had been a practical joke. Ta-da! It was, after all, 1 April. 'Bastards!' My uncle thumped the TV. Meanwhile, many people had got into their cars and sped towards the nearest border. Several people died of heart attacks, and at least one woman had a miscarriage. Our chicken was cold.

It was now six months later, with still no word from the Home Office. Clearly, they were considering our papers very carefully. My father went back to his job at the Technical Institute, which was no longer called Lenin. His monthly salary was almost enough – but not quite – to pay for a phone call I made to Jimmy in Colchester. What did I care for vulgar things like money when I had true love to deal with?

But my parents had other things to deal with. For example, the fact that my mother was suddenly diagnosed with a tumour and dispatched to hospital for emergency surgery. We didn't know whether the tumour was benign or not, and the hospital used newspapers (*The*

Worker's Deed, presumably) instead of sheets in the consultation rooms. The patients had to bring their own soap and towels.

I went to see my mother after the operation, but the hospital staff told me she was in no shape to receive visitors. I walked out a blubbering mess, my world flaking away like a house of cards in a nuclear gale. But everybody else's world was falling apart too, so nobody took any notice of me. Except a bedraggled homeless dog outside the hospital, who stopped her aimless trot and gazed at me pitifully. A pink, skinned rat hung from her mouth. We looked at each other for a while, then I ran.

As the power went out over the Youths, and we were plunged in darkness, my father sat in the kitchen by candlelight and filled in endless emigration papers in triplicate, while his hair turned grey. He was forty-three, and I had never seen him so old and so lost.

My mother miraculously survived the hospital ordeal, thanks to the wads of banknotes that changed hands between my father and the head doctor.

Meanwhile, Youth 3 had embraced capitalism. It had turned from the wild East into the wild West and it was hard to say which was worse. Tiny cafés and shops had mushroomed among the panels. People sold contraband cigarettes and suspect alcohol mixtures straight from their underground cellars. The elder Mechev son was a racketeer. He was charging people for parking their cars in our communal car park. But it's always been free, the bewildered neighbours protested. We've parked our Moskvich here for years. 'Well, things have changed. Pay up or piss off.' And he cracked the joints of his enormous fists. My once self-appointed protector was finally getting to rearrange people's faces. Yesterday's bully was today's entrepreneur.

My parents' friends were being laid off or were subsisting on salaries dwarfed by mega-inflation. My classmate Tedy was selling pantyhose at a street stall because her parents had lost their jobs. Beggars appeared on the streets. They were somebody's parents and grandparents. They were teachers, musicians, factory workers. I saw a dishevelled woman in the street, muttering to herself with a lunatic grin, and with a shudder of horror recognized a former teacher from the French Lycée.

And then there were the new rich. They were the kids of the old rich, but now they drove black Mercedes and called themselves businessmen. One thing was clear: money was king. Education, culture, and the life of the mind were for sissies, and sissies sold pantyhose on the street, walked the streets with a lunatic grin, starved to death, and were run over by speeding black Mercedes.

Real men, collectively known as *mutri* (gangsters) put together racketeering businesses, bought up government factories for small change and turned them into private businesses, trafficked drugs, weapons and women, laundered money, and felt like the winners they really were – until a rival racketeer shot them in the face. Real women, collectively known as *mutresi*, sold themselves to real men and rode in the passenger seats of the black Mercedes, wearing Gucci and a silicon pout.

The era of the gangster had dawned. Everyone else was drowning in a bloody sunset. It wasn't clear where exactly we would fit in this picture, except right outside the frame. Already the great mass exodus had begun. Everybody with a degree was filling in emigration papers.

Meanwhile, my sister was back at School 81, after two years in an

English school. And because academic standards in England had been much lower, she was now behind in every subject except English. Sensing the general climate of disaster, she did her best not to add to it with her school worries. She knew that we couldn't afford any more crises.

Just then, Jimmy arrived, bright and laden with gifts in the dirty snow of Sofia, like Father Christmas from a far-away land of plenty. In the dead of the Balkan winter, Jimmy heroically fought a blizzard from Youth 3 to the Central Post Office, to buy Christmas cards for home. If Jimmy was shocked at the misery of Sofia, he didn't say so. He was a proponent of the stiff upper lip, except when we had to say goodbye two weeks later. I'll see you soon, we kept saying at Sofia Airport. I'll see you soon, and we floated on a luxurious sea of eighteen-year-old tears.

The Home Office continued to consider our papers with such care that ten months rolled by, and our English future retreated further away, while our present remained suspended. Bored and depressed, I enrolled in a Spanish course, and sat there, conjugating the verb 'to go'. *Yo me voy, tu te vas, él se va, nosotros nos vamos, nosotros nos vamos, nosotros nos vamos*. Then one day I stopped eating. It was a protest – against what, I didn't quite know, but clearly something had to be done. And if you can't do anything to the world around you, you do it to yourself. I discovered that my cousin, the one who'd kept me company in the Suhindol fat farm that Chernobyl summer, had adopted the same strategy. We met from time to time, to discuss what had fewer calories: an apple, or a cup of coffee.

In the spring, I ran into Nikifor. I hadn't seen him since he disappeared into the Corrective Labour School. He had changed from a feral, snotty brat into a handsome man. A handsome one-armed man. We drank Nescafé in a basement and talked for the first time. What had happened to his arm?

'An accident.' He scratched his shoulder stump. 'When I was fifteen. I was in the factory where they made us work, and this guy pushed me. The last thing I remember before I passed out was seeing my arm on the floor. I had to relearn everything. I was right-handed, and now I'm left-handed. And what happened to you? Why are you so skinny? I heard you were in England.' And he added in English, 'Do you speak English?'

But there was no irony in his voice, and no bile in his heart. He was still living with his mother, who was still an alcoholic. 'It's a mess,' he said apologetically as he pushed open the front door of their apartment to reveal a humble one-bedroom dwelling. Full ashtrays and empty bottles everywhere. 'I'm the only person who cleans this place,' he said.

I remembered Jimmy's stoned friend raging against his parents in that town-on-the-sea, and I suddenly felt angry at everyone in Colchester, even Jimmy, who hadn't done anything wrong. But something was definitely wrong with the fact that they had castles to house their misery in, while Nikifor lived – literally – in a dump, and had nothing except one arm, a packet of cigarettes, and his stolen youth.

These days my school friend Rado was a full-time Metallica fan. He too was in a hateful mood. We walked together in the Park of Freedom, now renamed again Boris's Garden, and held hands as he quoted suicidal lyrics in an American accent.

Meanwhile, my classmates at the French Lycée, from which I had dropped out, were graduating. Rado, starched, polished and on his best behaviour, escorted me to the seventh form ball, where everyone looked grown up and serious. Grégoire, Maxim, Rado and many others were talking about studying law or medicine in France. Law and medicine scared me witless, but what if England didn't work out? I was then stuck with France, and maybe it took law and medicine to get there.

But it never came to law, medicine, or France. The Home Office finally remembered us. The passports arrived, three of them with visas, one without – the one that belonged to the eighteen-year-old in our family, no longer 'a legal dependent'.

My parents announced that they were not going to England without me. We were going to New Zealand instead. 'Where is that?' I asked. 'Near Australia,' they said. I fainted on the kitchen floor. It helped that I hadn't eaten for six months.

I would never see Jimmy again. I would never go to Leeds University. I consulted my world atlas, and there was New Zealand, two small accidental splashes of land at the bottom of the world, just above Antarctica. There was only one alternative: staying behind. Should I cut my veins now, or wait until we arrived in New Zealand?

'Go, for heaven's sake,' Rado said, 'And don't look back. It's the chance of a lifetime. I don't intend to hang around much longer either.'

'New Zealand?' Maxim said. He was going to study economics in Sofia. 'Classy. The further away from here, the better. And they speak English. Very classy.'

Jimmy maintained his stiff upper lip and vowed to emigrate to New Zealand as soon as possible. But something told me that he wouldn't.

Tedy was practical about it. 'You always wanted to be somewhere else. Just don't forget your friends.' How could I – it's not as though I had any friends in New Zealand. Did anybody live there?

Grégoire thought they spoke Dutch in New Zealand. 'So you'll have to learn a new language,' he said, 'but it could be worse. I'll write to you from France, I promise.' He didn't intend to hang around much longer either.

Nikifor was not surprised to see me go – nothing surprised Nikifor – and promised to write. 'I've heard they have penguins there,' he said. 'Send me a photo.'

Esther said, 'I wish I could go too…' and then, quoting from *The Hitchhikers' Guide to the Galaxy*, 'But don't let me depress you.'

Our luggage took up the trunks of two Skodas – ours and my uncle's – but when we arrived at the airport with my uncle and his family, somehow, in the chaos of tearful goodbyes, the keys to the second car were lost.

We missed our plane to New Zealand, and drove back to the empty Youth 3 apartment with its disconnected phone and empty bookshelves, where we holed up for two days in suspended animation, living out of suitcases, avoiding the people we'd said goodbye to, eating Ordinary Biscuits, and repeating something that closely resembled the carrot dialogue from *Waiting for Godot*. I'm hungry. Do you want a biscuit? No, thanks, I have some breadcrumbs in my pocket.

Three days later, the two-car procession and the tearful goodbyes were repeated. My cousin, who was ahead of me in the self-starvation race and had graduated to a skeleton, waved wanly from the other side of the glass pane separating the lucky departures from those who stayed behind. My uncle, always the cheerful macho, was crying, his bespectacled face smeared on the other side of the glass. I was completely numb. A sick, dumb relief was all I felt.

That was it, then. Goodbye England. Goodbye France. Goodbye Bulgaria. Goodbye Youth 3. I don't know where the hell I'm going, but I never want to come back.

PART TWO

Other Misadventures

'I love my country. Because
it is small and I feel sorry for it.'

An unnamed Yugoslav child
in the 1990s

8 She Grows but Never Ages

Getting reacquainted

And here I am again, fourteen years after that decisive farewell, waiting for the tram and inhaling the mountain air of Sofia, thick with pollen and pollution. Nothing is quite so decisive any more. In fact, since leaving, life has been a series of indecisions.

I have lived in France and in reunified Berlin, I am living in Britain as a putative New Zealander, and I haven't listened to Morrissey for a long time. But I also haven't felt settled anywhere since we left Youth 3. Someone else lives there now, and someone else lives in my grandparents' apartment in Emil Markov, which is no longer called that, of course.

In fact, when I look at the latest map of Sofia, I find all sorts of strange new names replacing the strange old names. First to go were street names like Machine-building Street, Hammer and Sickle Street, 11th Congress of the Bulgarian Communist Party Street, The Great Turning Point Street, Socialist Victory Street, Barricade Street, Heavy Tank Street. Next to go were the names of Communist Fighters and Heroes. Many street names are now prefaced with Prof., Dr, Gen., Tsar, Princess, etc. Some of them I've never heard of, because they have been resuscitated from the pre-Communist pantheon. Some of them used to be Fascists, Monarchists, Capitalists and Enemies of the People not so long ago.

In the renamed streets of central Sofia, orange trams and red buses lurch along a patchwork of old and new buildings. They're over-shadowed by giant posters of sultry goddesses advertising perfumes, 'mobiphones', leather sofas, and bio-active yogurt. The façades of *belle époque* buildings peel like damp wallpaper.

Down on street level, Sofia's women are thoroughly epilated, manicured, hair-dyed, tailor-dressed, perfumed, and pouting.

I am taking a tram to the National Palace of Culture. A bird-like woman with a messy nest of shopping bags looks me straight in the eye and smiles beatifically before she gets off at her stop, 'This weekend there's a convention for people who believe.'

'For people who believe in what?' I ask, helping her with the shopping bags.

'In God, of course. A belief that there is a better life than the one we have here. Do come if you can.'

And all these years I thought the misguided belief in a better life was simply called emigration.

'Thank you,' I lie, a bit disturbed that of all the people on the tram she chose me.

Ah, the National Palace of Culture! It squats across the tram line, its black and white eighties design blurred into dirty grey. It's the biggest convention centre in the Balkans, and perhaps the ugliest. I spent many happy formative hours there, gaping at festival films and classical concerts, and there is, of course, the plush café where Keti played the piano. The National Palace of Culture is approached through a gloriously long row of malfunctioning fountains, punctuated by a giant grey wreck of a monument originally called '1300 Years of the Bulgarian State'. Now it's known by various less stately monikers, including 'The Fallen Messerschmitt'. It was supposed to resemble a flag, but it always resembled a chunk of asbestos encased in granite. It was built in record time in 1981 for the 1,300th anniversary of Bulgaria's founding. And in record time, only a month later, letters started falling from the poetic quotes glued around its girth. Today, only one word remains, 'reborn', from a nineteenth-century song line about identity and revival: 'Go, reborn people, go towards the bright future!'

And here, in the bright future, the reborn people (pensioners) sit in the shadow of the fallen Messerschmitt by a mural of exploding graffiti art, complaining about their blood pressure and the price of bread. Next to them mothers with babies talk about poos and manicurists.

I sit beside them and wonder: Who do I call? Who is there left to see? What has become of my old friends?

Toni is married, with two daughters. Like his father, he is a physicist at the Academy of Sciences. I'm a coward, I know, but I don't call him from fear that we'll have nothing meaningful to say, except, 'Do you remember Comrade Gesheva…?'

Nikifor is married, and has two offspring. I'm relieved for him, but I'm also relieved that I don't have his phone number. What would we have to talk about? We had written a few letters, then stopped because he couldn't afford the stamps to New Zealand, and I didn't have a camera to take that penguin photo for him.

Tedy is an optometrist. The country is full of diabetics, she tells me, and many of them are going blind. Although we don't have much in common, over the years we have never missed each other's birthdays.

Maxim is an investment banker who lives between Paris and London. His languages and his brains served him well. He married a French woman, developed an expensive-looking bald patch, and rarely goes back to his home country. Every few years, we catch up in Paris or London and swap sardonic notes on our lives.

Boris is an underpaid surgeon in Sofia and thinking of emigrating to Canada. His time in the morgue across the road wasn't wasted.

Esther's mother died of cancer soon after we said goodbye, and Esther emigrated to Canada where she now lectures in literature and hopes for tenure. She returns to Bulgaria once every few years. 'I'll never feel particularly Canadian,' she emailed me, 'but I'll never go back to Bulgaria, and after ten years away, in what way am I actually Bulgarian?'

Right now, that's a question I can't answer for her, or even for myself. Right now, my deep suspicion is that it's possible, perhaps even inevitable, to live between – no, among – nationalities. It's a bit like wearing different suits, all of them the wrong size, all of them slightly ridiculous, either too baggy or too tight. They don't make the right size any more, it's been discontinued. But I also suspect that the

Bulgarian suit was never the right fit for me, or for Esther.

Fortunately, I have more urgent things to do than navel-gaze or gaze at the remnants of the fallen Messerschmitt. I'm catching up with Grégoire, who lives in France and is briefly in town to see his parents. Will we recognize each other?

Eight years ago, at the luggage belt of Sofia Airport, I instantly recognized Grégoire among the cluster of bedraggled émigrés disgorged by Air France. We were both visiting for the first time since emigrating. That winter in Sofia was glum and slushy, and I was glad to have a return ticket.

'Do you remember that time when I asked you out?' he said. I did. 'You saved me then by turning me down. I was so relieved when you said no. Because at that point I realized that I would never be attracted to girls. It was a turning point in my life.'

L'essentiel est invisible pour les yeux. Finally, it made sense.

'If only Bulgaria would have me back, I'd return,' Grégoire continued. 'I'm sick of French prejudice. I can't get a job in dentistry, despite my qualifications. I'm not making many French friends. My boyfriend is a Moroccan. But I can't return to live in Bulgaria until I'm thirty, because of national service in the army.'

Now we are over thirty, the sun is out, the trams creak towards a blue Vitosha Mountain, the chestnuts are blossoming, the beautiful people strut their backsides and fake Gucci sunglasses along Vitosha Boulevard, and Sofia looks decidedly liveable. Grégoire is sitting in an outdoor café by the tram line: a chubby, bespectacled Gregorian monk sipping an espresso.

There are so few moments in my life when the past and the present connect in the right place that I am overcome by a grinning happiness at the sight of Grégoire. But he isn't grinning.

'All the good men in Paris are taken, or don't fancy me. I'm on anti-depressants which make me drowsy. Paris is not a city, it's a meat-grinder. I yearn for Bulgaria. When they show a programme about Bulgaria on French TV, I bawl my eyes out like an idiot. But how can I come back? The gay scene here is all transvestites and freaks. And I still can't tell my parents. They still ask about girlfriends. Hello, I've never had a girlfriend! If I came back, I'd be coming back to a lie.'

'Remember how much we wanted to go to France?' I try to cheer him up. 'I was even prepared to study law or medicine!'

'Well, I did, and look where that got me.'

Along the chestnut-lined Boulevard Patriarch Evtimii, we're getting closer to the French Lycée. Time shrinks buildings and people, everybody knows this, but I'm still shocked by how tiny the Lycée looks. On the front steps, the new generation of French students smoke in morose silence or mutter sweet nothings into their mobile phones. They are fully occupied with the vanities of adolescence. I remember how that felt. We go inside to have a look.

'Yes?' a doorman greets us inside. 'Can I help you?'

'We're former students, we just want to have a look,' I say.

'OK, no problem.' He waves us in.

We look into the common room and the teachers' rooms. A teacher we don't recognize is marking student papers at one end of a long Politburo-style table, tapping his cigarette in a giant, fag-filled glass ashtray.

'We're looking for Madame Taleva,' I say. 'She was our French teacher.'

'Madame Taleva? Never heard of her. How many years ago is this?'

He laughs. 'Are you kidding me? Fifteen years ago I was a university student.'

We walk back down the stairs. The faded, bare-breasted Liberty is still on the wall, leading a faded people. The guard looks up from the pastry he's busy eating and wipes his mouth with a tissue.

'So, did you find what you were looking for?'

We shake our heads, then nod – yes, no, *da*, *ne* – confused by two different body languages and the tricky question.

Then we go stand in the Lycée courtyard, where the latest graffiti art greets us: '2006: Tits and Joints'. I look up to the classroom where we sang '*Ma Normandie*' with the now vanished Madame Taleva. '*C'est le pays qui m'a donné le jour…*' There is a broken window.

'Were they happy years, do you think?' I ask Grégoire.

'Well, if I'm not happy now, I must have been happy then. When I was at the Lycée, I wanted to be in France, to be free, to be myself. Now that I'm in France, I wish I could come back here, to be at home again. I feel more connected with the past than with the present. Is that normal?'

'I don't know,' I say. 'Probably not. But at least you feel connected with something.'

We hug and he waves as he disappears into a chipped underpass.

For now, I feel connected with hunger, and I drop in to see one of my closest remaining relatives in Sofia, hoping to get fed.

Auntie Lenche still lives in her darkened ground-floor apartment, just off Vitosha Boulevard. Across from her is a modelling agency called Visage. Three years ago, a small bomb went off outside the 'agency': one bunch of 'businessmen' blowing up another. The bomb was small but Auntie Lenche's kitchen windows shattered. She had to pay for her own repairs, of course.

'But we haven't had any problems since then,' she tells me cheerfully. 'I just stand at the window and enjoy the nice-looking girls and boys who go in and out of the agency doors. You know, two of them were kissing outside the other day. They saw me looking and became shy. I shouted to them, "Kiss away while you're young. Look at me, old and useless!" They liked that.'

Auntie Lenche's hair is thick and white like sheep's wool. She went white at the age of twenty-five, long before her life was blighted by an unpleasant husband and the terminal illness of her daughter, Pavlina.

Pavlina died twelve years ago. Auntie Lenche stopped wearing lipstick and fortune-telling with coffee cups. Now she is kept company by friends and neighbours, and a nameless turtle in a tank on top of her fridge. She opens the fridge and begins to extract salad, goat's milk, crumbly white cheese.

Auntie Lenche graduated from an American college in Sofia, but can't remember any English, except 'Would you like some tea?' It was all several lives ago, before the Communists, before the war.

She has always been religious. She stood her ground, even in the early 1980s when young thugs working for the secret police stopped her on the street at Easter and demanded, 'Hey, comrade, where are you carrying this candle?' 'To church,' she said. 'We advise you to put it out,' the thugs said. 'Is it illegal to carry a candle? If it's not illegal, then I'm not going to put it out,' she said. 'Now excuse me, comrades, but I have things to do today.' The thugs couldn't think of anything to say and let her pass.

Auntie Lenche has a corner of the dead in her chilly living-room. There she lights candles and gazes at the portrait of the smiling Pavlina in private moments so far down in the pit of grief that it's hard to imagine how she ever crawls out into the light. Her life revolves around death anniversaries and religious festivals. Yet she is the least morbid person you'll meet. 'God and the Virgin look over me,' she explains matter-of-factly, the way she does everything. 'Now, I've made lamb soup, your favourite.'

At this point, Auntie Petrana arrives. She is my grandfather Alexander's sister. Even after sixty years in Sofia, she remains a quintessential Bulgarian peasant: energetic, pushy, free of self-pity and complications. She has a house in her native village, where she goes every other weekend, and brings back for Auntie Lenche fresh milk, a chicken or two.

Auntie Petrana and her husband were proper peasants in a past life but, like the Mechevs in Youth 3, they were proletarianized and forced to work at Kremikovtsi Factory near the Youths, for decades exposing themselves to noxious substances. This resulted in her husband's early death from cancer and Auntie Petrana's close brush with the same fate. She partially lost the use of her right arm after surgery for breast cancer, but this doesn't stop her from cooking.

Today, she has brought an enormous tin of mince-stuffed pastry.

'Auntie's child.' She gives me a tearful, bristly kiss. 'It's been so long. Your Auntie Petrana made you a mince pastry, let's see if you like it.' And she wipes her tears and sweat with a large man's hankie.

I've forgotten that she's deaf, and that she sometimes speaks of herself in the third person. We eat salad and mince pie and, without further ado, Auntie Petrana downs half a water glass of home-made rakia, strong enough to knock out a herd of bison.

'Here's to the child's visit!' She suddenly gets tearful again. 'Ah, your grandfather Alexander, how I miss him! How I miss my brother!'

'I miss him too,' Auntie Lenche says. 'He used to come every day, after lunch at the Veterans' Canteen. We had coffee and discussed the

Healer newspaper. I subscribed to it, and he came to read it. We were like brother and sister.'

'Why did he do it, huh? Why did he have to do it?' Auntie Petrana cries out, her eyes red.

'An accident, it was a tragic accident,' Auntie Lenche hurries to say. In her Christian world, suicide is not an option. I'm about to join in the tearful chorus, but Auntie Petrana has moved on.

'They showed New Zealand on TV,' she goes, 'and it's all water. By God, nothing but water! How does your foot ever get a grip on dry land, tell me? And I look at the houses there, and I go, that's where my family are, in that nice house!' And she smiles at me with a couple of random teeth.

'Auntie,' I say, 'what happened to your teeth?'

'Ah, don't talk to me about that! I'm so mad at my dentist. She took 200 lev, and gave me a set of teeth big enough for a horse, I can't put it in! A horse, I tell you, a bloody horse.'

'Now.' She turns to me. 'When are you going to give birth.' It's not a question, it's an accusation. 'It must be about time, how old are you now? Twenty-five? Twenty-eight?'

I choke on my meat pie with laughter.

'Leave her alone!' Auntie Lenche protests. 'It's her business if she wants to have kids or not. The main thing is to be healthy.'

'Ah, ah, that's right,' Auntie Petrana shouts. 'It's time to think about these things. I want great-grandchildren before I die. Don't you wait for me to die!'

'The mince pie is delicious, Auntie,' I say.

'That's right, don't you wait for me to die!' She wags a finger at me and downs another half-glass of rakia, then reaches for the wine bottle. Auntie Lenche sighs and looks at me.

'She's deaf and stubborn like a mule. But she's the only friend I have left. All my friends have died.'

'What?' Auntie Petrana leans across the table in a cloud of booze. 'Speak louder, I can't hear!'

'I say you are my best friend,' Auntie Lenche shouts.

'Ah, ah, good. I'm glad you like it.' She pats her on the arm and peace is made.

In the afternoon, I go to browse books in Slaveikov Square. The book market here is encircled by trams, and flanked by shopping streets. The 'American Embassy', as it's known here, displays its scarily grinning red-and-yellow clown and Макдоналдс sign.

On the book stands, vintage porn mags rub naked shoulders with foreign dictionaries, classic novels, *The Tibetan Book of the Dead*, *Kama Sutra*, Secret Societies and Underground Movements, Dan Brown, John Grisham, illustrated recipe books and – at a stall manned by a lank-haired bookseller – a toxic collection of anti-Semitic literature. After an unpleasant exchange in which the man accuses me of being brainwashed and tells me that, actually, he's a Buddhist, I move on and another bookseller mutters to me, 'He's selling rubbish. It lowers our standards.' His own stall offers an extensive selection of Bulgarian *Playboy* back-issues, including the inaugural one, featuring an astonishingly smooth-bodied sixty-year-old Lili Ivanova, Socialism's greatest pop star, naked apart from a fake tan and some strategically placed roses.

I step into a shady courtyard and discover a huge antiquarian bookshop. This is where I have my first taste of the expat's rip-off. It's about time anyway. The shop is piled with the literatures of lapsed eras and discarded schools of thought, and overstaffed by unshaven men with bursting shirt buttons who sit on plastic stools and exhale cigarette smoke.

But the main operator here is a middle-aged woman with a hawk's eyes. She spots me fingering a book by an Italian academic about the salvation of the Bulgarian Jews.

'A rare book,' she says. 'You'll be hard pressed to find it elsewhere. Twenty-five lev.'

This is about three times the price of a regular book. When I protest, she protests back that it's the only such book on the Bulgarian Jews. I protest that it's not. Dimitar Peshev, one of the key public figures at the time, wrote about the anti-deportation campaign in his memoirs. Tsvetan Todorov too...

'And who is he?' she asks lethargically. He's one of France's foremost modern thinkers, I say patronizingly, and he's Bulgarian.

'I'm glad for him.' She turns away from me and lumbers off. 'You can take that book or leave it.' I leave it.

At one end of the square, near the traffic lights, a blind accordionist in an undersized jacket sits on a chair. He is a fitful virtuoso with the keys, and his urgent voice from the past is drowned in the traffic noise of the present. I've seen him before, once here, another time in Varna, once even with a blind band. He gets around. Right now, he's singing 'Exiles', a poem by the early twentieth-century poet Peyo Yavorov:

> And the time will never come
> for us to make it back:
> an infinity of water and land,
> the world will be a dream to us.

One of the booksellers, a man with a tired pony tail, comes up to him.

'Uncle, I'll give you one lev to stop singing these dirges. Sing something cheerful.'

The accordionist smiles with a black mouth, as if to say, 'I can do that, young man, but you are a philistine', and changes the minor key to major.

At the other end of the square, an old tramp with plastic bags sits on a bench next to two bronze statues, gentlemen with hats and canes. They are the Slaveikov father and son, two of the classic Bulgarian authors on sale here, and they have the avuncular smirk of historic detachment. What do we care? they are saying. We did our best a century ago, and you went and made dog's breakfast of this country. Idiots. Now you sort it out.

The tramp next to them mutters in agreement as he crumbles some stale bread for the square's fat pigeons.

Happy news: today is Palm Sunday. Here it's called Tsvetnitsa, All Flowers' Day. People with flower-related names celebrate their name day, and since Kapka means a drop of water, I decide to join them from the more marginal ranks of dew-related names. In the muggy, overcast morning, I head out to Alexander Nevsky Cathedral to watch the festivities.

Several hundred people crowd in the giant gold-domed cathedral underneath enormous crystal chandeliers, while a choir chants mellifluously from the balcony above. The overfed priests in gilded robes, led by a goggle-eyed patriarch, swing incense and chant '*Boje pomiluy*' from atop their luscious beards. '*Boje pomiluy boje pomiluy boje pomiluy.*' God save us. Several women with used-up faces and nervous systems wipe quiet tears.

Everybody carries or wears branches and flowers, and the

enterprising Gypsies outside are doing a roaring trade with all things green. A bunch of Gypsy kids follow me, and ask what's inside my camera. You, I say, and they collapse into giggles. An old beggar with a long white beard and rags wrapped around his feet is doing an impersonation of a nineteenth-century Russian serf, and small coins fall into his tin from generous festive hands. He mutters something about Judgement Day. I adorn myself with a laurel wreath and take a walk along the yellow tiles of central Sofia disguised as a mad bacchanalian, eyes running with hay fever.

The antiquarians outside Alexander Nevsky are selling painted icons, Soviet-era memorabilia, matrioshka dolls, wild animals skins, wind-up watches, German antique cameras, silver filigree jewellery, Baltic amber necklaces, fur hats, Socialist militia hats, leather cowboy hats, feathered hats for art deco damsels, photographs of smiling black and white people, gramophones from the thirties, and small busts of Lenin.

Behind me is the deafening gong of Alexander Nevsky's festive bells, all 100 tons of them. Before me is the glittering new Grand Hotel Sofia, and across, the former King's Palace. And between them is the empty space where the mausoleum of the Great Leader Georgi Dimitriov stood before it was blown up in 1999. Three generations of bewildered school kids passed through the marble catacomb and gazed at the moustachioed mummy lying inside, wondering, like me, if he was plastic. It turns out that sometimes he was.

Every year and a half, the Great Leader would be lowered into an underground laboratory, where he was re-embalmed by a team of experts trained by Soviet colleagues already experienced with Lenin. The Great Leader's gutted body took a bath in 300 litres of embalming fluid, was stuffed with fluid-soaked towels, and dressed in a new suit made by his personal tailor. Meanwhile, a plaster dummy was displayed in the cabinet upstairs while the lights were tested. Who knows — and who cares — whether I saw the mummy or the mummy's dummy.

By 1999, when the mausoleum was dynamited by the army, it had had an eventful series of second lives: as an opera prop for *Aida*, a shelter for drifters, squatters and junkies, a public toilet, and a giant graffiti board. As the mausoleum was prepared for destruction, two astonishing things were revealed.

One, the mausoleum was a labyrinth of corridors, passages and underground shelters as sturdy as the Civil Defence bunker we visited at school, complete with surveillance cameras. It had been built by the army to house the entire Politburo in a nuclear emergency. Just how sturdy it was became clear to onlookers when the same army that had built it had to blow it up not twice or thrice, but eight times, over the space of several scorching August days. As the explosions went on, the surrounding streets struck up a cacophonous orchestra of car alarms, a last salute to all those decades in which school kids had worshipped the mummy of a murderer.

Two, before the army came to remove the body in 1999, the scientist in charge of the mummy surreptitiously extracted the Great Leader's brain. He wanted to test it for mercury, and the forensic analysis suggested that the Stalinist murderer was likely murdered by Stalin himself. The theory goes that Dimitriov was urgently called up to Moscow in 1949, where he was exposed to mercury fumes. He died in Sofia two months later.

But not before thousands of Sofia's decadent capitalist bourgeoisie, previously known as the middle class, had been executed at swift kangaroo trials with Dimitriov's blessing. Thousands more were dispossessed and interned in the provinces: 23,399 people, to be precise. When the ban on these families was lifted in 1953, they were free to live wherever they wanted. Except in Sofia, Plovdiv, Burgas, Blagoevgrad and Varna (then called Stalin) or any other city. Or anywhere near the borders with Greece and Yugoslavia. This ruled out most places, which was the idea. The lucky ones were allowed to stay in their own homes, which were no longer theirs but the State's, and pay rent to the State. The luckiest ones were allowed to occupy a single room in their own house, for free, and share the rest with strangers who paid rent to the State.

Could Stalin have killed his protégé Dimitriov for being too soft on enemies of the people? Easily: Dimitrov was just a small squiggle in the grand Stalinist design. And since the Bulgarian State couldn't investigate its big brother at the time, the awkward question was suspended for fifty years.

Meanwhile, it's lunchtime, and across the yellow-tiled square outside the Presidency the guard is changing. Two uniformed guards ceremonially march away from the gilded gates, and two fresh new guards march in. I walk past them and look at the four faces squeaky with youth. They were born around the time when East Berliners were pushing their way through the Wall.

For them, Sofia has always been like this: the café over there outside the archaeological museum, charming with ivy and Roman ruins; the gleaming, anatomically explicit, gold and bronze statue of Sofia with a crown bearing the city's motto 'She grows, but never ages'; the glamorous shopping arcade opposite. It is still called Central Universal Store but it's unrecognizable from the store of the children's red boot stampede. I go in.

It's a glittering, air-conditioned, clinically tidy emporium with an escalator snaking up its middle. The girls at the perfume stands offer me the latest Givenchy with toothpaste smiles. Upstairs, in the spot where my sister had put on those miraculous red boots, a shop sells sophisticated natural cosmetics: perfumes in large glass bottles; natural sponges built into translucent soap bars. I buy a bar of soap with rose petals trapped inside. The fragrant shop assistant offers to gift-wrap it. I'm the only customer. When I step outside, I glance back at the Party HQ. The red star and the portraits of Lenin and Georgi Dimitriov are long gone, of course, but the building still looks sinister. I'm not the only one to think so, because for years it's been empty. They can't decide what to do with it. Personally, I see a large red KFC sign at the top...

I head for the plump-naved St Nedelya Church to check out the action on Palm Sunday. Among much chanting and swinging of censers, a displeased one-year-old girl in a silk white dress is baptized by bearded priests. Everybody in the baptism party is wearing their finest clothes today, 16 April. But they are glum and sombre with their candles, and they may as well be holding a funeral.

The sixteenth of April is a memorable day. On this date in 1925, a bomb went off right here, in the biggest terrorist attack in the country's history. Six hundred souls were gathered in the church for the funeral service of a general assassinated two days earlier by a Communist terrorist. The assassination had been only a pretext for the real attack, which targeted the government of Tsar Boris III. The Tsar himself was away that day, attending the funerals of those who had died in the latest attempt on his life, ironic for a man who refused to sign death sentences as the constitution required of him. But the bomb went off anyway, and the collapsed domes of the church buried 150 people, not one of whom was a government minister.

The priest is now sprinkling the ever-more displeased baby with a gilded cross dipped in holy water. And now exit the baby, the priests, and the candle-carrying believers. I straighten my laurel headdress and follow them out. I'm off to the Synagogue for a change of scene.

The Synagogue gate is locked, and when I buzz the bell, a middle-aged guard opens it. 'We always lock it, you know how it is these days.' He's glad to have company in his solitary kiosk. On the little table is a notebook in which he has scribbled Hebrew words with Bulgarian translations.

'I'm not Jewish,' he catches my glance, 'but I meet so many Jews that I became interested in their culture and thought I'd learn some Hebrew to pass the time. They come from everywhere, you know, America, Australia, Israel. Some tell me incredible stories. Some grew up here. They say they'll always be grateful to their fellow Bulgarians, even if they can't speak Bulgarian any more.'

'So why did they leave?'

'Ah, well, because they could. Israel was a better place to live than Bulgaria in the sixties and seventies, wasn't it? And maybe even in the eighties and nineties...'

He buzzes in another visitor: a dazed-looking Italian with a cloud of frizzy hair. The Italian stops dead in his tracks and points at my wreath. He speaks Italian only. The guard and I manage to explain in a mixture of pidgin Italian and English that this is a pagan Bulgarian festival. When the guard gives him a kippah to wear inside the Synagogue, he seems surprised and questions it with wild gestures. 'For respect,' says the guard in English. The Italian shrugs and stumbles into the Synagogue. Inside, we discover – or I do anyway – that the century-old Synagogue has been wrenched out of disrepair with donations from Jewish foundations, mainly in Israel. The largest Sephardic synagogue in the Balkans is splendid, and splendidly empty.

The Jews – the 2,500 who remain in Sofia – are fairly invisible. It was partly this invisibility and lack of enviable financial success that made them indistinguishable from their average struggling countryman, and meant that when anti-Semitic propaganda infected Europe in the 1920s and '30s, Bulgaria remained largely immune. After all, Bulgarians had plenty to worry about, for example recovering from the First World War, during which they fought on the losing side at the cost of nearly two hundred thousand lives. As well as coping with Macedonian terrorists, Communist terrorists, and the police terror of the tsarist government. Really, Bulgaria was psychologically booked up far in advance, there was no room for anything more.

So when the rest of Europe was dispatching its Jews to the trains, and Hitler was putting pressure on the government of Tsar Boris III to join in, city Jews were displaced to the countryside and forced to wear the Star of David while doing heavy labour on roads and railways. But when the trains and boats were prepared, public figures and ordinary people stood up against the deportation.

In a curious triple stroke of ignorance, self-deprecation, and Semitic apathy, Bulgarians don't celebrate – or often even know – the fact that all 58,000 Jews in the country were saved thanks to letters and public speeches from progressive and sometimes Communist politicians. The Metropolitan of Plovdiv vowed personally to lie on the rails if the trains left. And so the trains of the Holocaust never departed, although it was a close brush. Later on, the trains of emigration did depart, leaving behind only 16,000 Jews.

The dazed Italian and I walk to the Hali market together. Our language barrier is too great to explain ourselves to the other, but I manage to establish that he is from Bologna and he's here on a three-day holiday. What makes an Italian from Bologna come to Sofia for a three-day holiday? He shrugs his shoulders, as though he's surprised to be here himself. What else should he see? I point to the big blue mountain looming over the city. Vitosha, I say. 'Vitosha,' he memorizes. He kisses my hand with a florid gesture, and extracts from his trouser pocket the kippah he has nicked from the Synagogue. He waves it at me with an impish wink as he walks away, and I wish I could speak Italian. Now I'll never know whether he's newly released from a psychiatric ward, won a trip for two to Sofia but had no one to take along, or wants to invest in property.

The neo-Byzantine Hali is a covered market that sells Greek olives, oriental pastries, Bulgarian honey by the vat, German delicatessen items, Italian clothes made in Turkey and Greece, domestic appliances made in Spain… It's clean and tidy like the Central Universal Store, and not nearly as smelly and exciting as it was in its early days in the 1900s. Nobody is shouting or proudly slapping the carcasses hung from hooks. The butcher used to hack off the chosen part, then make a finger-sized hole in it. The customer departed with a piece of meat hanging from his index finger, brushing away the flies.

For a taste of good old squalor, I drop in to see the much cheaper Old Wives' Market behind the Synagogue. There's no meat, but the mountains of fruit and veg, the string of nargile shops, the sellers gossiping on low stools and eating sunflower seeds is the closest you can get to old Sofia's oriental vibes.

The mosque of the Baths, Banya Bashi, is just across from the Hali. A Turkish boy wraps me in a green mantle and flicks the hood over my head. I rejoice in my religious promiscuity. Inside the carpeted mosque, a single man reads the Koran, back against the wall. The mosque is bare and minimal, with the predictable orange and blue Koranic flower motifs. Until the early twentieth century, Sofia was an

Ottoman backwater with muddy streets, oriental markets, and dozens of mosques, but Banya Bashi is the only surviving memento of those times.

Outside, a well fed, middle-aged Arab addresses me in Bulgarian. He looks familiar. Then I remember.

'You are Abdel,' I say.

'Yes, Abdel. How do you know?'

I know his name because I met him here two years ago. He came from beneath the oak shade to chat to me outside the mosque. He told me he was Palestinian, but had a Bulgarian wife, a Bulgarian passport and a Bulgarian business – 'import-export' – here in Sofia, which wasn't doing so well. He was thinking of leaving, for Switzerland or Italy.

But now he doesn't remember me.

'How's your business going?' I ask.

'Business is OK. Better with European Union now.'

'And you're still living here…'

'Ah, still living here. I love Sofia too much. But maybe I go Switzerland, Italy…'

'Abdel,' I say. It's a long shot, but it's worth trying. 'Do you know a man called Fadhel? Algerian. Must be about your age now.'

'Fadhel? How he looks?'

'He looks… good. With glasses.'

He blinks.

'I know Fadhel in Lyon.' Abdel looks at me. 'With glasses. He have three childrens. He live in Sofia before. You know him?'

It must be him. How many bespectacled Fadhels from Algeria have lived in Sofia?

'But he not looking so good.' Abdel mimics a paunch bigger than his own. 'I looking better.' He laughs and pretends to smooth his thin grey hair. Then he points at my wreath. 'All Flowers Day,' he declares, and shakes my hand. The conversation is terminated, and he returns to his job as a full-time dweller in the oak shade of the mosque. I walk away in a daze, my delicate memory of Fadhel dislodged collectively by the paunch of an Arab in Lyon, three teenage kids, and a wife with a covered head.

A mellifluous chant distracts me from these thoughts. Actually, it's two chants. The muezzin is calling for prayer, and someone else is calling from loudspeakers behind the Sheraton Hotel across the road.

I peek into the excavated courtyard where some of Sofia's Roman life lies scattered about. The voices of angels are coming out of the pink-hued St George Rotunda. It's evening vespers. I walk down a white-tiled street towards the church, the only remaining street from Serdica, the Roman city that stood here.

They found Roman Sofia in the 1950s, when the authorities decided to remove the old heart of the city, with its narrow streets and bazaars, and erect a brave new centre in its place. This would have giant modern buildings, like the Party HQ and the Central Universal Store, which was built on the site of a flea-market and a popular Bohemian hang-out, the Armenian Café.

The only building they spared was the Mineral Baths, with its medicinal healing waters. In the course of the digging, the workmen hit a mineral water spring which burst onto Vitosha Street and flooded it. It was the middle of winter, and all along the city's main artery, the Gypsies of Sofia removed their shoes, rolled up their trousers, and paddled in the warm water.

The St George Rotunda is not quite as old as the Roman ruins – it's from the sixth century. In the sixteenth century, the Turks under Sultan Selim painted over the Christian saints and angels with flowers, and called it the Rose Mosque. Three centuries later, the Bulgarians stripped the Koranic motifs to reveal the saints and angels again. The result is a piece of layered time-art.

Inside the bare-stoned, high-domed church, a gaggle of downy-faced black-clad seminaries, as young as the presidency guards, chant the prayers of eastern orthodoxy around a pulpit. They take turns reciting the self-deprecating words in their unformed, timid voices. 'God instil me with fear of your heavenly might, I who am unworthy and unholy, your everlasting slave…'

The people standing in the audience cross themselves repeatedly and bow down to the floor. Searching for symbols of identity and nationhood, post-Communist Bulgaria is clinging to the beards of eastern orthodoxy. These days every public occasion is accompanied by an overweight priest in embroidered robes, swinging an incense-burner, and every politician, from the Socialist president to his contender in the far right party Ataka, makes sure that they are photographed kissing the hand of some gilded patriarch, either here or, even better, in brotherly Russia.

A woman with a careworn face wipes quick, mechanical tears and mumbles desperate prayers with pale lips. Her two young daughters, dressed in jackets and trousers they've outgrown, imitate her movements. All three cross and bow, cross and bow. It's not so much a prayer as a lament.

An angel from the ninth century gazes down on us from the dome way up above our heads, with something like pity on what remains of his face.

*

It's hard to believe that the busy American Bar and Grill was formerly The Hungarian Restaurant that provided both my first experience of dining out and a fight scene involving my father, a rude waiter and a plate of meatballs. Now, waitresses in mini-skirts and dyed hair smile 'enjoy' as they serve steak and fries.

My grandfather Alexander liked the American Bar and Grill – he liked the bland food and the waitresses in mini-skirts. He brought me here for my twenty-ninth birthday lunch, and we were joined by Auntie Lenche and his best surviving friend, Ljubo. Ljubo gave me a book of his mother's poems translated into English. My grandfather gave me a synthetic fur coat, to keep me warm in the future winters of my life.

Just across the road is a tinted-glass pavilion. It used to be the War Veterans' Canteen. At exactly twelve o'clock every day, my grandfather, Ljubo, and Nikolai Gaubich met here for chicken soup. They were all snappy dressers. In their beige coats, scarves, leather gloves, berets over silver hair, and gentlemanly manners, they were the last messengers from the old Sofia of the 1940s, before the new Sofia was hammered out on the anvil of Communism. After lunch, they would sit on the benches outside the canteen, bask in the afternoon sun, and talk politics.

Ljubo was the only son of Bulgaria's first famous woman poet and independent spirit, Elissaveta Bagryana. Tall and classy, he liked wearing gloves and telling naughty jokes. He had been a career officer in the King's Army, and had got as far as occupying the coveted Macedonia to the west before the tide changed and Bulgaria declared war on Germany – while briefly remaining at war with the Allies. Not bad for a little country with everything to lose.

My grandfather Alexander had been a reserve officer until the Red

Army absorbed the Bulgarian Army in 1944, at which point his unit was dispatched to rout the Nazi occupier in Macedonia – except the Nazi occupier had been helped by the Bulgarians until now. Either way, to Alexander the war was an extended holiday from adulthood. It sounded as if they spent their short time in Macedonia looting houses and getting drunk. Some of his soldiers were so dense that one time when looting a wealthy house with a piano in it (without his authorization, my grandfather stressed), they wrenched the lid off and made a bench out of it, hilarious fun. 'They'd never seen a piano before, can you imagine, they looked at it and they saw wood!'

If grandfather was the episodic soldier, Nikolai Gaubich was the artiste of the three. A renowned opera singer in his day, he had toured the world, and spoke a smattering of languages. He conducted an elegant, old-fashioned correspondence with me, the way he had corresponded with my grandmother Anastassia during trips abroad. His letters started or ended with '*ma chérie*', and were accompanied by an epigrammatic poem. His wife had died of cancer years ago, and his only son was killed in a car crash. Towards the end of his life, his poems turned maudlin and I filed them away in a drawer. Nikolai's sudden death was a shocking blow to my grandfather. The countdown had begun.

I take a long walk by South Park, along the boulevard whose length I travelled a hundred times on the buses of my childhood, because at the end of the bus line was Emil Markov and my favourite place in Sofia – my grandparents' apartment.

One side of the apartment looked towards Vitosha Mountain and the outlying houses of the village where the Fighter for Freedom Emil Markov was shot by the Monarco-Fascists. I mean, when the Communist terrorist Emil Markov got shot by the police.

The other side looked out onto a green children's playground, where my grandmother Anastassia sat on benches chatting to neighbours who would ask me with greasy smiles, 'Who do you love more, Mummy or Granny? Granny or Grandad?' I suspected these were trick questions, so I always replied, just in case, 'I love everybody equally,' which didn't satisfy the neighbours at all.

On my thirtieth birthday, which I celebrated in New Zealand, my grandfather was preparing for the arrival of his daughter, my mother, for her annual visit. His life had become narrower and lonelier since she had been there last. He was a cautious man. He disliked travel, change, noise, and risk, which in the end meant human company. He had stopped going to the War Veterans' Canteen because he was afraid of slipping on the winter roads. Besides, there was no one left to talk to – Gaubich was dead, Ljubo in hospital. Grandfather maintained order at home, read a lot, and wrote his comments in the margins of books. A professional accountant to the end, he loved organization. But now there was nothing left to organize.

The neighbourhood was quiet that morning. He stood in his old rubber flip-flops, leaning out of a window to shake the dust off some blankets. Perhaps his thoughts wandered across to the visitor on her way from Singapore. He was a tall man. Perhaps he slipped and the weight of the blanket pulled him out. Or at least he had planned it to look that way – a well-organized death, an accountant's death. They would arrive on time to bury him. He would not become a burden to his only daughter abroad. Either way, he fell from the window with the blanket, like a flying man in a Chagall painting. A child found him lying on the pavement seven stories down, carefully covered by the blanket, his flip-flops still on his feet.

A day after his death and my thirtieth birthday, in far-away New

Zealand, he appeared to me in my troubled dreams. 'Stop worrying about me.' He waved his hand irritably. 'I'm fine where I am, things are simple now. You think about yourselves now, your lives are complicated.' The subconscious was fixing the conscious.

But now, standing underneath the balcony, by the bench where my grandmother had sat, in the spot where my grandfather had been found, conscious and subconscious merge into two horrible human-shaped stains of absence. I quickly start walking away and soon break into a run. Two stray dogs stir from their afternoon nap among the spilling rubbish containers and bark after me, bedraggled, homeless creatures from the underworld of the past.

When exhaustion finally stops me, I find myself outside a '2 to 200 lev' shop. I go in. It sells packets of soap bars, threadbare towels, and plastic flowers. Three men in socks and rubber slippers sit on low stools around a small fold-up table, drinking tea and speaking Arabic. I reach for the most accessible things on the crammed shelves — a packet of pegs and a small glass teapot in a plastic frame.

'Very beautiful when tea is inside pot.' The youngest of the men gets up from the small table and wraps my loot in newspaper. Where are they from? They are Syrians.

'We have childrens here,' says the young man by way of explaining the strange phenomenon of three Syrians in Sofia. 'We are marry to Bulgarian women.' I compliment him on his fluent Bulgarian. How long has he lived here?

'Nine,' he says, and grins mysteriously with a golden tooth. His T-shirt says 'You are not alone,' the motto of the campaign in support of the Bulgarian nurses and Palestinian doctor in Libya condemned to death, for nearly nine years now, on false charges of infecting children with HIV.

My purchases cost me a grand total of 4 levs. Just as well, because the moment I try to use them on the balcony's clothes line, every one of the pegs breaks, and as soon as I pour tea into the glass pot, it shatters on the bench-top and hot water floods the kitchen floor. Incongruous tears fill my eyes, as if this crappy pot was a family heirloom. We don't have an heirloom. And right now, it feels as if we hardly have a family. My parents are in New Zealand. My sister is in London.

Grandmother Anastassia fixes me with a Gioconda smile from the folds of her pink shawl. How did that saying go? The living close the eyes of the dead, and the dead open the eyes of the living. In any case, she knows something I don't.

I should have bought some plastic flowers instead, I say to her, vengefully dumping the teapot, the ridiculous gift-wrapped soap, and the wilted pagan wreath in the bin.

True, they are hideous, but they last for ever. You can't ask for everything.

9 Freedom, Perfection or Death

Macedonian misadventures

In an old box of photographs at Peach Street, I find a photo of an exotic-looking woman with black hair, dressed in oriental garb and reclining on cushions. Someone has scribbled on it 'Ohrid, 22 April 1943'. This is my grandmother Anastassia, aged nineteen, at a costume party in her Macedonian home town, where she could have stayed and enjoyed a comfortable provincial life. But history and personality interfered.

It all started when, in 1932, in the lake-town of Ohrid some 300 kilometres from Sofia, a tailor called Kosta Bahchevandjiev got into a spot of trouble with the police. This was my great-grandfather. On a moonless night, he smuggled himself in a boat across Lake Ohrid and into Albania. From the Albanian coast, he sailed across to southern Italy, and after travelling the length of the country, he entered Austria, then Hungary, then Romania. It took him a couple of years, but he finally reached his end destination: Sofia.

Why this insane itinerary when he could have just crossed the border into western Bulgaria in a matter of hours? Because he was on the run. He was a man wanted for multiple debts, a man facing gaol. In Ohrid between the two world wars there was only one way to get out of paying yours debts: become a Serb and stick 'ich' at the end of your surname. If you insisted that you were Macedonian (-evski) or Bulgarian (-ev), you faced several options starting with gaol, and, if you really insisted, ending with murder. Kosta insisted, and then got the hell out of there.

It so happened that Ohrid, and all of today's Republic of Macedonia, had been annexed by Greater Serbia following victory against an aspiring Greater Bulgaria in the First World War. Bulgaria under Tsar Ferdinand had sided with Germany and Austria-Hungary in the hope of regaining western and Aegean Macedonia. These were historically seen – by Bulgaria, not by her neighbours of course – as Bulgarian lands. Why?

In the 1877 Russo-Turkish war, Bulgaria was liberated from the Ottomans. But before the news had time to sink in, this longed-for independence was cleaved in two by the Great Powers with one neat stroke of the pen. The 'big four' swiftly drew up the new borders of the Balkan region well before they invited the Balkan nations to the Congress of Berlin.

In the fateful and hateful Treaty of Berlin, independent Greater Bulgaria was dismembered and large chunks of it given back to the Ottomans: Vardar Macedonia (today the Republic of Macedonia); Pirin Macedonia (the south-west); and the whole of the south. With just a few signatures overseen by the dyspeptic German Prince Otto von Bismarck – who referred to the Balkans as 'places of which no one has heard' – the Great Powers made sure that the Balkans became places of which much would be heard in the following century.

So in the First World War, the Bulgarian army occupied and reclaimed all Macedonian lands, but the tide turned and it had to withdraw. The tide turned in such a way that, far from regaining anything, Bulgaria lost even more land, sustained the highest per capita casualty rate in Europe, and was left bleeding and deranged with loss. In other words, it was set to make new Macedonia-bound grabs in the next world war, which it did, also with disastrous results.

Meanwhile, great-grandfather Kosta saw himself as a Bulgarian, and viewed the brisk Serbianization of Macedonia as a crime. He resented his children going to Serbian school, and he resented people being imprisoned for refusing to say they were Serbs.

So did his wife, the switched-on and buttoned-up Ljubica, from one of Ohrid's prominent families. The personal motto of her famous relative, writer and educator Grigor Prlicev, was 'Perfection or Death'. Ljubica applied this principle in her own life with alarming energy. But now, in the wake of Kosta's desertion, Ljubica had more prosaic worries, such as how to feed her three children. Families were suffocatingly close knit, but once you were married, you were your husband's problem. Ljubica put on a widow's black frock to mark her husband's fiscal death, just in time for her own parents' real deaths which left her with nothing. After all, she was only a girl. Out of the inheritance her two brothers shared, they magnanimously gifted her a sewing-machine. This way, she could at least make clothes for Ohrid's bourgeoisie, to which she no longer belonged.

Three years later, she and the three kids joined Kosta in Sofia. He tried to set up a tailor's shop, but times were hard and they had no family to help them out, and now lacked even a sewing-machine. They lived in Banishora, a notoriously poor quarter near the railway station where tens of thousands of Macedonian refugees from across the border lived in cramped misery.

Sometimes they had nothing to eat. Ljubica, always one to keep up appearances, laid the table at dinner time, to give the landlady the correct impression. But the plates were empty. Kosta would get drunk and aggressive on just one glass of cheap wine. The more helpless he felt, the more he drank. Once, while Ljubica was in hospital, Anastassia came home and informed her father that she'd been diagnosed with malaria. This distressed him so much that he hit her on the face, knocking her to the floor where she remained for some time.

Every family must have its bleak winter, and this winter in Sofia was theirs, just as 1991 was ours sixty years later. Anastassia and her younger brother Slavcho amassed so much hunger and misery in those years that they spent their adult lives eating themselves into oblivion.

And now the dark vortex of European politics was churning, and Bulgaria was being sucked in, dragging the Bahchevandjiev family with it. In Banishora, Macedonian families like them endured brisk midnight visits from unshaven men with small foreheads and pulled-up collars. They were 'collecting funds' and they were the foot soldiers of the VMRO or Internal Macedonian Revolutionary Organization, which has the distinction of being Europe's first terrorist group. Actually, there were lots of groups, all at war with each other over the fate of Macedonia, and they operated on the principle of the mafia's state-within-a-state. This many-headed political monster was the offspring of the Treaty of Berlin. Their banner read 'Freedom or Death' and depicted a crossed dagger and gun, with a bomb for good measure. By the mid-1930s, the VMRO were responsible for 1,000 political murders, including two Bulgarian prime ministers and King Alexander I of Yugoslavia. In Sofia, Macedonian became synonymous with violence, conspiracy, and sinister disappearances, and the saying went:

> Where is Mitre the Macedonian?
> The moon swallowed him.

Great-grandfather Kosta was an urban Socialist and a nationalist, and it's certain that he sympathized with the VMRO cause. What is not so certain but quite possible is that he was a VMRO agent. A killer he was not, this much we know. There were plenty of angry young men for that. All we have is his disgusted mumblings, later in life, about the savagery of VMRO's 'punishments' of 'traitors' which featured removing the heart of a living man.

Meanwhile, on her street in Banishora, seventeen-year-old Anastassia met a dashing blue-eyed man called Alexander. He spotted her jumping over a puddle, and exclaimed 'Whoops!' – clearly a winning chat-up line. She looked at him, he had a nice blond face, and the rest is history. Actually, the rest was the Second World War.

As war broke out, the Bahchevandjiev family left Sofia and went back to Ohrid, now safe for them courtesy of the occupying Bulgarian army. It looked set to become part of Bulgaria once more. But the family's hopes were dashed when the town was retaken by Yugoslavia a few years later.

Kosta kept a low profile now. He was too old to die for lost causes. Finally exhausted of his political fervour, he was once again a small-town tailor. Ljubica continued to read the papers and talk politics, but in public they kept their mouths shut, so as not to injure their children who were making their way in life as young Yugoslavs.

Their plates were full, but their spirits were broken: Bulgaria and Macedonia were now living separate lives and would never be reunited. Until the end, Kosta continued to hum a dismal little song that went like this:

> From the top of Pirin Mountain
> I hear a sorrowful voice.
> Macedonia is crying:
> Be damned, oh Europe,
> Babylonian whore,
> bloodsucker of Macedonia.
> The French, the English, the Italian, the German
> Want us to be slaves.

He replaced Italian with Serb to keep with the times – after all, the song had been written in the wake of the Treaty of Berlin a century ago, and a few things had changed. But in this family, as in many others, the song seemed timeless. Even grandmother Anastassia used to hum it in her homesick moments when the shadow of the Yugoslav border loomed darkly.

*

The orphans of political divorces are always people. And in the Bahchevandjiev family, that person became Anastassia. In the mid-1940s, Anastassia was one of Ohrid's prettiest eligible young women. She was Sofia-educated, vivacious, olive-skinned, and strong-willed.

She looked like a movie star. But she wasn't a movie star, she was a bored school teacher, and Ohrid was a claustrophobic little town where the gentry's eyes were always on you. Having tasted the excitement of Sofia, Anastassia felt that her life was on hold here.

She was also in love. The blue-eyed man from Sofia started writing to her at the end of the war. Her yearning to be with him merged with the urgent need to discard her small life in Ohrid for bigger and better things. She couldn't set foot on the town's cobbled streets without stirring gossip: that hothead Kosta has been shuttling the family across the border for twenty years now. Like father like daughter. Such a pretty girl, so many suitors, but no, it won't do. God help her. But unlike her mother, Anastassia didn't care about God or public opinion. She didn't care about reality either.

In the box with the photo, I also find a typed letter addressed to Anastassia, dated September 1947, months before she crossed the border and threw in her lot with a man she hardly knew. The letter is from that man, and it is chilly enough to freeze the blood of the most inflamed romantic. Over two pages, he convincingly lists all the reasons why she should forget about him instantly:

> We have had permission from the Ministry of Foreign Affairs and the Directorate of the Militia for your visa. In two days, we will also have the decision of the Balkan Commission.
>
> I received your two letters and the photo, full of hope and love. You remain an idealist, unwilling to consider the ugly side of our decision.
>
> Your arrival won't be greeted by anything pleasant. You will find me completely unprepared for marital life, morally and materially. There is love, but will love be enough to shelter us from the dark forces of dire need and privation? I think not.

My salary is decent, but not after you take out my expenses for cigarettes (two packets a day) and pubs. You see, in the years we haven't seen each other, the war has changed me for the worse. The irregular and miserable life I have led has given me every imaginable vice. I drink heavily, and knowing of your bitter experience with this in your own family, I shudder to think of what awaits you here.

It is up to your feminine artfulness, perseverance and selfless love, strengthened by the legal bounds of matrimony, to make our marriage bearable, to shelter me inside it. It is a heavy chore, but once you have taken it upon yourself, you must bear it without complaint and regret. Don't misunderstand me: I am writing this in all honesty, as I do not wish to be accused, one day, of being the coward who dragged you into the abyss of his own life. Think carefully, objectively and sensibly before you take the fatal step.

Anastassia, aged twenty-three, thought carefully, objectively and sensibly, as you do when you're twenty-three. Two months later, she took the fatal step. After all, her interpretation of the famous family maxim was 'Romance or Death'. Never mind if the man she had chosen didn't have a single romantic bone in him.

In drab, impoverished post-war Sofia, where you bought everything with coupons and even coupons were in short supply, she had no money, no friends, no family, and no way back. All she had was her high-maintenance new husband who was a good man, but after four years of war he was a good man with a stomach ulcer, one deaf ear, a taste for drinking, and a cynical outlook. Now she discovered how painfully honest that letter was.

They lived in a house previously owned by a wealthy banker. That banker was now an Enemy of the People and pounding rocks in a labour camp. His house was turned into a tenement and rented out to the People. The young couple had a room, and shared a communal toilet with other families. There was no bath, so once a week they made a trip to the flat-roofed Mineral Baths, courtesy of the Romans. In their street was a row of bombed-out houses, courtesy of the Allies. Soon, a baby was born, which quickly proceeded to develop a pre-tubercular cough, followed by kidney disease. This was my mother.

But Anastassia was blessed and cursed with a surplus of romanticism. My mother, when asked by people whose child she was, was instructed to reply 'a child of love'. Anastassia lived simultaneously in the wrong time and the wrong place. She was a summer thunderstorm in a dark winter of the soul. Her taste for drama, her exotic looks and poetic notions of life clashed with a singularly unpoetic era. The regime strived to maul precisely such people and spit them out as 'work cadres'.

In the 1950s, Anastassia became a cadre at Radio Sofia, where she broadcast a programme for the Macedonians in Yugoslavia. The idea was to remind them of their true (Bulgarian) heritage, and it was blatant revisionist propaganda by the State. In the sixties, in yet another bewildering about-face, the State decided that the Macedonians didn't exist at all (because they were in fact Bulgarians), and the programme was scrapped. Now she broadcast a programme for 'Bulgarians living abroad'.

As relations between Yugoslavia and Bulgaria soured, the border was sealed off. Propagandist murals appeared on Sofia's buildings, featuring a fat-faced ogre in black holding a cleaver dripping with blood: Tito. Anastassia couldn't see her family, and in the space of twenty years she only called them three times: when her brother got divorced; when an earthquake flattened Skopje; and when her father died.

If Anastassia ever felt that the blue-eyed man she'd chosen had dragged her into the shallow abyss of mediocrity, she never let anyone know. He was not the knight in shining armour she had dreamed of, that much was clear even to her. He was an accountant from a sensible peasant family. She chose to see his emotional incompetence as a 'bedrock of strength' and wrote him poems, but he never found it in him to bring her a flower for her birthday. She yelled at him in fits of jealousy, and he slammed the door in boorish silence. He had no taste for drama – or affairs, for that matter. She wrote radio plays, and he could only sing one tune, the painfully simple hymn of the peasant: 'When I was a shepherd/and grazed my sheep/I was grateful for my lot/though I was a poor sod.'

But when, aged fifty-something, she fell into the abyss of illness, he followed her there loyally, like a humble, voiceless Orpheus in the underworld. And when Hades swallowed her, like a mute shadow he wandered the world of the living, until his own demons devoured him.

After several hundred euros' worth of border levies, Rado makes it to Sofia in the new Peugeot. He brings me flowers – real, not plastic – and we assure each other that we haven't changed since we last met five years ago. Or even fifteen years ago. I tell him many things, but I don't tell him that I still keep the first – and last – letter he sent me after I left Bulgaria. It was for my nineteenth birthday. I was by then moving slowly, skeletally, in an arctic chill of the soul at the bottom of New Zealand's South Island, which was inhabited, but only just.

'For your birthday,' he wrote, 'I booked two tickets to a screening of *The Wall*. The cinema was packed. Only one seat was empty, the one next to me.' Then he had signed off with a stanza from Metallica's latest hit ballad about trusting who we are and how nothing else matters. I didn't know who or where the hell I was, but I kept the letter, a message from a far-off land.

The next day, we borrow his father's beat-up old Renault, and head out of town for a few days. Cultural objective: to have a look at Pirin Macedonia in southern Bulgaria. Personal objective: to meet again and find out who we have become.

We are now standing outside the huge gates of Rila Monastery, where our bespectacled family was photographed a dozen times in the eighties alongside grinning French, Dutch and Japanese scientists in horn-rimmed glasses. Rila was the number one officially sanctioned attraction to show visitors from abroad. True, it was a monastery – slightly awkward for an atheist regime – but as the largest monastery complex in the country, it was also 'a cradle' of Bulgarian identity.

'The object is observed by cameras,' a typed-up sheet in a plastic pouch greets us. Rado finds this sign so amusing he wants to get photographed with it. Inside the courtyard, the gallery vaults explode in a symphony of colours. The velvety ranges of Rila rise on all sides. It's heart-stoppingly beautiful, but we are distracted by the frescoes. They are the work of nineteenth-century artist Zahari Zograf who painted half of Bulgaria's monasteries. Here, he has drawn graphic scenes from purgatory, replete with hairy devils and round-bellied sinners. On another side of the church, every sin is scrupulously depicted and defined in old Bulgarian, for example 'Sodomites or those who sin with man or woman unnaturally'.

'Beware sodomites,' Rado warns the courtyard, and people turn to look at the madman in denim jacket and dark glasses. I suddenly see that in the seventeen years I've known him, he has grown into a Clive Owen lookalike – dark, deadpan, destructively attractive to women. But blink again, and he is seventeen, awkwardly rocking along with Metallica in his fake denim jacket.

We're told that Father Varlan is responsible for the 'reception' at the monastery. Three humble provincial women pilgrims with battered travel bags stand in the courtyard patiently, waiting for him. Father Varlan appears on the third-floor veranda, his black cassock sweeping behind him. He's a young bearded priest with a businesslike manner. The three pilgrims speak up timidly from the ground. They'd like a couple of rooms for the night, please, father. 'Yes, yes.' He waves them away. 'I'll come down in a moment. Yes, back up those files and download the images,' he yells across the courtyard to another monk and vanishes into a cell, not to be seen again. Rado's guess is that he is surfing the net between the four bare walls of his cell.

Bearded priests in black cassocks shuffle around with a purposeful air. I ask one of them, a chubby-faced man with bug-eyed glasses, when the ethnographic museum will open. He stares at me myopically. The two villagers he is talking to also stare. 'Will it be open soon?' I repeat.

'No,' he nods, baffled by my impertinence. 'They're renovating it.'

'Yes, but when will it reopen?' I insist.

'Whenever they finish renovating it.' He shrugs self-evidently, astonished as much by my vulgar directness as by my ignorance. I thank him and move on to another priest who hovers around the gates.

'When do the monastery gates close, Father?' I ask. He gives me a mistrustful glance.

'When the sun goes down,' he mumbles, slipping away from my obnoxious presence. 'Or later.'

We drop into the monastery museum to stare at the Rila cross, a minutely wood-carved cross with 1,500 tiny figures that took a devout monk called Rafael twelve years to carve with a needle, and then took his eyesight. We also find an original document from 1378, the monastery's charter, written in the hand of Tsar Ivan Shishman, the last king before the Ottomans decapitated the Bulgarian state. At the mere mention of Ivan Shishman, I hear the soothing radio voice at 7.15 a.m., 'Bulgaria: Deeds and Documents', and feel a wave of sleepiness wash over me.

In vain, we look for the monastery's famous relic: the hand of the eccentric Ivan Rilski, the tenth-century founder of the monastery. Turns out it's been put safely away since a particularly devout pilgrim a century ago tried to bite off a chunk. Not surprising – Ivan Rilski tried to embalm himself while still alive by drinking special potions, and his disciples were so impressed by this, they believed his dead body to have healing properties.

'Still, I wouldn't go so far as to take a bite,' Rado remarks, earning an unsympathetic look from the heavyweight female museum guard.

Inside the church, which implodes with exquisite walnut-carved iconostases, more fabulous frescoes, and countless priceless icons including a reportedly miraculous one of the Virgin Mary, we spot the tomb of Tsar Boris III. Well, tomb is not quite the word – because here, underneath the sand, is buried a jar containing his heart, his only physical remnant. After being buried here at his own request in 1943, only two years later the tsar's body was disinterred, and the floor tiles of the church hurriedly rearranged. This brainwave emanated directly from the Great Leader Georgi Dimitriov who wanted to ensure that the popular tsar's tomb didn't become a site of pilgrimage.

In the same wave, and seemingly unaware of the undercurrent of saintliness they were allowing to run between saint and tsar, the authorities tried to remove Ivan Rilski's hand from the monastery grounds. But the lorry 'miraculously' didn't start on that occasion, and the hand stayed put inside the monastery. The tsar didn't, and his remains, together with the truth about his death, were lost in the shifting shadows of post-war conspiracy. Some believe he was poisoned by Hitler for being too soft on the Jews, others that he died of a heart attack. Some say that his ashes were scattered in a gorge, others that he was buried at his Vrana Palace outside Sofia, then disinterred. By then the new royals of the day were already living it up at Vrana Palace, and they might well have liked to dance over the dead body of a decadent monarcho-fascist. Either way, in the 1990s the heart was 'accidentally' found and reburied here.

But the most haunted place in the entire monastery is the refectory. Soot-blackened chimney, giant cauldrons, stone ovens. It's a medieval hovel of hunger and warmth. I smell the thousands of litres of bean soup, the tons of soda bread. I hear the crackle of candles burning, the bubbling of wild boar stew, the rustle of cassocks and scratching of itchy beards, the slurping and toying with worry beads, the long, holy silences. No downloading of files, no intrusive visitors with cameras. Just God, the sun rising behind the velvety mountain, and the Turks lurking outside the gates.

Outside the gates, Rado opens the car trunk to reveal a whole crate of sandwiches made by his mother, and enough fruit provisions for a month. We picnic heartily and then, fortified like plump monks, we wave goodbye to the humble pilgrim women who are still waiting in the courtyard, and trek up a tranquil wooded path to a well-groomed grave.

James Bourchier, Balkan correspondent for *The Times* for thirty-three years, peace activist, and defender of the losing side in the Balkan Wars (Bulgaria) and in the First World War (Bulgaria), asked to be buried in Rila. Unlike the other distinguished dead around here, he had the good fortune not to be dragged away posthumously in an army lorry. During his twenty-odd years in Bulgaria, he often came to walk in Rila, in the company of Tsar Ferdinand, Boris III's father, the man who loved Bulgaria and especially Greater Bulgaria so much that he dragged it into two catastrophic wars. I wonder what Bourchier, an Irishman, would make of the plaque at his grave, which carefully explains in Bulgarian that he was a 'great English friend of the Bulgarian people'.

We drive south along the straight, empty highway to Greece, and soon we enter the landscape that Tsar Ferdinand's army had so bitterly fought for. The snow-capped, jagged peaks of Pirin Mountain shimmer in the blue distance like a mirage. Our next stop is near the Greek border, at the foot of Pirin.

As we approach the border, bilingual signs begin to appear on roadside cafés and shops. We stop at a stall selling jars of home-made ewe and ox yogurt, and green, translucent fig jam. A soft-bellied waiter stands by the stall, a napkin folded over his forearm.

'Is there any goat's yogurt?' I ask him.

'It exists,' he says gravely, gazing into the distance. 'But it's runny, you can't cut it with a knife. Ox is better.'

'So where can we find goat's yogurt?' I insist.

'You'll have to ask the people with goats.' He shrugs in that deeply Bulgarian way — resigned, fatalistic, almost mystical — and waves vaguely towards the hills, his stained tea-towel flapping in the breeze. We pile back into the Reunault.

'Where are the people with goats?' Rado wants to know, but before we work out this riddle we reach Sandanski, world famous in Bulgaria for its medicinal air and mineral springs.

As an asthmatic child, I spent holidays here with my grandparents, Anastassia and Alexander. I ate salty corn on the cob in a wondrous white town with a chatty fountain in the middle. Sandanski is also allegedly the birthplace of the Thracian gladiator and slave leader Spartacus. When in the eighties Hollywood's *Spartacus* was screened on TV, no doubt because the broadcasting censors saw in him a worker fighting against the capitalist-imperialist machine, I gaped adoringly at the muscular Kirk Douglas. Why, he was almost from Sandanski. He was almost one of us, with a delay of about two thousand years.

We stop in the middle of town and buy food from the street stalls: dried cherries from Iran; dates from Turkey; cashews from India. Apart from the crunchy sesame seed bars and the fig jam, there is hardly anything local for sale here, despite the fertile soil. But luckily, a National Fair of Manufacturers has set up camp in the chipped Socialist-era cultural centre in the main square, and we browse the cheap clothes, shoes and cosmetics. 'Fancy some boots?' Rado picks up a stilettoed, fake snakeskin creation. 'When in Rome, you know...' And it's true, when we see the locals passing down the long, leafy pedestrian street leading to the park, they are dressed up to the nines in fake brands, every woman teetering on high heels.

The alpine flanks of Pirin rise on the edge of town like a tidal wave of memories. A small, broken fountain sits dejectedly in the main square. This is it, this is the magical white town. In a sudden lurch of vertigo, I sit on the edge of the chipped fountain and fixate on the tidal wave in the distance. Inside it, I see swirling my clueless asthmatic childhood, my glamorous grandparents Alexander and Anastassia, a blue Skoda, an orange Skoda, my scattered family, and fragments of things I can't quite make out. The chipped, monolithic Balkantourist hotel overlooking the square is where we stayed.

'Cheer up,' Rado says. 'Look how chirpy the locals are in their stilettos, eating their corn on the cob.'

We climb into the car and leave Sandanski behind, to fester with memories.

We nibble salty, firm-fleshed corn while we drive through dirt-poor villages without a soul on the potholed streets.

'Doncho for sale,' announces a scribbled sign pinned on a cart in the deserted village of Hotovo.

'Who or what is Doncho, I want to know?' Rado chuckles. 'Is it a donkey or an unwanted grandson?'

Another scribbled sign – '2 lv' – is pinned to the wire fence of an unfinished house sunk in weeds. Rado pulls over and we contemplate it for a moment.

'They're selling the house for 2 lev!' I guess. 'Bulgarian property prices hit rock bottom.'

'Or some cunning peasant is renting his rooms for 2 lev. So that when some hardcore backpacker goes back to France or Britain, he can boast that he stayed in a room for 1 euro. Groovy.'

What is happening, of course, is that the few remaining residents of Hotovo are selling their stuff out of desperation, down to their donkey carts.

We arrive in Melnik, endearingly known as 'Bulgaria's smallest town'. The river is lined with a hundred handsome stone houses, their upper storeys jutting out, in the nineteenth-century Revival style. It's all so small that if the snaking river went in a straight line, you could see the far end of it, and it's not very far. Why not call it a village?

Because this is not just the smallest town, it's also the saddest. For centuries, it was a plump wine-trading hub of some 20,000 souls — Greeks, Bulgarians, Armenians, and Turks — living, drinking and trading in contented prosperity. When the Treaty of Berlin gave this region back to the Ottomans, the new borders cut Melnik off from its trading partners. It was the beginning of the end. In the Balkan Wars of 1912 the Turkish army felt that if they were about to lose the town, they could at least gut it, and gut it they did. Those who weren't slaughtered fled south into Greece as refugees, and Melnik not only ceased to be a town, it ceased to be altogether.

These days Melnik is a tourist destination, but right now it's the off-season. We know it from the eerie emptiness of the main and only street. The local madman, a gentle muttering soul, wraps himself softly like a carpet over an iron press-up bar. Invisible cats mew with human voices. The river is thin, and the strange natural sandstone pyramids called *mels* lean over the huddled houses from the top of the hills, breathing raspingly in the dusk like asthmatics. Houses along the river greet us with signboards: 'Rooms to sleep', 'Rooms for sleep' and 'Sleeping rooms'.

Rado and I take two sleeping rooms at Complex Trayan. Trayan himself is oppressively chummy, and tells us that we can have fifty showers if we want to, because the water never runs out. And would we like dinner, they've just spit-roasted a tender little lamb.

Over tender little spit-roast lamb, Rado proceeds to get drunk on three 'single' rakias, which come in water glasses and together amount to half a bottle. I look at him aghast and he laughs it away. 'I'm a budding alcoholic, I know. No need to lecture me. Anyway, where are we at?'

Last time we saw each other, he was living with his Scandinavian girlfriend in France and studying law. With his eloquence and charisma, he was cut out to be a defence lawyer. I was going through bad relationships like bouts of flu, living in stark solitude, and making myself unemployable by writing a novel in Auckland. Five years later, Rado is going through a painful divorce from his Scandinavian wife, and working as an insurance broker after discovering that only French citizens are allowed to practise law – something foreign students of law in France are left to discover in their own time. He is now, finally, a French citizen, but it's too late. I've moved countries three times, found love which I'm going to lose catastrophically but don't know it yet, and become completely unemployable.

'Seeing you makes me feel seventeen again,' Rado says. 'Lately I've aged, emotionally and in every way. I mean, I'm thirty-two, and it's happened so suddenly, don't you find? Jesus, my friends are disappearing into nappies and mortgages, never to emerge again. I feel as if I've bungee-jumped into a world of grown-ups where I don't belong. No time of grace in the middle, no golden age.'

'Maybe our golden age is yet to come,' I offer.

He laughs cynically. 'I love your optimism. But I don't share it. No, I think our golden age was then. Of course we didn't know it, we never do. But think about it, it was simple. We knew what we didn't have, we knew what we wanted, and we went to get it. We wanted the world. We wanted to go and speak our languages. We wanted carnal knowledge. And now we've done all this and complicated our lives beyond repair... Now we've lost our innocence. Oh, I don't know...' He prods furiously at the rice-stuffed lamb.

'And now we don't know what we want,' I offer.

'I don't know what I really want. Do you?'

But we don't have time to ponder this, because our host Trayan plonks himself down at our table with a glass of rakia and treats us to a salty portion of politics.

'You are young people, and you should know some history. We are in Pirin, Macedonia. Ah, but we gave away our other Macedonian lands, idiots that we are, dumb idiots, slaves to the end…'

'Ah, but we didn't exactly give them away,' Rado interrupts. 'We fought for them and lost them because our army was pitted against the Serbs, Greeks and Romanians. It was a tad uneven. Besides, the Bulgarians attacked first and sparked off the Second Balkan War…'

But our host is not interested in military facts.

'How could we give away this land to the Greeks!' he bangs his fist on the table. 'Never! I'd give my last drop of blood to hold onto what's mine. Now they come here like kings with their euros, and throw money at us. No, I won't let my people go across to work in Greece and be Greek slaves! Over my dead body!' His face darkens, his mouth froths at the corners. He reminds me of someone, but I can't place it. 'I'll pay them double, but I'll keep them working here, not working like slaves abroad, like second-class citizens. We are a people of slaves, five hundred years of slavery, I tell you. Letting ourselves be crushed like fleas!' He crushes an imaginary flea into the folkloric tablecloth with his thumb. 'I won't let it happen! I won't be a flea!'

'No!' Rado agrees gleefully. 'Over my dead body will you be a flea!'

I laugh at Rado's mock-concerned face, but Trayan doesn't. Next thing, we're watching the news on the mehana's – or taverna's – TV, and we hear about a Bulgarian girl who was sex-trafficked in provincial Greece. When she managed to escape and drag herself to the police, the five policemen on duty gang-raped her. They will be sacked but not prosecuted. The Bulgarian ambassador in Greece makes a po-faced statement about trafficking being under control and working closely with the Greek police. After all, she was only a whore, runs the text between the lines.

'What did I say! The filthy Greeks, they think we're trash!' Trayan cries out to us and the other customers, two local men who smoke in silence. They shake their heads and look into the ashtray, lost for words. Trayan disappears into the kitchen, swearing under his breath.

Rado and I continue drinking, he especially. 'Ah, the filthy Greeks.' Rado grinds his teeth, and we laugh. We feel rotten for that girl, but we don't want to side with Trayan and foam at the mouth. We are so far above his neurotic patriotism we're practically from another country. But which country is that exactly?

'It's funny,' Rado says, 'I can only be Bulgarian when I'm in France. Here, I'm semi-French. Everything is funny and bizarre, and I laugh like someone watching a Beckett play. Except I'm a Frenchman with Bulgarian memories. I remember being inside that Beckett play. In France, I'll never be a Frenchman, despite my accent-free French. I'll always be *Rado le Bulgare* to them. At work, they think it's exotic, which is why I bedded all my female colleagues at my last job without moving my little finger. Flowers all around! OK, I know you don't approve, it's just an example. But I'll never be one of them. Ah, the filthy French!'

We laugh ourselves into a nervous exhaustion, and I retreat to my room, where I discover the meaning of the fifty showers Trayan promised: they're of the cold water variety, all fifty of them. In the morning, when Rado emerges, looking heavy-lidded, we inspect some local jams and peanut butter displayed at Trayan's 'mini market'. Trayan himself hasn't calmed down at all. He seems to live in a permanent state of patriotic paroxysm.

'This is fig jam,' he explains. 'The dumb foreigners don't know what jam is. Do you know that the French don't have a word for jam? *Confiture*, they say. *Confiture*, my arse. It's jam, jam, but they don't understand. The English don't have a word for jam either!'

'They do,' I say. 'It's jam.'

'No they don't!' Trayan shouts, raining spittle on us. 'They're a hundred years behind us in some ways. No, damn it, two hundred!'

'Make it five.' Rado winks at me and we collapse mirthfully.

'Five hundred.' Trayan agrees. Suddenly I realize who he reminds me of.

A sweat-stained, pot-bellied Greek man called Alexandros, with a gold medallion on his hairy chest and a long nail on his little finger, that's who. The medallion was in the shape of Alexander the Great's head, and Alexandros was the owner of a squalid one-star hotel in Thessaloniki (Greek Macedonia) where I once stayed for a week. Alexandros was given to pounding tables and shouting things like, 'Makedonia always Greek! Alexandros is Greek, Philippos is Greek. Four thousand years Greek civilization in Makedonia! We are childrens of Alexandros!' He was also given to referring to my family in the Republic of Macedonia as 'Skopjan Gypsies'.

Trayan and Alexandros don't know it, but they are brothers in chauvinism. The only thing that divides them is the wretched border.

We buy some fig jam, and get out of Trayan's spitting range. Despite Rado's hangover, we must do what everyone does in Melnik — taste the local wine. This, and the sandstone *mels*, is Melnik's reason for being.

Shestaka's Winery is perched picturesquely above the village, near the dreamy *mels*. We enter cool, dark caves full of wine barrels. Shestaka puts on some folk music for us and proudly answers my questions. Of course they serve meze with the wine, how can you drink wine on its own? He puts out a platter of sausage and home-made cheese. I glance at his hand for the six fingers that have given him his nickname. Shest means six.

A Bulgarian couple come in, the man long-haired, with a stud in his ear. 'Do you make rosé?' he asks.

'We don't consider rosé to be wine. It's water,' says the plucky Shestaka, his hands moving too quickly between bottles and plates for me to count the fingers.

'In Belgium, they drink rosé with their soup,' announces the visitor.

'They can do what they like in Belgium.' Shestaka is a stocky man with a face almost handsome in its rare moments of repose. 'They make raddish soup too, and they can have it with rosé all they like. Here, we drink real wine.'

I ask about the famous Melnik grape. And do they have other types of wine from around the country? I ask dimly, insensitive to local pride.

'No, there's only red Melnik wine here, you confuse things. And you don't even drink wine!' He flashes me a disapproving look. It's true, I'm allergic to red wine. I'm pretending to drink, but the wine is thick and rich like ox blood. It's only eleven in the morning and even Rado is restrained.

'That's why I'm asking you questions.' I smile, determined to break him with sheer psychopathic friendliness, like a Jehovah's Witness. I can afford to be friendly, I don't live here, I reason callously.

'You're a journalist.' the Bulgarian woman turns her beaky face to me accusingly. 'Journalists twist facts. I don't trust that stuff they show on TV.' She sits down righteously.

Rado and I thank Shestaka profusely and head out.

'You're very welcome.' He sees us off with a flourish, softened by our admiration for his wine. 'Come again.'

'You have to be nice to these guys,' I explain to Rado outside. 'They're jumpy like that because they're insecure. It's the region's history. It's not easy living here. Trayan needs…'

'What Trayan needs is fifty cold showers,' Rado wraps up.

From the lookout point above town, we survey Melnik's memento mori. The wilderness at the end of town conceals the thousands of wealthy houses from the bustling eighteenth and early nineteenth centuries, their ruins now overgrown. Then there's the Roman bridge, the ruins of the Turkish baths, the medieval ruins of the *bolyarska* house where the powerful ruler despot Slav lived. Of the seventy churches, only three are still standing. Even in times of peace, even on a fine spring day, border towns in the Balkans are ambiguous with melancholy.

The passing armies for some reason spared the Kordopoulova House, the largest Balkan private home of its time. But Turkish soldiers slaughtered the last Kordopulos descendants, ending the region's viticultural happiness. The elderly caretaker in a knitted shawl gives us handfuls of postcards and begs us to bring more visitors.

'This is one of the most beautiful houses on the Balkans, but we need more visitors to keep it going, to keep the town going.'

Inside the creaking house, an ambitious motto startles us from our seediness: TO LIVE MEANS TO STRUGGLE: THE SLAVE FOR FREEDOM, THE FREE MAN FOR PERFECTION.

The author is Yané Sandanski, a Macedonian freedom fighter from one of the VMRO factions, who gave his name to the magical white town of my childhood, and his blood to lofty ideals like freedom and perfection.

'I guess I'm not a free man,' Rado observes darkly, 'because I'm nowhere near perfection. I'm not even sure I'm striving for perfection. Are you?'

'I think I'm still striving for some sort of freedom. That makes me a slave, technically.' And an unworthy descendent of Ljubica's family, where striving for perfection was obligatory.

'But only technically.' Rado raises a cautionary finger.

We lunch in a riverside restaurant on a 'pork-made dish', eat the meaty Bulgarian tomatoes known as 'ox hearts' drizzled with Greek olive oil, drink Turkish coffee; and a fine, indiscriminate Balkan rain accompanies our meal instead of wine.

Large, comical *kratunki*, gourds, hang from house porches – a local souvenir. 'Want a *kratunka*?' Rado offers, and before I say no, he's buying in bulk from a hunched old man in rubber loafers. He smiles toothlessly and waves goodbye from his gate as if we were his long-lost grandchildren finally come to visit from the city.

We head up the hill loaded with fig jam, *kratunki*, and a peculiar Melnik blues that throbs in the head like a historic hangover.

The Sandanski trail takes us up to Rozhen Monastery, rich with a history of multiple sackings and burnings since its beginnings in the early thirteenth century. And a view as surreal as its history: in the foreground, a ring of golden-white sandstone *mels*, in the background, the snowy peaks of Pirin. And before the monastery, the tomb of the flamboyant Yané Sandanski, which may or may not contain his remains.

Sandanski was the Balkan Che Guevara; he even looked the part, with his spatula-shaped revolutionary beard. He is now a Macedonian national hero, and even pops up in the anthem of the Republic of Macedonia. He is also, naturally, a Bulgarian national hero, though the Bulgarian anthem wisely avoids names.

Sandanski led one major faction of the VMRO, but he differed from his brothers in terror. He supported the Young Turk Revolution and believed in a brotherly Socialist Balkan federation where all ethnic groups would be equal. In other words, he was a tragic utopian. But he was also a kidnapper. In what became known as the infamous Miss Stone Affair, Sandanski scored two firsts: the first kidnapping of an American citizen for political reasons; and the first recorded case of Stockholm syndrome. After the ransom was paid and the staunch protestant maiden Miss Stone was released, she became an ardent supporter of the Macedonian cause against the Ottomans, something that caused the American government acute embarrassment.

In his last years, between the devastation of the Balkan Wars and the devastation of the First World War, Sandanski took refuge here in Rozhen. The monastery was deserted: the Greek clerics were gone and the Bulgarian monks hadn't arrived. His nunnish sister was his only company. The free Macedonia his entire generation had fought for was now carved up between Serbia and Greece. Only tiny Pirin Macedonia remained in Bulgaria. When Franz Ferdinand was assassinated in Sarajevo, Sandanski saw a new disaster looming and wrote a letter to Tsar Ferdinand of Bulgaria: 'Your Majesty... you want to push Bulgaria onto the side of the Central Powers against the Entente, but... this will bring such disaster... that even the Danube won't be able to contain you.' He was right, but fortunately didn't live to see it as he was assassinated by VMRO agents with the blessings of the 'crowned wolves' (the royals) he so reviled. He was shot thirty times not far from where we stand now, at the monastery's bullet-ridden gates.

Rado and I watch an impeccably tailored and coiffed elderly French couple who look like the ambassador and his wife. They emerge from a diplomatic car and tiptoe gingerly through the mud, while a young translator briefs them on local history.

'*Mais c'est magnifique,*' the French woman exclaims, '*toute cette histoire.*'

Oui, madame, I feel like saying, the Great Powers ensured there was plenty of 'history' here. They also ensured that the psychotic shifting borders cut right through families and minds, generations into the future. I sense that Rado is having similar thoughts.

'You know,' Rado says suddenly, 'my mother's entire family came as refugees from Aegean Macedonia at the end of the First World War when it was reclaimed by Greece. They saw the Pirin ranges from the other side, as it were.'

'I wonder if they met any of the Greek refugees going the other way...'

'I don't know, but the more I meet clowns like Trayan, the more I feel that the whole idea of nationality is a stupid joke.'

Yes, but this stupid joke is deadly serious to some. Last time I saw Rado in Sofia, I was returning from a painful family visit to the Republic of Macedonia. There, fresh from my visit to northern Greece and Alexandros, aka 'four thousand years of Greek Makedonia', I made some startling discoveries about the malleable nature of ethnicity. Uncle Slavcho in Skopje was retired from the university, and overflowed with unused energy.

'You've just spent time in Greece and you've noticed that the Greeks are prone to delusions of national grandeur,' he said sweetly, and proceeded to brief me on the history of Macedonia, as conceived by the latest crop of deluded nationalistic historians.

'The ancient Macedonians of Alexander were proto-Slavs, and thus ancestors of today's Macedonians,' he explained.

I pointed out that the Slavs arrived several centuries after Philip and Alexander died, and that grandmother Anastassia would have laughed at this theory.

'Ah, yes.' He became rueful. 'I adored my sister, she was a very intelligent woman, but on this point she was wrong. She was a *bugaromanka*, a Bulgarian supporter, and so were our parents. But now we know who we are. We are descendants of Alexander and Philip, and the Bulgarians are, well... with all due respect, descendants of some Barbarian tribes from Mongolia.'

'Uncle, are you saying that you and I are ethnically different?'

'Well...' he waved his fork vaguely and reached for a second piece of baklava '... we are different in some ways, not exactly ethnically, but historically speaking. Still...' he patted my hand reassuringly '... the Macedonian blood flows in you. Look at you, so clever, and your hair is like Sijka's. And see how well you speak Macedonian.'

I was in fact speaking Bulgarian with a few tweaked words, but perhaps some forms of madness are better left undisturbed. This new Macedonian revisionism reminded me of the Soviet engineering of history. By Stalin's decree, all the richly mixed, migrating populations of central and eastern Europe from 1000 BC onwards had been 'proto-Slavs'. The writer Neal Ascherson calls this revisionist construction 'a skyscraper of chauvinist imbecility'. And it's a skyscraper because so many, across so many borders, are perched on top of each other, trampling those below, reaching for the stars of an imaginary national greatness.

The Macedonian region has been a hotchpotch of cultures for many centuries, and today one-third of Macedonia the country is

Albanian. But in their frantic effort to create a new national consciousness, the new Macedonians have engineered themselves a glorious history, to replace the bizarre tragedy of their past. A century ago Bulgarians, Macedonians, Serbs and Greeks were oppressed peoples united against the Ottomans. That day, in my Uncle Slavcho's kitchen, we made peace over baklava and Turkish coffee. But I didn't point out any of this, in case he saw me as a threat to national security.

In Ohrid, everybody in my family bent over backwards to make my stay pleasant. When someone mentioned in passing Anastassia the '*bugaromanka*', I kept smiling benignly, thinking that if she were alive now, this new travesty of identity would be enough to kill her.

Rado and I begin our journey back. We pass villages chewed up by last year's flood, half-houses missing here and there, but many lovingly rebuilt. Dogs and old folk stop in their tracks, startled by the passing car. Rusted signs from Communist times greet us eerily from the walls of houses, placed there thirty years ago for some visit from a Party official:

> Let us give a true Socialist aspect to our settlement by ensuring exemplary cleanliness.
>
> Observing personal and public hygiene is a sign of high culture.
>
> Greetings from the Central Committee of the Communist Party!

We drive past the town of Bansko, once the plumpest wool-trading town in the region, and now Europe's fastest growing ski resort. Mushrooming from the small cobbled lanes of Bansko's centuries-old heart is a giant construction site of hotels and apartment complexes for sale to foreigners and entrepreneurs.

Here is the ugly, brave new Bulgaria, dwarfing the rural charms of old Bulgaria. Here is the young, ravenous capitalism, hungry for a quick buck, chomping into the mountain forests which are this country's deepest wealth, nibbling at the Pirin biosphere with a hungry maw, not looking back. Chomp chomp, go the cranes and lorries.

Behind us, the snowy peaks of Pirin stand like a family of white-aproned giants. They have seen it all: Bulgarian armies; Greek armies; Turkish armies; Macedonian rebels; caravans of wine, tobacco and wool trotting along on the European road of prosperity. And now this sweeping grab for quick dosh. Chomp chomp.

'Forget Freedom and Perfection,' Rado mutters. 'This is Profit or Death.'

10 Balkan Blues

Surviving in the Balkán

The map of Bulgaria looks like an animal hide spread out, with the head end looking to Europe and the rear end sitting at the Black Sea.

The Balkán ranges are the spine, running from Cape Eminé on the sea side to the border with Serbia. This is the country's historic heartland, where medieval tsars reigned, revolts were fomented, revolutionary guns fired, cliff-top monasteries built, independent Bulgaria got its first constitution, and the peninsula got its name.

Bulgarians call the ranges, and mountains in general, simply Balkán, with a stress on the second 'a'. Their fondness for mountains in general and the Balkán in particular is summed up in the saying: 'The Balkán gives birth to people, the plain gives birth to wheat.'

Which is not a nice way to talk about my family, who happen to live in the plains just north of the Balkán. There is nothing grain-like about them.

Uncle and Auntie arrive in their Moskvic from Suhindol to pick me up at the railway station. It is 1999. Auntie has squeezed herself into the rusty husk of the car. She puts the gear into second for Uncle, and he presses on the accelerator. We go in second gear all the way. Donkey carts piled up with hay and kids overtake us. Uncle manages to drive into all the potholes in the road, which is not difficult since the road is like Emmental cheese. All is well while there is no other traffic, but as soon as a car shows in the distance, Uncle snaps into action and goes straight into the oncoming traffic lane.

'Christooo!' Auntie shrieks. 'What are you doing, you want to kill us!' And she fumbles with the steering-wheel. They have always driven in tandem. I close my eyes and pray for us not to die here, on this godforsaken road.

Auntie's white hair is a cloud of petulant authority, though her legs are dead. Uncle's 1970s brown suit is missing a button or two, and he has a three-day stubble, or is it a week's? Hair grows more slowly when you're old, he says. We stop at a petrol station and when I insist on paying for the expensive petrol, a quarter of their monthly pension, Uncle protests, then gives in dejectedly.

'We always wanted to provide for you kids.' Tears leak from his eyes. 'I never thought it would come to this.'

After dinner, with a heavy heart which might just be a heavy stomach, I go for a walk in the village. The inhabitants are bored children and hairy-chinned old people. The handsome, peeling, turn-of-the-century houses in the main square have been returned to their original owners, but there is no one with the money to restore them. Gypsies are squatting in the house of great-grandfather Nikola Munkov. Literally squatting: the stench of latrine is overpowering when I step into the courtyard. Nikola's daughter, grandmother Kapka, now owns the house, but she lives a few miles away in Pavilenki, and it's too expensive to do this place up just to rent it out.

Nikola had several houses. In the early 1900s young Nikola spent ten inebriated years in Heidelberg studying viticulture. On his return to Suhindol, he sobered up and helped set up one of the first wine cooperatives: Gumza. The wine industry boomed, the region thrived, workers flocked to Suhindol's vineyards, and Nikola became mayor. But when the People's Courts came into power in 1944, Nikola became an Enemy of the People. His lands and houses were nationalized and he spent his last twenty years living with his widowed elder daughter in a small apartment in Sofia, stripped of income and pension but counting his blessings for not ending up in a labour camp or an unmarked grave.

The streets are busy with animal traffic. A girl with the face of an angel, dressed in a rough sweater and tracksuit pants, is herding a cow with a muddied rump. I look for wings behind her shoulders.

'Is this your cow?' I ask.

'Yes.' Her eyes sparkle unnervingly.

'And where are you going?'

'Home.' She looks at my long city coat and finds me entertaining.

'Where are *you* going?' Her tone suggests that she knows the answer. The cow turns around and trumpets out a bored 'moo'.

'Nowhere.' I shrug. 'Just wandering.' And off we wander into the muddy sunset.

A few years later, I stand again outside the peeling yellow house. This time I have brought Michael. The creaky wooden gate opens to a vine-shaded courtyard. It's very quiet. The grapevines are ripening. Inside the house, they greet us with feeble cries of joy. Auntie has become completely crippled. Uncle is bent over in his favourite brown suit. A young neighbour called Dobrinka comes to help every day, and she giggles nervously over the stove when I introduce 'the foreigner'.

This is the first time I have brought along a boyfriend to meet them. The names of foreign boyfriends have circulated in the family over the years like rumours of exotic diseases; nobody knew how they manifested themselves.

'Go down in the basement,' Uncle says, fluffing about in his trade-mark ineffectual style, 'show Michael, what we have, the potatoes, the wines, see what you can find. Take what you want. Where did I put the torch?'

In the damp darkness of the basement, we find hundreds of dusty wine bottles, some from the 1970s, crates of sugary 'beverages' – the reason for Uncle's dental devastation – and sacks of potatoes, onions, chicken food. It is as if a ten-year-long siege is expected to paralyse Suhindol any day now.

'Did you see the potatoes, the wine? Did he like the basement?' Auntie wants to know. Now she can't cook any more, all she can offer is the basement provisions. Uncle opens a wardrobe and starts extracting old, carefully unopened gifts and laying them out on a bed.

'Take this,' he says, 'and this. We have no use for these things. Look at these teaspoons, they're excellent. This tea-towel is brand new, what does it say? Is it English, German, I can't see.'

It says 'Welcome'.

'Look, Lux soaps. This flannel, it's pure cotton, to keep you warm. Look, it fits Michael, excellent!'

Uncle beams. 'And now,' he says, 'let's disclose a fresh box of chocolates to celebrate your arrival.'

'Uncle, how are you going to chew them, you've got no teeth left!'

'Aha – I have my denture! But you're right, these chocolates are not good for the health.' He chuckles, and proceeds to disclose a box.

In the evening, we watch a documentary about Bulgarians abroad. The director has artfully collated people's homesicknesses to form a home-affirming narrative.

'I feel like a nobody here,' says a woman in Germany. 'As an immigrant, I'm nothing.'

'I am invisible,' sighs a man in Canada.

'I have been successful here,' muses a bespectacled scientist in America or Australia, 'but I miss my language.' He chokes on his words. 'What are we without a homeland?'

'Is that how you feel over there?' Uncle asks, suddenly worried. 'Do you feel invisible? Do you miss home?'

'No, don't worry. I have a good life there. But of course I miss you and Auntie.'

'We miss you too,' Auntie says. 'Why don't you come more often, stay longer? We'll feed you up...'

They have never asked for anything in return for giving everything and, indeed, they have never been thanked. All they want is not to be forgotten – the occasional postcard from an exotic location, the occasional phone call. They never forget our birthdays, and with flawless timing, a month later a formal, old-fashioned card will arrive, handwritten by Uncle over pencil-drawn lines: 'On the joyful occasion of your birthday…'

Overnight, Michael is eaten by cat fleas, and I lie listening to the crowing rooster. I always shared this huge bed with my sister, cousin, or both. It's a crossing of time wires. Between the small, confused person who sat here anaesthetizing herself with cakes and the impossibly foreign Richard Chamberlain in *The Thornbirds* and the grown-up person lying here with a 'foreigner' and two passports, there is no common language. They can't meet in time, they can't speak, they can only lie in this bed, very still, without touching.

When we leave, we discover that Uncle has prepared a parcel for us – honey, apples, wine, salami. He is distraught when I explain that we can't fit any of it into our backpacks.

'I understand you're modern travellers,' he says after a brief discussion, 'but next time come by car so we can stock you up. You can't leave with empty hands.'

Auntie pulls me to her. 'Did he like the house? Will he come again?'

There is only one correct answer, of course. I kiss her and she clings to me for a desperate moment, as if drowning. We get into the taxi and Uncle waves to us from the empty street outside the yellow house, pausing to dry his eyes with a crumpled hanky, until he shrinks into a homunculus in the dust.

A visit to Suhindol means a visit to nearby Pavlikeni. At the bus station where the local layabouts wait for something to happen, we are met by grandmother Kapka and her companion. He was my grandmother's colleague at the local school where she taught German. I've never seen her like this: relaxed and flourishing. Her legs form an arthritic arch, and we walk at a snail's pace. While her companion regales me with tales of his prostate problems, Michael strikes up a conversation with her in German. She is delighted by this and the prospect, finally, of great-grandchildren.

We trudge past the park where we used to pick mulberries. It is overgrown, the swings broken. My grandmother tells me, almost with relish, that it's full of thieves and stray dogs. The zoo has been closed due to lack of funds. The animals were dying, nobody wanted to work there.

'How are they?' she asks after Auntie and Uncle. She is gratified to hear that Auntie can't walk.

At the sepulchral apartment, full of dust, faded photographs, and the smell of old sorrows, she starts pulling crumpled clothes out of a wardrobe and offering them to me. It's an old trick of hers: recycling as gift-bearing.

'A lovely dress.' She holds up something made from toxic green polyester that could be used to frighten small children. 'Green is back in fashion.'

Then we eat a lunch of meatballs in a cold sauce. She's been busy all day cleaning the house from top to bottom, she says, and it's now 'sterile'. Hearing her churn out the old lies with such conviction, and seeing her presiding over the table while her benign companion chuckles at her musty old jokes makes me happy. Perhaps it is never too late to claim a little bit of happiness.

'Are you healthy, do you eat enough?' Grandma Kapka leans over.

'Yes, Grandma.' I smile, but her mind is already elsewhere.

'Do you know that your friend Malina has a lovely child?'

Malina still lives here, but somehow I can't bring myself to look her up. Then Grandmother suddenly switches to German, for Michael's benefit, and to practise her German. She has only been to East Germany once, on a school trip in the sixties. She tells Michael about the good old times, when I was little and spoke about myself in the third person. 'Kapka will now begin to cry.'

And she slaps the table mirthfully, causing the slumbering meatballs to jump in their congealed sauce. Then she shows me her latest collection of epigrams and we laugh some more – she because she thinks they're funny, and I because I'm so glad for her.

When I visit again two years later, the mood is less mirthful. Her companion has had a stroke and is about to go into a nursing home. She will live out her days alone. We sit in the living-room and I ask to see some photos. I browse black and white pictures of a smiling, full-faced young woman in a beret and tailored coat walking down a street.

'This is in Sofia. My sister and I lived there with an aunt before the war. I wanted to study German philology in Berlin, but the war came and my father forbade me from going. He was afraid I'd get killed. We had enough bombings in Sofia.' In another Sofia photo she beams, surrounded by men. 'Cousins,' she says vaguely.

'I had a lot of suitors. But I was stupid. I made a bad choice. This…' she points at a man in an elegant coat '… was my fiancé, an architect. A great love. But a silly misunderstanding drove us apart. Through the war, we wrote to each other, I waited for him. But when he came back, he saw a photo of a cousin in my room. He thought it was a new man in my life. He didn't contact me for six months. Then a marriage offer came. A distinguished Suhindol family, a good match.

We were betrothed before we even met. A single decision ruined my life.'

She has never spoken openly about this or anything else. She has finally decided that she is too old to be afraid of anything, even the truth. Her companion keeps quiet.

'Life was difficult. He was a regional vet, I was a teacher. We didn't have money for heating. Our first baby boy died from the cold at three months old. But soon the twins came.'

I pick up a family album, its leather binding gold-stamped with '25 Years of People's Power'. The photos here were arranged by my grandfather, which explains the absence of women. Two startled boys in identical coats look out from a frozen, black-and-white day. My uncle is chubby, my father thin, a hunted look in their eyes. Their sleeves are too long. They look like underage conscripts in the siege of Stalingrad.

'He was a very angry man, I could never do right. And he had other proclivities later on. One day I found him fooling around with youths. When I challenged him, he took a knife and stuck it in the kitchen table. Either you get used to my way of life, or you die, he said. And so time went on.'

I look at her companion. But this is no news to him.

'Well,' he says gently, 'everybody knew he had a bad temper. It was obvious that Kapka suffered.'

'I saw the architect many years later,' my grandmother continues. 'He was divorced. Pride, stupid pride, and our lives blighted. We could have been happy.'

'My wife and I were happy,' her companion suddenly says, 'for thirty-eight years and not a bad word between us. One daughter and all we needed.' Tears spill from his eyes. 'Then she got cancer. Do you know what her last words were? She said "I love you". I think of her every day.' He breaks into big, choking sobs. His tears fall onto his crumpled brown trousers, and my tears fall onto the scary green polyester dress I'm clutching.

'Stop it,' my grandmother snaps at him harshly. She's displeased that he's upset her favourite grandchild. 'You're not going to bring her back.'

Heartless, I think, but then she's jealous. She too wants thirty-eight years of happiness. I realize that I've never seen her cry.

My most recent visit to Suhindol. The creaky wooden gate opens to a vine-shaded courtyard. Auntie is bedridden. 'She gets drowsy' is the operational term, which in this family could mean anything from tired to comatose. But this also helps Uncle maintain the illusion that she will get better.

'Come come, we're waiting for you.' He hugs me hastily and shuffles ahead. He's so bent over his chest is parallel to the floor. The favourite brown suit jacket looks oddly lopsided. I am unprepared for what I find. Auntie is not drowsy, she is a living corpse. She is paralysed and has dementia. She doesn't recognize me at all. I remember how she whispered, in that Chernobyl summer 'the worst, the worst might happen'. But death is not the worst.

'Look who's here,' Uncle says tenderly, stroking her hair. But I've come too late.

Over the next days, while my own sanity crumbles, I discover that Auntie has two main states: howling like a wounded dog, and catatonia. Occasionally, she comes to and utters coded messages from some place halfway between this room and the grave.

'Leave me alone, what do you want from a dead person?'

'What are you going to have for dinner? Get some take-away grill.

What do you mean, they're not open on Sunday? And they call that commerce!'

'You're too late! You're too late!'

Every time she says something, Uncle lights up. 'Did you hear that? She's coming to. You'll see, I'll get her up again.'

After a day, she recognizes me. 'Kapka, is that you? Where are the others?'

Then we lose contact again. Dobrinka is still helping them after work, acting as nurse, cleaner, and gardener. She has a teenage daughter I haven't met yet.

One day, we go together to the local store to buy a frozen chicken and pallid tomatoes for dinner. We walk across the deserted village-town, past the culture hall named 'Sobriety', *circa* 1871. Someone has renovated and repainted it. There is hope.

I ask Dobrinka about her daughter Vera.

'She went to Germany this year and got sold. She's back now.'

'She got what?'

'Sold. For 1,000 euro.' Dobrinka laughs at my dumb expression, but it's not a cheerful laugh. 'As soon as she arrived. Thank God she could think on her feet. I'll send her to you, she can tell you herself. Do you know German? Because they sent her letters from court, and we don't know anyone in town who speaks German. They've been sitting there for months…'

When Vera arrives with the letters still in their envelopes, I sense I've seen her before. It takes me a moment to rewind, and when I do, I see the angelic face and the muddied cow. 'Where are you going?' Nowhere. Nowhere is Vera's destiny – no father, no education, no prospects, and this destiny she tried to challenge with her trip to Europe. What happened in Germany?

'I know this guy from the village down the road, he said I'll give you a ride to Germany, I know some people who can give you work in a bar.'

Vera was warmly welcomed by a Macedonian man who put her up and took her passport. On the second day, she found herself in a Frankfurt bar with three men and an Albanian girl with a bruised face. The helpful acquaintance from the village down the road had vanished. The men spoke Turkish, and she knew enough to understand what they spoke about: her price.

One thousand, one man said. Too much, another protested. She's young and fresh, the first man said, you'll get a lot out of her. The Albanian girl sat there like a zombie. Sensing imminent doom, Vera asked in Bulgarian if she could go and call her mother. For some reason, they let her. She stepped outside the bar, and grabbed the first Turk that came her way – thank God there are so many Turks in Frankfurt, she chuckles – for she spoke no German. She begged him to call the police on his mobile, and within ten minutes the three men in the bar were in handcuffs.

Vera and the Albanian girl, who had been immediately raped and forced into prostitution, were given translators and asked to testify. Then the police escorted them back to their countries. 'I felt like a criminal,' Vera says sullenly. 'I only wanted to work in a café and earn euros.'

Painstakingly, with Uncle's 1960s dictionary, I decipher the three letters from the German court. They didn't mess about. Within weeks, the three men were tried and convicted to fifteen years on numerous charges of human and drug trafficking. Vera was only the latest hapless girl from Eastern Europe to be lured by a Euro-job 'in a bar'. The names of the three men are Turkish, but they come from Bulgaria,

Macedonia and Turkey. Nations once at war, and now, a century later, peacefully united by international trade.

'It's all very well,' Dobrinka clatters in the kitchen. 'But what happens when they come out? They can track her down and kill her, and they wouldn't bat an eyelid. How can I protect her against those criminals? I'm on my own.'

Vera is embarrassed by her mother's anxiety. 'My boyfriend will protect me.' she smiles confidently. Her boyfriend is a local Turk from 'down the road'.

'He'd better marry you if he wants to protect you,' her mother snaps. Later, Vera tells me that her boyfriend wants to take her abroad to earn euros, but her mother won't let her. 'I can understand your mother,' I say. Boyfriends of village girls have been known to become pimps. I wonder if I can say this without hurting her feelings. I can't. I ask Vera about the local contact who so helpfully drove her to Germany. Why wasn't he arrested?

'Oh, but he just drove me there,' she says. 'He drives to Germany all the time for errands.'

Errands. I stare at her. In the angelic cherry eyes, I glimpse the true depths of provincial innocence. It's the innocence of Suhindol, the village of old people and children. The same innocence that stopped Uncle and Auntie from adopting 'foreign blood' for fear of being judged. The same innocence that makes Uncle believe that Auntie will get better, and that made them squander everything so that now they are destitute. An innocence that springs from the poisoned village-well of ignorance, conformity and fear.

When I am about to leave, Uncle opens the wardrobe and extracts the obligatory small gifts. Among them is an ancient compass on a leather strap. 'Now, this is from my father, a quality compass. You're a modern traveller, I know. Still, you never know when you might need a compass, it's good to have one just in case. Let's see, does it fit your wrist? Oh, excellent.' The compass must have sat in this wardrobe for sixty years – Auntie and Uncle never travelled.

Auntie is not there to say goodbye. She is transfixed by something on the wall.

'She's drowsy,' Uncle explains. 'We'll let her rest.'

He sees me off outside the house. A burly local man nicknamed the Lump comes to pick me up in his taxi. Taxi is an overstatement: it's just his old car. There are no taxis in Suhindol. Dobrinka is here too. In a pitiful last attempt at being helpful, I tell her to send Vera to nearby Veliko Tarnovo, not Germany again. She smiles with a golden tooth the innocent smile of Suhindol that breaks my heart.

I hug Uncle and his voice fails him. Mine too, so I just give him the cheeriest smile I can manage, and we drive away. I wave, although I know he can't see me, until we turn onto the Emmental strip of the main road. Then finally I do what I've wanted to do since I arrived. I cry.

'Good people, the Kassabovs.' The Lump clears his throat, embarrassed by this show of emotion. 'Are you related?'

'Yes,' I croak, snot running over my lip, 'I'm their granddaughter.'

A year later, Auntie has died. I am already too late for the funeral, so I make a slow pilgrimage back to Suhindol, travelling up through the Balkán and giving myself time to prepare for the sight of Uncle alone in the big house. Again I have a backpack that will be too small to accommodate any gifts. But this time I'm carrying the ancient compass. Every now and again, passing through the familiar rocky landscapes, in a world forever empty of Auntie, I consult its gently flickering hands. I don't know what I expect to see there, but it gives me a strange comfort.

I pass through the small town of Karlovo in a taxi owned by the Balkán's most garrulous taxi-driver.

'On each side of Karlovo, there's glacial wind, but Karlovo's protected, and its temperature is five degrees higher than elsewhere. Where are you from? The people in this part of the country used to be hopeless. God saw their plight and out of pity he gave them the town of Karlovo. A gay English couple live here, nice guys. Where did you say you were from?'

Karlovo's main distinction, apart from the God-given climate and surreal 2,000-metre-high peaks looming at it doorstep, is that it is the birthplace of the national hero Vassil Levski who, before losing his head, spearheaded the national liberation movement.

As a child, four things struck me about Levski. One, the perfectly mnemonic dates of his birth and death – 1837 and 1873 – as if planned so that school kids could remember them. Two, he was so dedicated to the national struggle that he had neither a home nor a girlfriend. Three, the physical resemblance between him and Luke Skywalker, especially the nostrils. But when it came to courage and moral fibre, Luke was a pushover next to Levski. Four, his gnomic sayings, for example, 'If I win, so do the people. If I lose, I only lose myself'. In vain, I tried to work out whether he and the people had lost or won when he was hanged and when, three years after his death, the national April Uprising against the Ottomans was drowned in the blood of the people. Or 'Time lives inside us and we live inside time' – I pondered this one for years. But one key idea of his that school kids weren't and aren't given to chew over is 'In a free republic, everyone shall live together as equals, regardless of nationality or faith'. Somehow, this is unbecomingly pluralistic for a national hero.

Many thousands of words later, the happy driver drops me off in the country's geographic heart: the Rose Valley. Much of the world's rose oil is extracted here from *Rosa damascena* petals every June. For one kilogram of rose oil, which costs three times more than a kilo of gold, 3,000 blossoms are steam-distilled. As if these aromatic facts weren't enough, the Valley has recently been dubbed the Valley of the Thracian Kings thanks to the lucky archaeologists who keep digging up sensational Thracian tombs.

But when I arrive in the laid-back regional town of Kazanlak, this floral and antique state of affairs isn't immediately apparent. I'm told that most of the tombs in the region aren't open for visits and, anyway, their contents are displayed at the local history museum.

The local history museum, 'Spark', looks like a concrete bunker. A beefy security guard gallantly holds the door open for me, and the two women in the front kiosk rush to turn on the lights for the small bevy of visitors – me and two others.

We are led inside by an affable man with sweat stains under his arms. He is excited to have company. And we are excited to see the awesome regal gold-leaf wreath, found in 2005. Its delicate leaves cast a dazzling aura of light across its twenty-five centuries. The wreath belonged to King Seuth III whose curly-bearded bronze head was found at the entrance of his tomb. The Thracians knew how to have fun both with the living and the dead.

After Seuth III's death, they ritually beheaded his statue and buried the head alone, to ensure its smooth passage from the realm of the living to the afterworld. In a catacomb reached through a 13-metre-long corridor, they placed all the riches a man needs when dead: full body armour; amphorae full of wine; gold and silver dishes. There is no mention of his wife; perhaps he didn't value her enough to have her entombed with him, as was the custom. Then they sealed off the tomb complex, thus ensuring that something would survive of their greatest – and only – united Kingdom of Odryssian Thrace.

Because if Seuth's head has finally emerged from this fertile valley, his capital Seuthopolis hasn't. It lies 20 metres under water, at the bottom of a dam. The guardians of the British heritage industry would have a collective heart attack if it were suggested that Hadrian's Wall be flooded by a dam. And I suspect the archaeologists who in 1948 found Seuthopolis, Europe's best-preserved Thracian city, experienced a few pangs too. They were allowed to pick up whatever they could from the city remains, before the valley was flooded by the new dam. Communism wasn't about the past, it was about the future. Seuthopolis found itself at the bottom of the aptly named Georgi Dimitriov Dam.

But wait, there's hope: plans are afoot for revealing Seuthopolis in the middle of the dam and making it an attraction – boatfuls of tourists, hanging gardens, glass lifts, a Thracian Disneyland. The cost: 50 million euros. I must remember to look it up in 50 million years, when Bulgaria can afford such cultural indulgences. It's unfortunate that unflooding ancient cities costs so much more than flooding them.

None of this is explained by our sweat-stained guide, who avoids the painful fact of Koprinka Dam, and keeps pointing at the fabulous diagram of a Thracian Disneyland. This way, his pointing finger says, this way to the future, forget the past.

The second visitor in our group – who is a translator for the third visitor who is Dutch – can't think of the English for 'dam'. Dam, I prompt, and she explains about Koprinka and Seuthopolis. The Dutch tourist blinks with his white eyelashes, bewildered. He can't see why an ancient city was sacrificed for a dam. He thinks there's something lost in translation.

But another Thracian discovery survived the manly decade of dam-building. While digging in Kazanlak's Tyulbe Park, some soldiers hit upon the entrance to a small tunnel. At the end of the tunnel was a small chamber. They lit up some newspapers and squinted in the sepulchral darkness, as I'm squinting now under the artificial lights in the humming stone silence. A procession of toga'd people and chariots snakes around the vault in bright mineral colours. In the centre, a man and a woman sit around a low table, their faces mellow. Their contrasting wrists – his dark, hers white – are entwined in a poignant gesture. This became known as the Kazanlak Tomb. Some believe the scene is a funerary feast, others see a wedding feast. Either way, the couple were buried here together, and the sad expression on her face could be as much sorrow for her beloved as sorrow for her own imminent slaughter. I think of Uncle and Auntie. How will he live without her? Perhaps, when you've been with someone for sixty years without a single day apart, and even driven in tandem, there's something to be said for joint burial.

I hike out to a place grandly named the Institute for Rose Research and Rose Museum. Tramping along the hot dusty road, I have fantasies of sticking my face in rose-petal jam and pots of rose creams – the next best thing to rolling in the rose fields of June or whirling in a wine-fuelled Orphic feast. These florid thoughts quickly wilt when I reach the Rose Museum. For some reason – Thracian tomb imitation? – it's located in a dank basement. A basement that stinks of leaky sewage pipes which might well date back to the Romans.

'The museum has had extensive repairs,' the bemantled attendant informs me. She stands behind a counter strewn with faded goods: pallid soaps; forlorn creams; last bottle of rose liqueur. I wonder how it was before the extensive repairs: raw sewage in the corridors perhaps. Clearly, this is a State museum. If it were private, smiling maidens would be greeting you with rose jam, selling you your own grandmother made from rose petals and charging you the earth.

'We have plenty of visitors,' the hostess tells me proudly. She's right to be proud: it's a remarkable achievement to take something as romantic as rose oil, distil pure drabness from it, and still have visitors from Japan beating the doors down.

I spend a night in the boutique Hotel Rosa, musing on private versus state-owned business, while gorging on fruit. The watermelon slices are on ice. There are three varieties of grape. The internet is free. The breakfast could be a Thracian wedding feast. I'm tempted to take up permanent residence in the Hotel Rosa, but as a three-star hotel it's three stars over my budget. Besides, I have the Balkán ranges to cross.

Our bus is winding through the precipitous Shipka Pass, along the road from Edirne in Turkey to Ruse on the Danube. It's a glorious ride, but I'm too worried about our driver to enjoy it. Facial hair creeps up to his eyes from all sides, and a poster of a naked silicone diva covers most of his front windscreen. His eyes are in direct contact with the diva's pubic hair. I hope he's made small holes in her genital region to see through, otherwise we're in trouble.

The sky suddenly darkens over the sea of green ranges, and the bus stops for a cigarette break next to something that used to be, according to the chipped lettering, the Shipka Hotel. The Shipka Hotel now looks like a small nuclear reactor after a big accident. The passengers spill out and greedily begin to suck on their cigarettes as if plugging themselves into a life-support machine. The hirsute driver unwraps a greasy pastry. Our summer jackets are too thin for the mountain chill, and we shiver by the dusty bus with that peculiar, threadbare Balkan miserableness most noticeable at border crossings. And the Shipka Pass is a kind of historic border.

It's where Bulgaria passed from being an Ottoman backwater to being an independent backwater, thanks in part to a series of battles on Shipka Peak in the Russo-Turkish War. We look up that way, instinctively, to where we know a modest monument sits atop 894 steps. There, in the crushing August heat of 1877, 5,000 under-armed and overwrought Russians and Bulgarians fought off the 30,000 Turks of Süleyman Pasha, first with ammunition, then with rocks and finally with their dead mates' bodies. That the Slavs had found themselves in such straits was one of the many strategic blunders of a war some described as waged 'between the one-eyed and the blind'. But Süleyman Pasha was the blind one, and the Shipka battle became a turning point in the Russo-Turkish war.

'The Volunteers at Shipka' was the first epic poem we had to learn by heart at school, and the 'white bones and bloody moss' of Shipka are part of my mental furniture. So are the opening lines about Bulgaria's image in Europe as an oriental backwater: 'shame on our forehead, marks of the whip, signs of bondage, no place in history, our name a tragic one'.

But wait, our name wasn't always a tragic one.

We reach Veliko Tarnovo and I'm standing at the gates of the medieval citadel Tsarevets, watching a puppet show. There is a choice of Bulgarian or English, and I join a group of elderly American evangelists for the English version. Through the life-size puppets of the tsar, tsaritsa, and court jester, the puppeteer ventriloquizes the story of Tsarevets, glorious city of the Second Bulgarian Kingdom. He lists all the devious enemies and traitors punished by the equitable Bulgarian monarchs. For example, the self-proclaimed Latin emperor of Byzantium Baldwin I of Flanders who spent some time as a prisoner here before Tsar Kaloyan executed him in a paroxysm of rage. 'And the rest of Europe looked to the Bulgarian kingdom with envy and fear,' the jester concludes and bursts into neurotic laughter.

The laughter is, of course, not the puppet's but the puppeteer's, who like me cringes at this historical flexing of long-expired muscles. True, Bulgaria's medieval history is impressive. But I know, and the puppeteer knows, that today the rest of Europe looks to the Bulgarian 'kingdom' with either indifference or condescension. Still, the American evangelists are impressed.

'We love East Europe,' the cheerful pastor enthuses as he drops some coins for the puppeteer. 'It's so romantic.'

Over the road from Pip's Bar, where the English-speaking expats hang out, is Shtastlivetsa Restaurant, famed for its enormous pizzas. Shtastlivetsa is named after Aleko Konstantinov, Bulgaria's first travel writer and the creator of the devastating Bay Ganyu satire in which a hairy, grunting upstart with dubious hygiene goes abroad to trade in rose oil and happily embarrasses himself in every conceivable way, before he returns home to become a reactionary politician. Aleko Konstantinov wrote satirical columns about everything that was wrong with newly liberated Bulgaria (quite a lot), dubbed himself Shtastlivetsa or the Happy Man, and died aged thirty-four a most unhappy death. He was 'accidentally' assassinated by tsarist police. It was a symbolic death heralding what was yet to come: Bay Ganyu killing his creator. The philistine killing the cultured.

The two florid-faced, middle-aged Englishmen I'm sharing a table with must wonder why a retro-style portrait of a man with a goatee is overlooking us. But there is no time to explain about the Happy Man. They are busy celebrating the purchase of a local house. The proud new proprietor explains in great, tedious detail and a midlands accent where the house is and how cheap it is. (Somewhere near Veliko Tarnovo. Cheap as chips.)

'A bargain!' He leers euphorically. 'And the workmen too. I can pay them as little as £15 a day!'

The English Bay Ganyu's friend is more socially aware, or less drunk.

'He has four kids and his wife is on sickness benefit. Imagine a holiday house for them in Britain, no chance. Now they can enjoy real summers…'

'And the women are pretty!' The father of four nudges his friend. His friend nods at his stew. He already has a house or three here. Or five. An investment, he says, and glances at his gold-plated watch. It turns out he runs an online estate agency business for Brits buying Bulgarian property. They're not friends but client and agent, which explains the gold-plated watch. Selling property to foreigners is good business, because they make up a massive thirty per cent of all buyers. And most of those are British or Irish. That's entire villages.

Across the street, in a guesthouse called 'The House', my next-door neighbours are an Irish couple from the west coast. They've just bought an apartment in a building that's not yet built and a vineyard that's not yet planted. They find the language impenetrable (three genders and two verbal modes!), their only friend here is a British estate agent, and they're moving to Veliko Tarnovo now with their newborn. So what's wrong with Ireland?

'Oh, we luv Ireland. We just don't wanna live there. Bulgaria reminds us of Ireland thirty years ago, so we don't feel that far from home. This is a land of opportunity, like Ireland was.'

In other words, their euros go a long way here. I wish them luck and promise to come back and try their wine in five years' time.

There's one more place I want to see in the medieval capital: the ancient Forty Martyrs Church, now reopened after forty years of restoration. One of the stone columns that prop up its ceiling bears a curiously existential ninth-century inscription in old Greek, from the time of the Bulgar Khan Omurtag: 'Even if a man lives well, he dies and another one comes. Let the one who comes later upon seeing this inscription remember the one who had made it.'

The column's fate, I like to think, reflects the inscription: from the Bulgar royal town of Pliska, it was taken to the Forty Martyrs Church here in the medieval capital. When the Turks arrived, they turned the church into a mosque, but kept the supporting columns. I fancy that one fine summer evening, some time between 1400 and 1800, a philosophically-inclined imam sat with his worry beads to contemplate Omurtag's poignant message from the ruins of the Bulgar empire, written in the language of the ruined Byzantine empire.

This reminds me that it's time to go and pay my respects to Auntie. I flag down a taxi. It's a wreck of a Warburg, and the driver is unimpressed when I ask him to stop by the Roman town of Nikopolis ad Istrum.

'Nikopolis? The road there is like the surface of the moon.' And so it is. Every time we go inside a crater, it feels like the Warburg has deconstructed and we're sitting among its debris.

The iron gates are locked, so I do the obvious thing and climb over. Inside Nikopolis, I walk on Roman streets made of giant stone slabs.

It's eerie. Half-temples point at the sky with the stumps of their columns, half-agoras open up, half-streets end suddenly. Emperor Trayan built this town in 102 after his victory against the Dacians, and named it City of Victory on the Danube. For centuries, nobody took notice of this incongruous stone town in the middle of a field, until the Austro-Hungarian ethnographer Felix Kanitz found it in the 1860s. A few years ago, a gate went up, but by then the locals had already incorporated Nikopolis into their houses. We drive past holiday houses, and I swear I see a Latin inscription over a colonnaded doorway.

'It's called recycling,' the driver says. 'If the government doesn't care, why should we? Besides, if I didn't get a few stones for my house, the neighbour would've helped himself anyway.'

You can't argue with that.

It's exactly ten days after Auntie's death. The house seems derelict without her. Uncle is bereft and disoriented, and keeps looking for things – his glasses, his keys, his slippers – to distract himself from the ultimate, unacceptable loss that has made all other losses insignificant.

We pour crosses of red wine over the fresh soil of Auntie's grave, light long candles and wait until they burn down. There is little left to say but Uncle is trying to keep busy with constant talk of houses and wills. The house belongs in effect to Auntie's family. Uncle is terrified that he might be left without a roof over his head. After fifty years of prodigious accumulation and equally prodigious waste, Uncle has nothing, at least not on paper.

'We have no claims on the house,' I say, hoping to reassure him. I have the opposite effect. Uncle is hurt.

'What do you mean, no claims?' he exclaims, his dentures clattering indignantly. 'Fifty years we've been improving this house. And now you don't have claims! Now, where did I put my glasses?'

Uncle is raiding wardrobes and cupboards for Auntie's will. Then he has a brainwave.

'I'll call the village fortune-teller, she'll tell me where the papers are! Last time we lost those coins, we called her and bingo. Who knows, maybe I'm walking past Auntie's will every day.'

We sit in the vine-shaded yard, and eat roast peppers and watermelon. Dobrinka is here too. 'Cheers,' I say and my voice is hollow.

'You don't say "Cheers" when there's a dead person,' Dobrinka says in her matter-of-fact way. 'You say "May the earth rest lightly upon her". You know, just before she died, Auntie wanted to tell me something. I waited for hours, but nothing came out. She couldn't say it.'

'Once,' Uncle rejoins, chewing soft bread, 'I said to her, "Can you hear me, that I'm crying for you?" She said, "I hear you, and it makes me sad." She understood everything right until the end. I knew she did.'

Dobrinka nods. 'She did.'

Uncle wipes tears with his arthritic hand. I can't bear this, so I turn to Dobrinka. 'How's Vera?'

'Vera? She picks them up, I tell you. First that Turkish guy last year, then the Gypsy and his clan… All the hoodlums in the world, it's like they're lining up for her outside. At first I worried myself sick. But if I'd kept worrying, I'd have been buried long before Auntie.'

It transpires that Vera had taken up with a Gypsy 'down the road'. But when she tried living with his family, they mistreated her and she went back to her mother. Disaster struck during the funeral lunch for Auntie in the village restaurant. Dobrinka called the restaurant from home, hysterical: 'The Gypsies are at the door with pitchforks, they want to kill Vera!'

The Gypsy clan were indeed at her door, ready to claim the errant bride-to-be. What could the village men do but defend her honour? Spearheaded by my Uncle Vanyo, the bride-saving party got up from the funereal feast, removed the napkins from their distended bellies, picked up a few logs, and went to face the Gypsy clan at the village outskirts. The attackers fled and Vera was saved without bloodshed.

'You know...' Dobrinka's handsome face cracks into a smile, the smile of the unsung woman survivor. 'You travel the world for stories. And it's all here in Suhindol. You don't have to go looking any further.'

But I do: Pavlikeni awaits. Grandmother Kapka is living alone after the death of her companion.

'Do you miss him?' I ask in the kitchen while we pick at a suspect salad. She is surprised by the question. Come to think of it, emotions always surprise her.

'He was useless.' She looks blankly at the plastic tablecloth. 'I had to cook, ensure there was sterile cleanliness in the house.'

'So you don't miss him,' I conclude.

'Nope,' she nods, and with startling speed of reflex, she picks up a plastic swatter and stuns a fly dead on the table. She briefly examines it, then brushes it off and onto the grubby lino floor.

And at this point, I finally zoom in on the fuzzy space that is this woman. She has no emotional life. Emotion was wiped out at some distant moment in time, by an unknown evil hand. This is how she has survived everything life served her, and outlived her peers.

'You know that Malina has had two kids now,' she moves on. 'Two lovely blond kids. She's in the cooperation across the street now. Oh, and Ivo died last year. Hodgkin's lymphoma.'

I choke on the salad while she continues to chew pastry with the callous self-regard of old age, focused on her own survival.

Ivo's familiar cheery face smiles at me from the notice pinned to Malina's door. The *necrolog* is freshly printed for the first anniversary of his death. I think of our dance across that carpeted floor, our shy embrace, our socked feet. It's as if my own youth has suddenly dropped dead.

Malina recognizes me instantly, although we haven't seen each other since 1986. She smiles and I see the downy girl with grazed knees peeking from behind the woman's heavy body. Her white-blond children float around us as she tells me how Ivo died.

'It was a year before they diagnosed him. They'd been treating him for sinusitis. They still could've saved him, but you know our hospitals. The radiation machine in Sofia was broken. He actually died of meningitis in the end. It was the hottest summer I remember. Like hell.'

Malina is working as a supervisor at a local boarding school. She graduated in Bulgarian literature and has been earning a meagre salary. Her husband runs a bookshop.

'At first, he wanted it to be a proper bookshop. But soon it became obvious that people don't read apart from the tabloid *Shock*. So he got rid of the books and started selling stationery. It's the only way to survive. Under Socialism, whatever else was wrong, at least we read. Now I see fifteen-year-olds who can't read.'

We pledge to stay in touch and I step outside, dazed. I still can't believe that Ivo is dead. The woman from the corner shop shakes her head and adjusts rotisserie chickens on a grill.

'People are falling like flies. It's not normal. Ivo worked in a factory for faience. Run with American technology, but rumour has it that it wasn't safe. Maybe they poisoned him there. Or else it was Chernobyl. I think it all boils down to Chernobyl. Their father too, those years ago…'

The last thing I see from the bus leaving Pavlikeni is an English graffito sprayed on the wall of a cooperation: BRUTALITY IS MY REALITY.

To cheer myself up, I call Uncle on his new mobile phone. He doesn't pick up. I call his landline.

'I was waiting for the ringing tune to finish, it's such a nice tune I didn't want to interrupt it,' he explains. 'But by the time I answered, you were gone… Now, the fortune-teller told me where the papers might be. I told you, she knows these things. But I can't find them because I've lost my glasses… Now, I'd prepared some tomatoes for you. You left with empty hands again.'

On the bus back to Sofia, three loud men get on and spread out on the seats in front of me. Actually, only one of them is making all the noise, enough for three. He wears wrap-around sunglasses and swings a string of worry beads menacingly.

Speaking to strange men on buses is not the local feminine thing to do. You pout, look pissed off, or flirt. But you don't make conversation, which is why they're dumbstruck when I do. The boisterous one is the first to recover.

'Stoyan.' He shakes my hand. 'Pleasure. You speak good English. I heard you on your mobile before.'

I explain that I live in Scotland.

'I'm Ahmed.' A sunburnt freckly face smiles at me. Ahmed

could be only forty but his side-teeth are missing.

'Scotland,' Stoyan says. 'Cold up there, but stay there. My sister's in Italy. She calls and goes, I'll never come back. And I agree. If I leave, I'd never give this rotten country a thought. Look at it, seventeen years, and what has changed?'

He swings the worry beads furiously. The other two are quiet.

'I think quite a lot has changed,' I offer. 'Besides, fifteen years is not such a long time.'

'You have a point,' Stoyan agrees. 'I lived abroad too, I've been everywhere. *Gastarbeiter*. But without a language, it's hard. I always come back.'

'I've been around too.' It's Ahmed's turn now. 'Ten years in Greece, Istanbul. But I always return, I don't know why.'

'You don't feel yourself abroad,' Stoyan agrees. 'Even if you meet good people, it's not the same.'

'We've been friends for ten years,' Ahmed says. 'The three of us. You don't get that easily.'

They work in a factory for processing gold. They must have lots of it, then.

'Do we look rich? We don't get a gram of gold for ourselves.' Ahmed laughs.

'Not even a milligram,' the third one mutters.

When we arrive in Sofia, Ahmed gives me his sister's number.

'I'll be here for a week. Please call. We can have a drink, talk more, just talk. Women here are so demanding, they look at your wallet and that's it. It's not often that you meet a woman you can talk to.'

I like Ahmed but I squirm. Stoyan presses his much-worried worry beads into my hand.

'Have it. My lucky charm. To remember crazy Stoyan on the bus.'

He overrides my protestations. 'No, please. I'll get another one in Greece next time I emigrate.'

'And remember me too.' Ahmed smiles. 'Though I haven't got anything of mine to give you.'

I keep the number for weeks before I discard it. Ahmed and I inhabit different worlds. All we share is a bus ride through the Balkán, there's no point pretending.

But it feels somehow wrong, almost a self-betrayal. It feels like throwing out much more than a phone number. It feels like rejecting Uncle and Auntie's last parting gift. Like saying goodbye to the Balkán.

At least I have the ancient compass with its live, flickering hands and its worn leather strap. Come to think of it, it's the only thing of theirs that I have.

11 The Curse of Orpheus

A Rodopean story

Just as I'm about to conclude that the long-delayed bus from Plovdiv has fallen into a river, it shows up. Slowly, we wind our way up and down the narrow mountain road. We are in a realm of forests dripping with chlorophyll and legend.

The Rodopi Ranges are the country's most mysterious region. Pirin, Rila and the Balkán have higher peaks, but the Rodopi breathe with a strangely zoomorphic energy. Entering this brooding landscape is like entering a dark, enchanted labyrinth of live flesh.

At Smolyan's bus station, listless Gypsy men in soiled tracksuits smoke cheap tobacco and gaze at nothing in particular. A dull, habitual despair hangs around them together with the reek of unwashed bodies.

Smolyan is the Rodopi's regional centre but it doesn't look like a place bustling with job opportunities. In fact, it's sunk into a scenic slumber. The most interesting fact about it is that it's the country's longest and thinnest town. Ten kilometres long, to be precise. But precision is no use here, and everything in the Rodopi has more dimensions than meets the eye and the foot.

For example, Smolyan looks like a new town, thanks to the monstrous construction boom of the 1960s. But beneath the brick and concrete lies another story. In the seventeenth century, violent Islamizing campaigns swept the region and, like many villages in the Rodopi, Smolyan rose from its ashes. It was rebuilt from scratch by Islamized Bulgarian survivors (those who didn't get beheaded in *Time of Violence*) and named Pashmaklu. After Liberation in 1878, the Turkish name was replaced with the proudly Slavic Smolyan. And later still, the seventeenth-century buildings were replaced with proudly concrete houses.

I'm standing on the balcony of one such house which the enterprising owner has turned into a B&B and called 'The House of the Three Fir Trees'. The three fir trees are strategically placed to disguise the house itself, but not obstruct the view to the crags up above the town, one of which is called The Bride. In local lore, this is where a maiden betrothed to a *haiduk* (mountain rebel) jumped off before the local Turkish bei could take her for a bride.

The Bride joins a teeming population of ghosts in the busy hereafter that is Rodopean folklore. Rodopean ballads are surreal and existential – dramatic monologues, wrenching farewells, maidens plummeting from rocks, mothers who weep to the grave, shepherds swallowed by mountains, doomed lovers, floating brides, and yet more weeping mothers.

The ghosts live alongside another population in the Rodopean towns and villages. They wear brightly coloured shalvars, and they are the Islamized Bulgarians collectively known as Pomaks. In the 1960s and 1970s, the Pomaks were the first batch of Bulgarian Muslims to have their names 'voluntarily' changed.

But the Rodopean story doesn't begin or end with a medieval clash of civilizations. It begins, and hopefully ends, with a marriage of civilizations. The oldest of those were the Thracians, and the most enduring Thracian is, of course, the mythical singer Orpheus. He came from the Rodopi and his preternaturally beautiful voice haunted these parts, just as his doomed bid to save his beloved dead Eurydice from the underworld has haunted the imagination of the Western world.

Even Mature Socialism couldn't remain indifferent to Orpheus, and here I am, sitting by a fine specimen of proletarian plastic art at its most romantic. A rudimentary, seated Orpheus is plucking a string-less lyre and gazing to the heavens. An angular-featured Eurydice sits at his feet, leaning on his sinewy thigh and also gazing to the heavens – or is it the Bright Future? They look like Comsomol youth at rest during a dam-building brigade. It's amazing the artist didn't replace the lyre with a Russian accordion.

On the bench opposite me sit two old men with felt hats and rolled-up newspapers. It's late afternoon: gossip time.

'Do you know,' says one, 'there are 250,000 couples in the country who live together, kids and all, and unmarried?'

'No way!'

'I swear. Marriage is becoming an anachronism. It's not important any more. That's the way of the future.'

'My word.' The other one shakes his head.

'Let's ask this young lady here. Are you married to your boyfriend?' The extrovert turns to me. 'I assume you have a boyfriend…'

'Stop flirting,' his friend interrupts, flashing a golden tooth.

'I'm not married,' I admit.

'Ah, there you are,' the champion of the unmarried triumphs. 'Marriage is a thing of the past.'

'It is,' I agree. 'It's love that matters, not marriage.'

'Ah, thank you!' He turns to his friend, beaming. 'Did you hear that? Love is what it's about, not some stupid paper, rings, vows, all that rubbish. I can't get my ring off any more, it sinks into the flesh like a slave's collar.' He pulls at his wedding ring theatrically. 'They'll bury me with this piece of metal, like they used to bury the Thracians with their treasures. Take Orpheus and Eurydice here, were they married? Who cares? That's not what remains after us.' He punctuates the air with his rolled-up paper.

'True true,' I say. It's not often that you find octogenarians right on your wavelength. Even if they read that lowest of tabloids *Shock*. I glance at a headline: PRIEST CONVICTED FOR ARROGANT HOOLIGANISM REFUSED TO OFFER LAST RITES TO A DECEASED MAN AND BEAT UP A POLICEMAN.

'There you are.' He nods at me. 'And I hope that you always have plenty of it.' I hope he means love.

The other old man grins indulgently at Orpheus and Eurydice, at the dark mountains rising on all sides, at his friend, at me, with a mouth full of golden teeth.

I spend a day with a local taxi-driver who doesn't even try to rip me off. His name is Angel and it suits him. Angel is thirty-five, single, chubby, his fringe carefully slicked to one side. Diligent glasses complete the choirboy look. The Rodopi might be fitness freak heaven, but Angel mostly treks from his parents' fridge to the car and back.

We drive through Pamporovo, the winter sports resort of the Rodopi, where I learned to ski and later survived a spectacular ski-fall which nearly relieved me of my brain. Now it's all luxury hotels and fresh construction sites for more luxury hotels gnawing at the flesh of the forest like tumours. One sign at the edge of the forest proudly announces 'Hotel Extreme'.

'Extreme greed, that's what it is. Ever bigger, ever more luxurious. You know that all these hotels are owned by *mutri* big and small,' Angel says quietly, without anger. He doesn't do anger. 'So-called developers. Like at the seaside. Bulgarian, Russian, Greek, Turkish developers, some Westerners too. Greed, sheer dumb greed will eat the heart out of our beautiful country and then it'll be too late to be sorry.'

As if to match our mood and the increased elevation, the darkened sky suddenly begins to shed enormous rags of snow. In this fairy-tale blizzard, we reach the deeply fissured Trigrad Canyon. Giant cliffs hang over the road.

'I avoid coming here.' Angel adjusts his glasses nervously. 'I feel hemmed in. These rocks oppress me. The entire Rodopi oppress me. It's too much for me. I like the sea, more gentle landscapes...'

You definitely couldn't accuse the western Rodopi of gentleness. The river has dragged all manner of detritus along its distended bed: rags; stones; entire trees. The road has been patched up after the river ripped it up last year.

'You should have seen the river last spring. It swallowed a whole Mercedes, near the bus station. The owner didn't move it in time, too lazy. Then one day it just drifted away. He waded into the river shoulder-deep, hanging onto his Mercedes like a madman. They showed him on local TV. Later, the river spat it up, all twisted up like wet laundry. And he was crying like a baby that's just lost its mother.'

We stop at a deep abyss cave which enjoys not one but two hellish names: Devil's Gorge and Gate to Hades. And with good reason. Legend has it that this was the gate to the underworld through which Orpheus passed to look for Eurydice. Two divers in a 1970 expedition also passed through here but, unlike Orpheus, they were looking for the bottom of the abyss and, unlike him, they never came back.

Angel has never been to the cave before and he's not exactly thrilled to be inside a dripping, slimy, tomb-like world, deafened by a waterfall 40 metres high. It enters the cave from one end and comes out the other, and the fact that we hear it but can't see it makes it even more menacing. The Thracians who lived around here for thousands of years would throw their dead chieftains' bodies into the river, and since nothing comes out the other end except crystal-clear water, the bones remained inside.

I can't imagine why anyone who isn't unhinged by grief would dive voluntarily into this thundering, chthonic darkness, and, judging by Angel's steamed-up glasses, neither can he. This is simply not a human realm.

And yet, in a dripping alcove, a tiny icon of the Virgin Mary is overlooked by a faint stone relief of Orpheus with his lyre. Coins for good luck have been deposited all over the wet altar, and spring water leaks from the rock beneath Orpheus' feet. The red and white threads of *martenitsi*, deposited for health, add to this eclectic altar of paganism, Christianity, superstition, and simple hope in the ante-chamber of Hades.

Our next cave, the Yagodina or Strawberry Cave, is more cheerful. It's 10 kilometres long, but to Angel's relief, only one-tenth of it is accessible to sedentary bums like us. We are treated to an hour of brisk walking and talking through dripping galleries by a handsome, deadpan cave guide with a face wilted by cigarettes and sunburn, and terrible facial tremors. I wonder if he has Parkinson's or is simply a nervous wreck.

'See the Cyrillic alphabet here?' The guide points shakily to a shallow pool with strange formations. 'This is evidence that the cave is Bulgarian and not Greek.'

We are only a few kilometres from the Greek border, after all. Which is presumably why he sees fit to tell us a nationalist joke.

'Now, Turkey, Greece and Yugoslavia had earthquakes. They went to God and said, Dear God, can you arrange for the Bulgarians to have an earthquake too, it's only fair. God said, I'll see what I can do. And Turkey, Greece and Yugoslavia kept having earthquakes. They went back to God and said, Dear God, we asked you to visit earthquakes on Bulgaria, not on us again. God said, Hold on, let me check which map I was using.'

Angel and I laugh politely.

'This here is the wedding hall,' the guide runs ahead. 'We sometimes marry couples here; look, this is the celebrant's table. Out of nearly 300 weddings, we haven't had a single divorce. Those who want a divorce are sent straight to the Devil's Gorge. Now, see this stalagmite and stalactite? We call it the Incomplete Kiss. That's because they need another 150 years to meet up and form a stalactone. You're welcome to pop in then and see it.'

We'd rather pop out into the world of the living, and when we do, there is no trace of the snow. It's warm and sunny as we arrive in the protected village of Shiroka Laka.

Shiroka Laka was built by Christian breakaways from seventeenth-century conversions, and became a National Revival stronghold with its fortress-like houses and church schools. Last time I stopped here, I was trekking in the Rodopi with Michael. Actually, we weren't so much trekking as getting hopelessly lost in the hills and we stumbled into Shiroka Laka by mistake, all scratched by brambles, sunburnt, and delirious with thirst. The locals looked at us as if we were devils, or Turks at the very least. We only stayed for a few hours, to admire the fortified, whitewashed houses, but by the time we left, the locals were practically waving strings of garlic and crucifixes in our direction. There were no buses at the end of the day, and we hitched, desperate to get away from the bad vibes. A young army officer from the Alpine division in Smolyan saved us from our predicament and enlightened us.

'The locals are jumpy these days,' he explained, 'because so many foreigners and new rich Sofianites buy up the houses here for a song. They come with their jeeps and arrogance and prance around like they own the place. The locals are proud folk. They feel like they're being bought out of their own village. They like visitors, but not property buyers. They just want to be left alone.' We wondered how anybody could mistake bedraggled tourists for property sharks, but it wasn't that amazing. Most property-buying foreigners first come as tourists, and then return as owners. The most handsomely done-up house in the village bears a wooden sign saying 'Jack's House'.

Perversely drawn to the hostility of Shiroka Laka, I have decided to stay for a few days. I'm determined to see at least one person smile.

Angel and I arrive at siesta time, and the only people on the main street are a red-faced policeman fattened by too much rakia and too little work, and two local men with crumpled faces and distended bellies. They're discussing important matters: the long weekend. More eating and drinking. Angel and I sit down to a meal of smilyanski beans, famous in the Rodopi for their buttery texture. Except they taste like they were genetically engineered and transported from China in the hull of a very slow, damp ship.

'They probably were,' Angel says. 'This is what happens when small producers are bulldozed by big businesses.' He adjusts his glasses. 'No more authentic smilyanski beans. But let's not ruin your short visit. Just breathe in the pure air of the Rodopi because you haven't been here for ages. Recharge yourself. I haven't been outside Bulgaria, and I'm sure Scotland has nice air too, but there's nothing like home.'

And nothing like old-fashioned chivalry. I have hired Angel for the day and expect to cover all expenses, but he insists on paying for lunch. We argue over the bill until I surrender and he proudly picks it up. Only hours ago, he'd told me all about his expenses with the car, the high price of living, the meagre taxi custom in a small town, how he still lives with his parents because he can't afford his own place. But paying for lunch is another matter altogether.

After the bean soup and saying goodbye to Angel, things begin to go downhill. I discover that instead of the 'golf course'-sized apartment I was promised by the guesthouse owner on the phone, I'll be sleeping inside a roomy cupboard. The price, on the other hand, is the same. I politely ask for a cupboard discount, and the guesthouse owner politely tells me that if I'm not happy with the price, he can show me the door. But he knows, and he knows that I know: it's a long weekend and there isn't a free bed in the village. Not even a free cupboard. I decide to calm myself with a piece of sweet pumpkin pie in the folk-themed restaurant downstairs.

'No.' The dessicated waiter nods negatively. 'We don't offer it by the piece. You can order it for the next day and our chef can make you a tin of it.'

'Do I have to eat the whole tin?' I joke. But he isn't laughing.

'Well, you don't have to eat it all if you don't want to. But you have to buy all of it.'

I stare at the 'Rodopean pumpkin pie, 300 g, 3 lev' in the menu. How much for the whole pie, then?

'Let's see,' the waiter calculates. 'There are about five pieces in a tin. So that's 15 lev.' And no discounts for ordering in bulk? No, this is not 'bulk', he explains, this is just a tin. Just a tin with 1.5 kilograms of pumpkin pie that I must eat by myself. To hell with it, I'll take it.

'OK, I shall tell the cook to start hunting for a pumpkin,' the waiter says, and I almost get my first smile. Almost.

My cupboard looks out towards the local culture hall which has proudly hung out two flags from its windows: Bulgaria and the EU. In the evening, its windows light up and the squeal of bagpipes lures me in. All the locals under the age of fifty are on stage, rehearsing for the hall's grand opening at the end of the week. Those over fifty are in the audience.

'It's been derelict for twenty years,' a flushed old woman tells me, and hands me the script for the play, like a menu. I almost look for the price. It's a folksy comedy written by a teacher in the 1930s and based around a village gathering. 'It's being played by several generations of locals,' the woman informs me, as if she's running me through the specialties of the house. 'And we're finally opening our doors again. I didn't think I'd live to see it!'

During the rehearsals, a few Gypsy kids sneak into the hall to watch. They are well groomed but their faces are prematurely stamped with dejection. They smile at the slapstick and watch in awe the young women in jeans singing folk songs and the chubby young bagpipe player squeezing his goat skin to release Olympian sounds. A couple more kids come into the hall, and what they do takes me aback: they hug the Gypsy kids. It's an unusual sight, to see a Bulgarian and a Gypsy holding hands, even if they are twelve. Later, I learn that they are all from the local orphanage.

Over the next few days, I see the young faces from the stage at cafés in the morning and cheap mehanas at night, smoking in tight-knit cliques. They are here for the public holidays, otherwise they all work out of town. The orphans are too young to work, and hang around the single main street, looking bored and lost already.

'We're the only village in this region which has been 100 per cent pure Christian Bulgarian for ever. We have two Gypsy brothers, builders. But they're completely integrated,' the retired old nurse in the new pharmacy briefs me sweetly while selling me some mountain tea that treats everything from dry coughs to menstrual cramps. And, presumably, intolerance.

'You know in the seventies when I was a nurse at the local Mother and Child Home—' the generic name for orphanages in Bulgaria has always struck me as odd '—conditions were so basic that we'd sometimes have to ride a mule through the snow to reach Gela village six kilometres up the hill. Those who couldn't ride walked. Even so, in the old days, under Socialism, there was no ethnic distinction. Turks, Gypsies, Bulgarians, everybody got the same deal.

We cared for everyone. Nobody suffered privations like today. There was no hatred. It was a more humane system. Today it's man eat man.'

I've heard this one before, but who am I to contradict her? She is telling the truth, or some version of it anyway.

'Take me, for example. I've given forty years of my working life to the State. What did I get when I retired? A 100 lev pension. That's why I'm working here. This would never happen in the old system.'

She asks me where I live. I tell her the truth, some version of it anyway.

'See, you and your family, you too are victims of the new system. If it hadn't been for this man-eat-man society, you would've stayed. But you've been deprived of a homeland.'

I don't point out that it was the previous system, the humane system of man spy on man, that had made me want to leave in the first place.

'One teaspoon per litre of boiling water,' she instructs me with care. 'And don't forget Bulgaria. It needs you.'

Does it? Shiroka Laka doesn't give the impression of needing anybody. It would be easy to feel that even if no tourist set foot here again, the village would plod on and endure, stubbornly, ox-like, as it has always done. But the difference between now and when I visited three years ago is everywhere: in the revived culture hall; the spruced-up houses; the new mehanas; even this new pharmacy. Shiroka Laka needs me and other tourists despite all appearances.

And appearances are of an enclave bookended by small bridges arched like the backs of cats. Beyond each bridge is a densely folded land of canyons, caves, mosques, and women in baggy trousers. I decide to rent a car and explore.

At the end of the road to the south-west is Trigrad, the last big village before the border. The village shop sells everything from salami to shampoo and sunglasses, and the mehana is owned by a man so hairy he seems wrapped in a brown rug. He wears an intensely cartographic T-shirt of Greater Bulgaria *circa* the Middle Ages. 'Bulgaria on three seas!' it screams, the refrain of the nationalist revisionist, while its owner explains amiably why he has overcharged me for my sausage lunch. It's because in the menu the sausage is priced by the 100 grams, you see, and, without realizing, I'd greedily eaten the 200 grams they'd served me. It's the pumpkin pie all over again.

When I spot a lone minaret standing in a pile of rubble across the road, my first thought is that the Bulgarian on the three seas must have taken a bulldozer to the mosque.

A pockmarked man is chainsawing the wood from the mosque. A woman is working alongside him. I approach and they turn off the chainsaws. I ask when the mosque came down.

'Three days ago,' the man says, gruff and wary of the nosy city person.

'Ah, so recently,' I say, trying to sound neutral.

'Yes, but they're putting up a new, bigger one,' the man explains, examining my face for signs of bias one way or the other. Or maybe I'm examining him. 'A church on one side, a mosque on the other. And they'll keep the minaret.'

'Wow, that's very democratic!' I say. He blinks at me.

'We're like that here,' the woman joins in with a smile. 'We get on well in this village. There's no tension. Why should there be? The main thing is that people believe. Everybody should be a believer.'

'I'm not a believer,' I say. There's a pause of disapproval. 'But I believe that people should get on regardless,' I hasten to add.

'That's right,' the woman agrees, relieved.

'Where are you from?' the man asks, still suspicious. He can smell a Sofianite when he sees one. I confess.

'Sofia for you, here for us, that's the way we like it,' he declares, and starts up the chainsaw again to make a point. But then he turns it off again. He prefers to chat. I ask about the logs.

'We're cutting these up, then we'll sell them to old people as fire-logs. I work for a construction company, I do this sort of thing all the time.'

'And I work for the local forestry. We have to live somehow.' The woman smiles again. It's a smile that's quite happy with its lot, a rare sight in the countryside. A rare sight in this country altogether.

'I'll let you get on with it,' I say.

'That's fine. We don't mind, we have time here. Not like Sofia.' He smiles gruffly and puts on his ear-muffs. We've made peace. They start up the chainsaws again.

I stroll around Trigrad, greeting the gentry who are busy sunning themselves on benches, watering vegetables, feeding pigs, and gossiping: old men with walking canes; women in flower-printed headscarves and trousers under their blue work mantles. They squint, smile and nod greetings. White crags and pine forests rise on all sides.

The villages around here have palpable names like Chestnut, Pear, Leather, Strawberry, Dragon, Thunder. All the geopolitical and ideological brutalities of the last century haven't managed to whitewash the colours of the Rodopi or violate its mysteries. After all, humans of one belief or another have lived in the caves and river canyons of the Rodopi for as long as there have been humans at all. What are a hundred years? Not even enough time for the stalactite and the stalagmite to complete that marble kiss.

A hundred years is also how long it takes me to reach my

destination. It's in a deep canyon at the eastern end of the Rodopi, and it's called the Devil's Bridge.

I can see why: the devil's road leads down to it from a tiny village called Grandpas. The grandpas have clearly died off because the village looks derelict. But before Grandpas, I stop in the town of Ardino. I stop because I need to check that I'm still in Bulgaria.

The central square of Ardino is dominated by a huge, pigeon-covered mosque, travel agencies advertising in Turkish, and a loungy café called Bosforus where idle youth with sleek hair sip fruit cocktails. Everybody speaks Turkish. The slow-moving woman in the grocery shop seems lethargically surprised either by my purchase of a packet of Turkish-delight-filled Armenian sweets, or by the fact that I purchase them in Bulgarian. I have heard rumours that in some Turkish-majority towns down here, you won't be served unless you speak Turkish. You might even be attacked if you don't. I must admit I'm a little uneasy, both because of the rumours which I desperately want to prove wrong, and because I feel like a foreigner here.

But although the Bulgarian I hear is slightly accented, the ethnic Turks look indistinguishable from their swarthy Bulgarian cousins, and the vibes – if we can speak of vibes in a comatose mountain town on a public holiday – are benign. And since this is a marble quarry region, I'm definitively reminded of my whereabouts by a small marble slab resting in a garden next to the mosque. It's inscribed in gold letters:

01.01.2007

BULGARIA IN THE EUROPEAN UNION

I imagine the unveiling to general cheer by the smiling Turkish mayor. I wonder if anyone else has noticed that it's only the small gold stars encircling the letters that save the slab from looking like a fresh gravestone.

But on to Grandpas, and off down the devil's road. It's ten kilometres of steep, rocky whiteness plunging into the canyon of Arda River. The owners of private cars are easy to spot: they are walking; their hair isn't standing on end like mine; and they're not muttering through gritted teeth, 'This bridge had better be worth it.' By the time I reach the river, I'm as wrecked as the rented car. But one look at the river confirms that it was worth it.

A dream-like, three-arched stone bridge rises to twelve metres. It is so stupendously curved that it actually peaks at the top. Not a stone has fallen out of it since it was built – not by Romans, Byzantines, or the Devil himself, as some locals fancy, but by the Ottomans. On closer inspection, I find one possible reason for this endurance, locked in a hexagonal keystone in the centre of the bridge. This is what was known to alchemists as Solomon's seal, a symbol of earthly and heavenly vision popular with every major faith.

It was especially popular with Sultan Süleyman the Magnificent. Speculation about the date of the bridge's construction wanders wildly between the sixteenth and the eighteenth centuries, but it's very possible that it was built in the 1500s under the Magnificent one. The central stone then makes perfect sense. The Magnificent one liked to stamp himself messianically onto buildings with all available symbols of earthly and heavenly power, especially Solomon's seal which had both.

It also makes perfect superstitious sense. The seal protected you from evil, and since the bridge was used by camel caravans carrying cotton, wool, tobacco, rose oil and other earthly delights, travelling all the way from the Thracian plains to the Aegean in the south, you really needed supernatural protection to survive. Because the various bands of hirsute brigands operating in the mountains were enemies in theory, but united in practice by a desire for self-enrichment.

A gunshot startles me from my reverie. After I check that I'm not bleeding anywhere, I locate two teenagers further down the bridge, with an airgun. They flip-flop back to the wooden shelter on the edge of the river, where their fathers whack them edifyingly on the neck and beckon for me to join them.

Soon I'm putting away quantities of barbecued chicken, watermelon and baklava, overseen by an extended family of Bulgarian Turks – mute grandma in a headscarf, men in tracksuit pants, teenagers, and younger women in jeans who talk little but smile a lot.

'We often come here for picnics,' one of the fathers says, 'and now we have family over from Turkey.' The woman at the barbecue shakes hands with me. She doesn't speak Bulgarian, and giggles delightedly when I thank her in mangled Turkish for the second portion of chicken. They ask me which part of Sofia I'm from. Youth 3, I lie. Ah, the woman who made the baklava says, my sister lives there. Her brother, a man of few words, has worked in Sofia too.

'We all work in construction,' the more extrovert husband adds. 'But now there's more work here, and we won't have to go far any more. It was quite depressed before, but things are picking up.'

We chat for a while, and finally I manage to casually slip in my burning question: what happened to them in the eighties, during the Revival Process? There is a painful pause. Even the relative from Turkey seems to understand and freezes up, barbecue prod in hand. Then the extrovert father waves it away with an uneasy smile.

'Ah, it's all water under the bridge now...'

'We came back but some of the family stayed in Turkey,' the

woman with the baklava tries, but her husband cuts her off.

'It's all water under the bridge. Forgotten. Why talk about it now?'

She doesn't insist. Embarrassed, I quickly say the first thing that comes to my mind – what's the baklava recipe? She starts listing the ingredients (which include yogurt, of all things) and everyone relaxes. Then they load me up with one last lot of chicken, and I scramble back up to the car.

I'm reluctant to leave this charmed – or cursed, it's hard to tell – place. The more I look at the central arc and its twin reflected in the calm green water, forming a prefect mirror-like oval, the more I find all kinds of unlikely superstitious tales quite likely. When you have so much history, an old bridge is never just an old bridge.

There's the one about the master builder who had to build his own wife's shadow into the foundations, to ward off the devil. This made bridges durable and killed off wives. But it's too generic a story. Every second bridge in Bulgaria has a person's shadow built in. This is also the story of Ottoman Bulgaria in a nutshell. Build your shadow into the Ottoman bridge, it will kill you but what you build will live on. It's a suitable metaphor for a nation that lay low for centuries in order to survive. As the saying goes, keep your head down and it won't get chopped off. Those who dared lift their heads usually lost them.

The sky is packing up and I look back at the Turkish family who are beginning to pack up too. It was their Ottoman ancestors who designed the bridge, but I have no way of asking how they feel about this heritage, how it feels to be the descendent of the national oppressor, how it feels to see graffiti like the one in Peach Street in Sofia: 'Death to the Turks'. After all, the opening scene of *Time of Violence* was shot here, on this bridge: the cruel caravan of the janissary Karaibrahim filing into town to slaughter the locals.

And for as long as some Bulgarians have to believe it was the Romans who built the bridge before they can admire it, these questions remain hard to answer, and harder yet to ask.

Back in Shiroka Laka, I decide to part on a friendly note with the guesthouse owner. I sit at an outdoor table with a soothing mountain tea. He's pottering in the bar with his back to me.

'Your cook made a delicious pumpkin pie for me,' I say brightly. There is no reaction. He keeps his gruff back to me. I feel foolish with my forced friendliness.

Eventually, when I'm about to go, he turns a glum face to me, looks away, and says, 'It's been a hard year. Fires, droughts. I don't know how she found a pumpkin.'

This is his way of being friendly. This will have to do instead of a smile. I'm a bit lost for words and try to arrange my face into a suitable expression of glumness. Then I walk to the top of the village, watch the sun set over the rooftops, and dine on wild plums from the trees. After the pumpkin-pie orgy, I have neither the money nor the appetite for a more substantial feed.

From up here, Shiroka Laka looks like a bowl filled with broken brick fragments and set carefully in the middle of the canopy of hills. I think I get it now.

Like the houses, this is a fortified stronghold, first for the endangered Christian identity, then for architectural unity, and now… Now it's as if survival in hard times has hardened the very soul of the village. As if the quiet, stubborn will to survive unadulterated is written into the DNA of the locals, and lives on for generations after the enemy is gone.

Suddenly, a choir of undulating female voices rises from the bottom of the bowl, or rather from the culture hall, where rehearsals for the grand opening continue.

The otherworldly, high-pitched lament of the voices takes you straight back to those Orphean times of wine, blood, and undying love.

And caravans trotting along arched stone bridges, carrying the invisible cargo of a mountain spirit across canyons and centuries.

The next morning I am in Plovdiv. This is the country's number two city for population after Sofia, number two for beauty and history after Veliko Turnovo, and – for me – number one for home-made pies.

I stay at a small nameless hotel near Djumaya Square. My shower ejects lukewarm water in desultory spurts, just enough to flood the bathroom, but it's the cheapest hotel in town and every hotel room is booked up anyway. Most importantly, it's three minutes away from the Oriental Patisserie at Djumaya Mosque.

But when I arrive at the patisserie, greedily panting in anticipation of semolina cake, calamity strikes. The patisserie is no more. The street around the mosque is dug up, the mosque itself encased in scaffolding, and two swarthy men are poking with grim tools inside the cake shop. They are Turks, and answer my anxious questions with heavily accented gruffness. No, the cake shop won't be coming back. Yes, we're fixing the mosque. In my distress, I briefly consider turning my back on Plovdiv for ever. It's just not the same without the semolina cake. True, I'm glad they are restoring the Balkans' oldest mosque, here since the fourteenth century. But a mosque without sweets is like an Eastern Orthodox church without incense, a dull affair.

Still, heinous cake crimes aside, Plovdiv is looking its best. Above the excavated Roman forum, a bronze Philip of Macedon points victoriously to the heavens from a concrete plinth, reminding us that this was once the city of Philipopolis. Being the egomaniac he is, Philip stands as tall as the minaret, if not a few inches taller. High up in the old town, a Roman amphitheatre spills whitely downhill.

The International Jazz Festival is on and the pedestrian mall in the new town is buzzing with shops, shoppers, cafés, café moochers, buskers and artworks. A euphoric jazz orchestra is playing on a summer stage near a jubilant water fountain, people are sunning themselves on benches, and the colourful *fin-de-siècle* façades are being spruced up for the first time since the Second World War. Things are happening in Plovdiv, good things.

I meander up the steep streets of the old town.

Past the Puldin Restaurant which sits on top of Roman walls and inside a medieval monastery of the Persian Order of Whirling Dervishes.

Past the nineteenth-century Hypocrates Pharmacy full of wondrous jars and humming with alchemy.

Past the richly painted Revival houses lining the streets, the names of their old masters ringing brightly like chords in a cosmopolitan symphony of times past: Hindlian; Efosyan; Nedkovich; Balabanov; Danov; even Lamartine who only stayed here for three days in 1833, but Plovdiv so yearned for Europe that the name stuck.

Past the hallucinogenically painted church of Sts Konstantin and Elena where a muttering old witch with a moustache tells me to 'cover up your tits, girl', meaning that I shouldn't wear a vest-top inside.

Yes, past the charming people of the old town, all the way up the dead-end last street to the Nebet Tepe lookout point. Nebet Tepe sounds like an extinct volcano, and in a way it is. The hill underneath my feet is so packed with history that it's amazing it hasn't imploded from the sheer pressure of eras bubbling inside like elemental gases.

Here lie ruins from the Thracian settlement of Eumolpias in 7000 BC, a Hellenic citadel from the times of Philipopolis, Roman underground passages from the time of Emperor Justinian which lead to Maritsa River, medieval water tanks from when the town was called Puldin, and no doubt the odd Turkish stone from Philibe.

In the pink light of dusk, the rooftops of Plovdiv seem to shift, coming in and out of focus inside the long-zoom lens of time. A strange oriental tune suddenly rises from this open-air museum. I search among the detritus of Nebet Tepe and find a lonesome, barefooted hippie in a headscarf and long skirt. Turned towards the setting sun, her hair on fire, she is playing a flute.

Later, the night sky unleashes a warm thunderstorm on the city. I duck inside a late-night internet joint in the now empty pedestrian mall. It's at the top floor of a heavily graffiti'd, urine-smelling staircase. There are a dozen teenagers in the smoky computer room, playing violent computer games. They're pimply, aggressive, and speak with about five words, all of them obscene. I flee back into the warm rain.

It's technically impossible to get lost in the centre of the new town, but the combination of rain and darkness makes sure I do. I grope for my hotel in the tangle of semi-dark streets. The only noise I hear is the distant thumping of some disco and the lashing of the rain through blossom-heavy trees. I'm sodden and suddenly sad, and to cheer myself up, I hum an old song by the pop band Tangra: 'Yes, that's how it is in the small town/in this boring, old-fashioned town/You may as well fall in love/Or nothing ever happens.'

'You wouldn't happen to have a cigarette on you?' A ruin of a man materializes under a streetlamp in a whiff of alcoholic haze. He has eyes washed out by alcohol and rain.

'I don't smoke, sorry.' I glance around the empty street to confirm that if he attacks me, nobody will come to my help.

'Do you have 10 stotinki?' he tries.

'What can you buy with 10 stotinki?' I continue my brisk walk in a random direction, and he hobbles along.

'As much as I can buy with 10 leva or 1,000 leva,' he slurs. 'Nothing. The things that I've lost can't be bought with all the money in the world.'

'What have you lost?'

'I used to be an artist. Not any more. The muse died.' He burps and waves a vague, heavy arm: too complicated. The fly of his trousers is undone.

'I've lost my hotel,' I decide to confide in him. 'Can you help me find D— Street?'

'D— Street? Ah, that one changed. What's it called now? Street names have changed all over, one doesn't know any more where one is walking.' And he turns the corner, gesturing for me to follow. I follow. And there, to my relief, I see a flickering neon HOTEL sign. I leave him leaning on a wall to steady himself, his chest wheezing like an old accordion. I wonder how many degrees he has. I wonder what he painted before the muse left him.

I lie on the hard bed in my dark room, and listen to the rain outside, the distant thumping of the disco, an ambulance siren, the dripping faucet in my bathroom.

I know, it's probably just the sudden rain, the demise of my favourite cake shop, and the HOTEL neon sign flickering outside my window like an SOS signal, but tonight, despite the jazz festival and the singers in Shiroka Laka's new cultural hall, I feel isolated and lonely. Something has eluded me here. The Rodopi don't reveal themselves fully to smiling outsiders in rented cars.

All you can hope for is a shadow that will follow you from the underworld, like Eurydice followed Orpheus. But as soon as you turn to look at it, it vanishes. All I have succeeded in doing is to tune into the discordant growl of the land, crouching fawn-like, in some ancient Orphic curse that can't be broken.

12 Into the Memory Hole

Bulgaria, Turkey, and the Death Strip

In an Istanbul hotel, I am carefully mispronouncing the Turkish for 'thank you' to the hotel cleaner, when suddenly she speaks crystalline Bulgarian and puts me out of my misery. She is strangely pleased to see me, like long-lost family from back home. Except that Bulgaria isn't back home for either of us, and we're not family.

We stand on the landing, her bucket and broom between us. The French and Spanish guests of the hotel file past on their way to the breakfast terrace, trying to work out whether we are speaking Turkish or something even weirder.

'We're from a village near Burgas on the coast,' she says. 'We moved here in 1989, you know, with the name changes and all that… It was hard, but we've carved out a decent life. You can make a good living if you work hard. Even so, my husband keeps going back to Bulgaria. He doesn't work, he just collects the rent from our house over there. I don't know, he misses it a lot, his friends, the town. He can't get used to things here after all this time… He says he's going to retire there, on the Black Sea. I say forget Bulgaria. But he's stubborn, Bulgaria this, Bulgaria that. That's where all my memories are, he says. And his brother's family is there.

'Our youngest daughter,' the cleaner continues, 'she didn't want to come at the time. She hid at some friends' place for a week, we had to drag her out kicking and screaming.' She shakes her head. 'And now it's him that wants to go back. Go figure.'

Her family were in the convoy of Bulgarian Turks who went on that 'long holiday' courtesy of the State in the eighties. They had suddenly found themselves living collectively in Room 101 of the Ministry of Love. There, pregnant women were told that they couldn't give birth in the local hospital until they changed their names. People whose parents had just died couldn't bury them in the family plot because the family tombstone with the name Ahmed was translated overnight to Assen. Those same people had to confirm, on revised birth certificates, that their great-grandfather hadn't been called Hassan, but Ivan. Graduates who had the misfortune of being called Selin found that their diplomas were suddenly invalid, until they became Svetla. School kids had their certificates burned – since Aishe didn't exist, it wasn't possible that Aishe had passed from grade four to grade five. So Aishe disappeared from school for a week or so, and when she reappeared, the teacher told the class her new name: Ana. Ana-Aishe burst into tears at the sound of her new name.

Blind spots appeared everywhere, while people disappeared into piles of forms, militia headquarters, prisons, forests and border zones where they were sometimes arrested or shot for trespassing. The State's objective was to erase all traces of Bulgaria's Muslim past, present, and future (he who controls the past...). The State's method was to shove a million people into a giant memory hole. The State, in the words of Brecht, was dissolving the people and electing another people.

The scenes that followed three years later heralded the ethnic purges in Yugoslavia: families ripped apart as some wanted to go and others stay; children lost in the melee; furniture piled up in trucks; people running in tears after the cars of departing neighbours; pets released into the wilderness.

When we say goodbye, the cleaner holds my palm between her rough hands, wishing me all the best things in the world, and I thank her, in Bulgarian this time. I thank her for bothering to distinguish between people and ideology. A distinction Mature Socialism didn't bother to make.

The next day Michael and I leave Turkey. Between Istanbul and the border the bus gradually fills with Bulgarian Turks. Behind us is seated a tiny, toothless woman in faded black, no bigger than a child, travelling from some previous century with her two great-grandchildren. She wears a headscarf with the ends undone and hanging around her squashed face. She chews soft pastry with her gums, listens with dismay as Michael and I speak a strange foreign tongue, and stares at people's faces with the vacant eyes of history's unwitting survivor.

Next to us is a smiley teenage girl who speaks broken Bulgarian. 'I was only a year old when we left Bulgaria,' she says, chewing gum. 'I don't remember anything.' The middle-aged woman next to her smiles timidly, avoiding our eyes, remembering everything, and saying nothing.

As we get close to the Bulgarian border, the driver stops the folksy Turkish tape that has been playing for hours, and puts on a Bulgarian tape. The popular, vulgar pop-folk known as *chalga* is the ideal musical switch from Turkey to Bulgaria. *Chalga* is derived from a Turkish word derived from Arabic, and the result is Bulgarian turbo-folk with Middle-Eastern embroideries. Now, unfortunately, I can understand when the crooner Azis wails 'How it hurts, how it hurts'. The moustachioed twins in front of us, sunburnt to a crisp on some Turkish beach, sing along, loving it.

At the border the merriment quickly dies down. A thick-set border guard clambers onto the bus and collects everybody's passports. He doesn't miss the opportunity to abuse the Bulgarian Turks who twitch defensively by an old reflex. The uniform of officialdom can't disguise the fact that here is just a timeless common or garden Balkan thug, the type that in his twenties might have been among the 'official organs' of the Revival Process, reviving people with his fists.

He turns to the gummy old woman. 'Where is your Turkish passport?'

She produces her second passport, muttering Turkish curses.

'Speak Bulgarian, grandma,' the guard grumbles. 'You have a Bulgarian passport.'

The old woman resentfully shrinks into her headscarf. An unhappy silence hangs over the bus. Border crossings in the Balkans haven't been friendly places since the Ottoman Empire dissolved into a mess of cocky nationalisms, and people began to be herded across new borders like cattle. In a historical sense, the Ottomans only really left yesterday, which is why this thug is bullying their descendents.

The guard turns to me: 'You have another passport?'

'Yes. From New Zealand. Do you want to see it?'

'No, that's OK.' He waves me away. 'You can keep your New Zealand passport.'

He glances at Michael, as if to say, And your New Zealand lover too. Slut.

We are kept waiting for an hour, although there are no other buses at the checkpoint. The passengers smoke and bask in the sun. A Kontiki tour bus heaves out of the Bulgarian side, full of young Western travellers. They study us from the height of their superior vehicle like Sunday strollers watching flea-ridden animals in the zoo. Their passport checks are over in five minutes, and their bus continues on its picturesque journey.

Until seventeen years ago, this checkpoint was the most forlorn spot in the country. The only traffic was black Volgas with diplomatic number plates and tinted windows. Then suddenly, in 1989, 300,000 refugees flooded the gates: the first mass displacement since the Second World War, and the first exodus wave from the burst dam of Mature Socialism.

Finally, our mild-mannered Bulgarian-Turkish driver comes back with the passports and calls out each name. All names (except mine and Michael's) are Turkish. And one other traveller who doesn't make it across. It's the nervy, unshaven man in a threadbare jacket at the back of the bus. The driver shouts at the man in harsh Turkish and throws his tatty bag out of the luggage hold. The wretch catches the bag, slings it over his shoulder, and without a word turns back the way we had come.

'A Romanian.' The driver spits out a fat globule of phlegm. 'Trying to sneak in. With an invalid passport.'

The Romanian shuffles down the dusty road of no man's land, his tracksuit pants fluttering around his ankles. The hills rise forbiddingly on every side like walls of dark velvet. There isn't a village for miles either side of the border crossing, just mountain, dust, and road.

Only seventeen years ago, the sneaky Romanian might have been arrested or shot by a Bulgarian border patrol on sight. Many were. In the Cold War, this border zone in Strandja National Park was known as the Death Triangle. The Death Triangle was where the Fatherland and the entire Warsaw Pact bloc was protected by ever-vigilant patrol guards against the capitalist-imperialist enemy: Turkey and its NATO allies. Should Turkey attack, the soldiers would fire from their permanently entrenched positions and hold out until the Soviet army rushed to the rescue.

No civilians were allowed here, and the patrol guards had instructions to shoot any moving target, which usually assumed the form of young Bulgarians, Romanians and East Germans. The moving target believed, wrongly, that the border zone here wouldn't be as scrupulously guarded as the Berlin Wall. The moving target was bright, naïve and indestructible with youth, and the last thing he or she saw was the barrel of a gun. The body of the now-still target was relieved of its meagre possessions and dumped into an unmarked grave. If the moving target was an East German, the Stasi were informed by the Bulgarian State Security about the tragic accident: a drowning at the beach, a road accident, a heart attack, it's unfortunate that young people are so reckless. The Stasi passed on the news minus the body bag to the family, who had no choice but to accept it. It's not as if they could file a complaint. The number of East Germans who were killed along this border is higher than all other East German victims of border crossings put together.

The number of dead Bulgarians is unknown because no one has bothered to find out. And, anyway, now the files can't be found, and the comrades who gave the orders from above are too amnesic or too busy elsewhere to remember where they put them. When a German author recently asked for cooperation in his research for a book about these ad hoc executions, the Interior Ministry – an updated version of the old Ministry of Truth – kept silent. Perhaps it never happened. Without evidence, nothing can be proved.

I wonder who among those glamorous beach foreigners I spied from the corner of my eye were also spied on by the special coastal agents of Bulgarian State Security and the Stasi. Who among them threw themselves onto the barbed wire of the Soc Camp. Who is lying inside these hills, their youth buried twice: once by soldiers following orders, once by the slumber of this grass full of rusty tanks and memory holes.

Meanwhile, Michael and I begin to wonder why the only traffic we see on the lush back roads of Strandja is us. One reason is that the potholes are so big you could disappear inside them and never be found. Another reason is that even seventeen years after the Death Strip was deactivated, it still casts a long, barbed shadow. Villages here still bear bizarre names like Bones and Border Patrol.

We drive through a ghost town with the name Little Star and panoramic views over folding dark ranges and chipped, concrete apartment buildings purpose-built for the hundreds of border patrols once stationed here with their families. When Bulgaria joined NATO a few years ago, they went home, and the light of Little Star went out. I go into the town's only shop, to buy a credit voucher for my mobile phone. There are three people inside, and seemingly three people in the village altogether: a surprised shop assistant; a lurching drunk who's buying cigarettes; and a Gypsy teenager in a flamenco skirt who's grinning at nothing in particular with what appear to be several rows of dazzling white teeth.

The village of Brushlyan or Ivy has an ivy-clad charm about it. But beneath the ivy lurks the rot of depression. The houses are spruced up, mostly because they offer guest rooms. But what would guests do here? See the museums. One of them is the 'cell school' where nineteenth-century kids learned to read and write in sand-boxes while seated on animal hides on the floor. It was a primitive affair because Strandja, like the whole of southern Bulgaria, remained under Ottoman control until the First Balkan War wrenched it from the Turks. The First World War a few years later herded Bulgarians, Greeks and Turks across new borders. There is a charge of 1 lev for the cell school museum, but the sad thing is that you can see all there is to see – yes, a room with rugs and sand-boxes – from the doorway.

We poke our heads into another open-air museum in a pretty garden. It's a display of primitive nineteenth-century agricultural tools that elicits pity for both ox and man. It costs only 1 lev, but we decide against it. Agricultural tools are not our thing.

'Why?' the disappointed owner protests. 'Isn't the gentleman from England? They have a high standard of living there. What is 1 lev to them? Fifty cents.'

I protest that the gentleman isn't from England and, besides, we are on a budget. But the man doesn't believe me and sadly shrugs his round shoulders. I sadly shrug mine, feeling mean not to be supporting the agricultural initiative. But Michael takes a pragmatic approach. 'It's great that they have business initiative, but isn't business about selling something that the buyer actually wants. Such museums should be free.'

They should. Brushlyan is trying to survive not on business but on charity without losing face. It's busking instead of begging. Such museums are free in countries where local government supports local heritage. But here, it's the *mutra* from Sofia who supports himself by building a hotel with funny money.

We leave Brushlyan for a border village at the dead end of a dirt road. It's as close as we can get to the border. But we discover that there is something between us and the fruity-sounding Slivarovo, Village of Plums: the border checkpoint. After kilometres of green wilderness dripping with birdsong, a nasty barbed-wire fence looms suddenly, like a bad memory. It has just enough of an opening for the car to pass. A large black dog barks at us. A smoking soldier pats him calm and steps down from his kiosk.

'Hi.' He casually leans on the open-windowed passenger door, and grins with nicotine-yellow teeth, the only flaw in the kind of Antonio Banderas lookalike face you don't expect to see in this spot.

'We normally ask for papers, but don't bother.' He waves indulgently, amused by the double novelty of a woman driver and a foreign visitor. 'Drive on. But bear in mind that it's prohibited to go beyond Slivarovo. We have instructions not to allow people to walk down to the Resovska River. The boss is in the village and he won't let you…'

The scenic river is the natural boundary between the two countries and precisely where we want to go. But we can't argue with Antonio Banderas and his boss.

We leave the car next to a parked blue Lada in a vast clearing at the start of the village. From here, spectacular hilltop vistas open up over the blue and green ranges of Turkish Strandja. It's the mountain doing its own thing, mindless of borders, languages, and history.

Slivarovo (number of residents: ten) is green and creaking with abandoned houses and plum trees. As soon as we step on the village path, clouds of tiny flies encase our heads. The quiet is thick and oppressive, like walking through syrup. I feel like a First World War correspondent in the Balkans walking into a border village a day after the enemy army has passed through. I almost expect to see pigs feasting on unspeakable things.

Instead, we see three middle-aged locals talking in hushed voices, as if the open spaces might magnify their words. As if the hills have ears. We greet them, our voices loud and hollow, and they nod and examine us with a circumspect eye before muttering something that might be a greeting.

Next, we spot a man in a worker's overalls, and a squat, grey-haired woman with bosoms the size of small Strandja hills. She moves very slowly, as if stirring cement. She is, in fact, stacking up logs against a wall. The man is chopping them up in a primitive outdoor summer kitchen. A brew of aromatic mountain herbs bubbles in a tin on the stove. They're startled by the visitors, but when they get over the initial shock they loosen up.

'Yes, I grew up here,' the man tells us in a regional accent so thick that at first I think he's clearing his throat. 'There were a thousand people here. Houses there, there, there.' He points to the wild bush. 'This was my school.' It's the gutted, windowless house next door.

'Some Sofianites bought it and they're gonna do it up.'

'And do you live here?' I ask the bosomed woman.

'I live on the coast. But I'm doing up this house.' She smiles sheepishly. 'I want to get away from the coast, it's become a madhouse. Hotels and tourists everywhere. Are you out for a walk? Enjoy.'

We walk on. So far we've met five out of the ten residents.

'We might even be eleven since I retired here a couple of years ago,' smiles a rotund man in a woollen hat. He's fixing an antiquated scooter outside his house. 'I was a miner. And a bus driver. Mm, that's right. I know Strandja inside out. Do you want some of my honey?'

'Yes, thank you,' Michael says in Bulgarian, which pleases the miner no end.

'My man.' He shakes Michael's hand, his round face grinning like a full moon on a clear night. 'Where are you from? New Zealand! You know, many years ago, in the sixties, a guy from this village ran away to New Zealand. Mm, that's right. He and some other lads from nearby villages managed to sneak across the river down there. Then from Turkey into Greece, and somehow he ended up in New Zealand.'

'Did he come back?' Michael wants to know.

'He never came back. Never. He died there recently, we heard. Mm, and now, you know, now that we're in the EU, they're talking of pulling down the barbed wire. And just having a few border patrols here in Slivarovo. Mm, we're becoming an open door... Fifteen Kurds crossed the river last year. Refugees. They caught them.'

I ask him if he's heard of any shootings of runaways in the old days.

'Well, there were lots of young people down at the International Youth Centre in Primorsko. Germans, Poles, Czechs, Russians...

Some wandered down this way, mm… it's possible. Anything is possible.'

At this point, the muttering trio down the path call out for him to come over. They've been listening to our conversation. The hills do have ears. He waddles off in their direction. When he passes us later on his scooter, he doesn't smile at us any more, as if under instructions from the vigilante team.

Resident number seven is Bai Kolyu, a switched-on pensioner with rubber boots and a camouflage cap who retired to his home village to rear goats and churn butter. He is appalled at my suggestion about border police abuses in the old days.

'It's out of the question. Some young people would have been caught trying to sneak across, but that's all. There was respect for life back then. Everybody knows how difficult it is to bring a child into this world… You don't remember the old system, of course…'

'But I do!' I protest. 'I grew up in the old system.'

'Ah, so you did, but you're too young to remember everything. Many things have been exaggerated about the old system.'

So he's an old-timer. 'Well, it's nice that borders are now opening up, relaxing…' I offer breezily. Then I see his pained face. 'But there are other problems, of course,' I add.

'Serious other problems. The young people of Bulgaria must think about it very hard. See.' He points at the spilling ranges with a twig. 'That's occupied Strandja. Bulgarian lands lost to us for ever. But watch out. Just as the Turks colonized us before with brute force, they're colonizing us now with assimilation. Yes, with their birth rate. By buying up property. The entire coast is bought up by Turks.'

'Well,' I search for the right words here, 'Bulgaria has always had a large Turkish minority. It's just part of our heritage. And there were never any problems with them until our own moronic government chased them away in the eighties…'

Bai Kolyu disagrees. 'Most of them left of their own choice. Nobody chased them, nobody forced them. Now they have two passports and they use them well. There are illiterate Turks who vote in the Bulgarian elections, under instructions…'

Some of this is true. Bai Kolyu is a gentle soul and it's clear to both of us that it's time to move onto more neutral themes, for example the climate and topography of Slivarovo, where two currents combine, Bai Kolyu explains, to create a uniquely pure air.

'That's why I came back to live here. Away from newspapers with bad news. I milk the goats and feel better. More people should milk goats… You know, the EU inspector for veterinary health came to inspect us here. Because we're the southernmost village of the EU. I made him cappuccino, with goat milk. He liked it very much.'

We don't get to meet the remaining three residents, but we come across the first couple again. How can we get down to the river? we ask.

'Keep your voice down,' the woman hisses. 'Just go.' She points with her chin to the eastern end of the village. 'Go quietly and don't ask anybody. It's better not to ask.'

The last inhabited house in the village features a small, shy, slightly soiled Bulgarian flag, and a barking dog. We hear muffled male voices inside. Perhaps this is where the 'boss' camps when he comes to Slivarovo. We tiptoe past the dog and the voices, and plunge into a sun-spotted world of high grasses, butterflies, and fresh goat droppings. Down in the green ravine, the Resovska River gurgles invitingly: it's the natural divide between two countries, and it doesn't know it. But I do. I can almost hear the furtive steps and stiffled giggles of twenty-year-olds with bell-bottomed trousers and ridiculous sideburns. They were the lucky ones who made it. By now, the danger of the barbed-wire zone would have been over. They could relax.

But I can't. Descending into the river gully feels like walking straight into the sights of a Kalashnikov. 'What if they're patrolling the river?' I whisper and clutch Michael's arm. What I really want to say, but don't because I know it's absurd, is, I don't want to die here.

'They're not,' he says breezily, but puts his camera away. We may not look like we're about to cross the border illegally, but we definitely look like we're taking extensive photographic records of the border area.

I start walking back, almost running. A quiet hysteria grips me. But to Michael such old-world, cold war paranoia is completely foreign. He tries to wind me up.

'If the border patrol sees us in the village, how do we prove that we didn't cross from Turkey?'

But I am not amused. My heart is in my throat. And guilty and tremulous like real fugitives, we tiptoe back into the village. This time we avoid the house with the male voices and squeeze through a small, scratchy orchard.

'Ah, you're back,' Bai Kolyu greets us. One of his goats comes with familiar nonchalance to chew my bag, and he shoos it away. 'I'll walk you up to the top.'

We reach the high clearing where his Lada and our battered rented car are basking in the setting sun. He wipes his hand on his jumper to make sure it's clean of goat, and shakes our hands.

'It was a pleasure to speak with two intelligent young people. If you were staying overnight, I'd make you cappuccino, with goat milk.' He shrugs. 'But you're leaving. Go well and come again some time. Me and the goats, we'll be here. We're not going anywhere.'

Today, I arrive alone at Shumen bus station. This area in the north-east has a large Turkish minority, and I've never been here before. I've come to see the Shumen fortress and the ruins of the early medieval capital Veliki Preslav.

Unshaven men with bad teeth and worn-out jackets smoke outside the station, waiting. They all look like Vladimir from *Waiting for Godot* – nobody will ever come for them. I almost expect to hear 'Do you want a carrot?'

It's hard to imagine that a tsar's city stood here once. In fact, it's hard to imagine that anything at all stood here, other than these men inside this rusting bus station.

'Are you looking for a taxi?'

The man is bearded and middle aged, and holds a sodden cigarette.

'Yes, are you a driver?'

'I'm a driver in the sense that I have a car. Where are you going? I'll give you a good rate, I won't skin you like the taxi fellas over there. twenty leva. But...'

I knew there was a catch.

'You see, I'm waiting for someone on the next bus. Ten, fifteen minutes? Let's make it half an hour. Go and have a coffee, I'll be here.'

Suddenly, the skies open and spew out a violent warm torrent. Within five minutes it's a biblical flood. I watch the uphill street into town become a river and briefly contemplate abandoning my mission. Small waterfalls are now forming here and there, and on the other bank are lined up yellow taxis. I have five hours before the last bus back to Varna on the Black Sea coast. Meanwhile, my driver has vanished.

And then the rain stops as suddenly as it started. I walk up and down the street-river to see if the water level is better anywhere. It isn't, so I just hitch my trousers and wade in ankle deep, the water tugging me downstream. The taxi-drivers contemplate me with detachment from their open car-windows and blow out philosophical ringlets of smoke.

'Bravo,' says the first driver in the line and smiles with all the wrinkles of his face. Bingo, he's the only one not smoking. 'Crossing like that without a bridge, well done!' His warm brown eyes have the soft glint of someone who has given up all pretence. 'I'll take you there for 15 leva.'

A deal. We plough upstream, water splashing the sides of the car. I close my window.

'Ts ts ts, look at this river!' He fumes quietly, 'A river in the middle of town. You know why? Because the street drains don't work. They made it especially so it wouldn't work.'

But he isn't an angry man, he's just making small talk. He has a pleasant, soft Turkish accent. His name is Mehmed.

'Or Mihail. I was Mihail when they changed the names. But nobody called me Mihail, everybody knew me as Mehmet.'

I've never talked to a Bulgarian Turk about the Revival Process. I want to ask him questions, but I feel squirmy, uncomfortable.

'Was your family affected?' I try cautiously.

'Well, they changed everybody's name, if that's what you mean.'

Mehmet is friendly but guarded, and so we chat about the state of the roads and the recent rains all the way to Veliki Preslav, capital of the First Bulgarian Kingdom.

In old Bulgarian, Veliki Preslav means something like 'Greatest of the Great', which it really was for about a century during the Bulgarian golden age, from the late ninth to the late tenth centuries.

Under the unusually enlightened and progressive for his time Tsar Simeon, the kingdom reached the apogee of European medieval culture. It was perhaps the best time ever to be a Bulgarian.

Splendid buildings stood inside the double fortress walls each three metres thick. Simeon's giant kingdom – incorporating today's Romania, Macedonia, part of Serbia and Albania, half of Greece, and greedily lurching down to Gallipoli and Constantinople – made the Byzantine emperors very jittery. The life mission of Simeon was to become crowned as a Byzantine-Bulgarian emperor presiding over Europe's greatest dominion. He almost made it but a heart attack put an end to his grab for Constantinople.

We get out of the car and squelch through fresh mud on the way to the ruins. Mehmet pulls up his wide tracksuit trousers and wades right in. He is wearing battered old shoes without socks.

'Ts ts ts, and they want tourists to come here in this mud!'

Only the contours remain of the medieval capital, and some rusty signs. We squint to make out the partly missing letters. Mehmet is indignant again, like a true patriot.

'Ts ts ts, look at this. They should put proper signs. All these riches, this heritage, and all they've got is rust.'

We stand haplessly among the ruins, courtesy of the invading Ottomans who razed the place to the ground in 1388. I try, without success, to picture how the Balkans could have been governed from here. With an irony that probably escaped the victorious Turks, they named the village that stood in the place of today's modern town of Veliki Preslav, Eski Stambolchuk – old Istanbul. Tsar Simeon's dream of merging with Constantinople had finally, perversely, come true, if only in name.

'Veliki Preslav isn't very *veliki* any more,' Mehmet observes as a fine rain begins to fall over the ruins and we head back to the car.

We're driving over potholes again, and before Mehmet gets a chance to complain about the roads, I pick up some courage and try again. 'Was anybody killed here during the name changes?'

'No, not here, people just got smacked around, sometimes roughed up, that sort of thing. One guy in a village near by, he got himself killed. Didn't want to change his name. He said I've been Hassan all my life, my mother named me Hassan, and I'll die as Hassan. And my daughters and my wife are keeping their names too. He wasn't taking any shit. They messed him up, probably didn't mean to kill him, but he died anyway. In Isperikh up the road, there was this boy, a famous wrestler, he gathered a band of friends and stood up to the militia. They beat them up, then they sent in the tanks. Ten tanks, twenty tanks, just for a few guys. In another village, the mayor gave the Turks carnations with their new passports – a red carnation for each new Bulgarian name. Or chocolates. Flowers and chocolates from Mother Bulgaria.' He chuckles.

'Then, in 1990, we went to Istanbul. You know Istanbul? Ah, Istanbul! But not for living. Too hard. You know how the Communists said back then: All the Turks who don't want to change their names, go back to where you came from. But the thing is, we don't come from Turkey. We come from here. In Turkey, they're different, they cover up their women. So we came back ten months later. Bulgaria is nicer, life is easier. We haven't got much money, but then nobody's got much money here, and we have our friends and neighbours, we'll get a small pension. My daughter is studying. All that stuff is in the past, you know, I don't hold grudges. I hope it stays there. All in the past.'

All in the past. When I was growing up, the Five Centuries of

Turkish Yoke and the 'three chains of slaves' felt very recent. They were the holy cow of national folklore. An entire purgatory of poems and ballads about the evil Turk traumatized my childhood, but the ballad of Balkandji Yovo was a cut above the rest. When the Turks come to Balkandji Yovo's house, to convert his sister Yana and take her away for the harems, he says, 'I'll give away my head, but I won't give Yana away.' The beastly Turks cut off his arms, then his legs, and finally blind him, but he's still not giving her away. In the end, he turns to her:

> Farewell, beloved sister,
> I have no legs to walk you to the door,
> I have no arms to embrace you,
> I have no eyes to see you.

At this point, whoever was reciting the poem (my mother, for example) would break down. I had no choice but to break down too, hating the sadistic Turks for making my mother cry, and wallowing in collective self-pity somewhere at the bottom of some miasmic pit of history.

Now it occurs to me that the prominence of Balkandji Yovo's grotesque bravado in the school syllabus was part of a State-encouraged national pathology that carefully blended the myth of heroism and the myth of martyrdom. The dismembering of Balkandji Yovo is the undoing of the Bulgarian ethnos. But, of course, the main thing is that he keeps his head: the nation will survive after all. Which also means that the memory of suffering will survive.

Religion is secondary in these myths. Religion stood for identity, which is why in their declining centuries the Ottomans became so violent in their campaigns. Converting a young woman to Islam, calling her Fatime and taking her for the harems amounted, in the eyes of any Balkan Christians, to annihilating her. It was not just a violation, it was a spiritual death. The families of beautiful girls would sometimes tattoo them with a cross between the eyes, to mar their beauty and make them less desirable to the Turks. But nothing could protect young Christian boys taken from their families as 'blood tax', and trained into fanatical janissaries who then turned on their own villages, like the savage Karaibrahim in *Time of Violence*.

At least Balkandji Yovo and Yana have their ballad. There are no ballads about Aishe-Ana and Hassan-Ivan of twenty years ago. The inane cruelties of the Revival Process were inflicted by shadowy agents in the shadowy zone where minorities dwell. The guilty walked free, and it is hard to compose songs about unknown villains. At this stage, only the occasional film and the occasional taxi-driver tell the story of Aishe-Ana and Hassan-Ivan.

The Bulgarian Turks – those who remained and those who returned – have had all their rights restored, and more. There is a Turkish TV station, Turkish language papers, Turkish schools, the mosques are being done up, and one of the country's top politicians, the cunning Ahmed Dogan, is leader of the Movement for Rights and Freedoms which represents minorities.

In matters of historical vocabulary, the pendulum has swung the other way too. At school, I learned that Bulgaria had been under a Turkish yoke. Today, kids learn about a certain vague Ottoman presence. The 'three chains of slaves' have mysteriously disappeared from public view, and Balkandji Yovo's severed limbs have been packed away in some historical freezer. His suffering is not politically correct any more.

*

Back in the car, Mehmet is now talking at ease, with a kind of unguarded innocence. I ask if he has friends and family in Turkey.

'All my family are here, but I have friends in Istanbul. They visit sometimes. They like Bulgarian girls. They go with prostitutes here, but it's expensive, 150 leva for one hour. They pay for two hours. Two hours! Why do you need two hours? Just do it and go. Stupid men.'

'Well, I don't feel sorry for them,' I say. 'I feel sorry for the girls who have to sell themselves.' I almost add 'to Turks' but check myself on time. Mehmet goes quiet at my righteous remark.

I go quiet too and ponder bizarre questions: for example, if there is a war between Bulgaria and Turkey – a near impossibility – which side would Mehmet be on?

An anti-Semitic taxi-driver in Buenos Aires once shouted at me, spitting with rage, 'If tomorrow there is a war between Argentina and Israel, whose side would the Argentine Jews be on? Huh? Huh?' I noted that a war between Israel and Argentina was not very likely but, of course, that's beside the point. The point is about fear of the Other, real or imagined.

Then I turned the absurd question on myself: if tomorrow there is a war between Bulgaria and New Zealand – a farcical scenario – which side would I, a citizen of both countries, be on? Would I side with one and spy for the other? Or would I sit tight in Britain and pretend it's not happening? Answer: let's be glad that neither country can find the other on the map.

It seems primitive to ask people who are culturally divided in time, like Mehmet, or in space, like me, to have single loyalties. Come to think of it, there is something suspect about single loyalties anyway, since they lend themselves so easily to Revival Processes like head-chopping in the mountain village of *Time of Violence* and name-chopping in the same village three centuries later.

'Do you mix with Bulgarians?' I turn to Mehmet.

'Yes, of course we mix, we live together, we struggle with the same problems. But you know, some people want trouble. Some people divide us. We all grew up together, no difference, but now some politicians… Those troublemakers, the Ataka guy and that Turk who talks about southern Bulgaria going to Turkey, they should lock them up together, let them be buddies!'

The far right Ataka is a paranoid and xenophobic ultra-nationalist party in the best European tradition. Its leader Volen Siderov has declared many ludicrous things, but among them is that just as the demise of the great USSR was brought about by the Zionists, and the Holocaust was invented by the Jews, so the 'long holiday' of the Bulgarian Turks was brought about by Turkey. Because they really needed half a million penniless refugees from the Soc Bloc.

The wounds have barely begun to heal, the stories of loss and separation barely told, but already the strident voices of revisionism are loud and crude, just like those busybodies with 'spontaneous' placards in the distant Sofia of 1989. Which is no surprise: they are the same voice, the same continuous screech of fear and hate, and today's paranoid Siderovs are the malformed offspring of yesterday's paranoid Jivkovs.

We reach the top of the hill and get out of the car. Only the foundations are left of the mighty medieval Shumen fortress. We skip along the contours of stone rooms where people lived their small lives in the mountain air, here on top of this small, green world. Thracians, Romans, Byzantines, Bulgars, Turks, they all enjoyed the lush views from here.

'Everybody passed through here,' Mehmet muses, as if overhearing my thoughts. 'So much folk passed through, and everybody destroyed. Destruction, destruction. I came here from school. School trips. They told us the Turks destroyed it, but we liked coming here because it was a day out. We never thought about the history.'

We're standing at the lookout point at the end of the fortress. Unreal, chlorophyll-green hills rise above the town huddled below like a handful of pebbles. Clusters of tile-roofed houses at one end, ugly monolithic buildings at the other.

'What's that?' I point across the valley to where a gigantic granite monument squats on top of a hill.

'The Monument to the Creators of the Bulgarian State. Built to commemorate 1,300 years of Bulgarian statehood,' he recites.

My *Lonely Planet* swears that out of many ugly, conspicuous monuments in Bulgaria, this one is the ugliest and most conspicuous, and I have to agree. Only Stalin deserves a monument like this.

'We all built it back in 1981,' Mehmet continues. 'They told us to take time off to work on the site. It was Lyudmila Jivkova's idea.'

'Did they pay you?'

He laughs, amused by my naivety, and a couple of golden teeth glint in his mouth.

'Not only did they not pay us, they took money off our salaries because we weren't turning up to work.'

'Did everyone work on the Creators?'

'Everyone. Every able-bodied man in Shumen was up there, mixing cement.'

'So who's up there?'

'Oh, all the Creators. Khan Asparuh, Khan Tervel, Khan Kroum,

Khan Omurtag, all the khans. And a big lion at the front...' he does a lion's paws impression with his hands '... guarding the Bulgarian State. Guarding...' He trails off.

I laugh and after a moment's hesitation, he joins me.

I am laughing at the Creators of the Bulgarian State with a Turk, and do I care? The nomadic Bulgars and their khans were an Asiatic people anyway, a bunch of talented barbarians who cleverly merged with those other talented barbarians, the Slavs, to form a hardy little nation of survivors.

And after so many centuries of bad blood and mixed blood, after so many five-year plans and so many tons of cement, after so many tears and so much water under the bridge, it's good to laugh together. After all, it isn't the original State we are laughing at, it's *that* State, the one which tried to dissolve the People into cement and built monuments like this with their sweat and blood. *That* State loved me, the child of 'poor engineers', as much – and as little – as it loved Mehmet.

We get back into the car and slide down what feels like a vertical road. Mehmet drops me off at the Tombul Mosque. He asks for a bit more than the modest agreed price.

'It's still reduced price for you. Out of the generosity of Mehmet's heart, reduced price.' He winks and puts his hand on his heart, and I put the extra money in his palm. We shake hands and keep the peace.

Tombul or the 'plump' Mosque is the biggest in the Balkans and the prettiest in Bulgaria, and it is prayer time. The smartly dressed teenager at the entrance gives me an explanatory folder typed in several languages, and asks me for money.

'How come,' I protest, 'all the churches and mosques in Bulgaria are free, except yours?'

'This is a heritage monument,' he says pointedly. 'It's listed.' But

I'm not having it. Something about his cocky manner bothers me. He behaves like he owns the place. Like he owns the *country*.

'So is Rila Monastery.' I force myself to smile. 'And still it's free.'

'OK, you can go in for free,' he relents and smiles too. I suddenly feel mean. 'But hurry because it's prayer time.'

The mosque is splendidly decorated and renovated, and above the gate a poem in Arabic immortalizes the builder. Next door is an enchanting courtyard, an expired school for dervishes, and a library. The imam's voice quietly summons the faithful to prayer, and when I peek inside the mosque again, I am greeted by the bottoms of twenty or so men and boys, a strangely disarming sight. I close the gate quietly, and rush back to catch the last bus out of town.

The unshaven men in worn-out jackets are still at the bus station, smoking and glancing at their fake Rolexes, as if Godot's arrival were now imminent.

'Ah, here you are, I've been looking for you.' The bearded driver *manqué* from this morning suddenly materializes again. 'Do you still need a driver? I'll give you a good price. Where are you going?'

Back out of the Memory Hole, please. How much for that?

13 In the Enchanted Garden

On the Black Sea

On the train from Burgas to Sofia, I sit in a full second-class compartment with Michael. An extrovert elderly couple sit by the window, facing each other. The man reads a tabloid newspaper and supplies a running commentary for the benefit of the compartment.

It's 2004 and Bulgaria has the most eccentric prime minister in the world: His Majesty Simeon II of Saxe-Coburg Gotha, the exiled tsar. He made a triumphant return from Spain in the nineties, wooed the desperate population with vague but grand talk of 'fulfilling my historical duty to Bulgaria', formed a party modestly called the National Movement Simeon II, and won the elections in 2001.

'Listen to this,' says the old man. 'King Simeon went to Athens for the Olympics. And there, in downtown Athens, he ran to catch the bus, leaving his wife behind. What a gentleman! Is that why he studied how to be European for fifty years in Spain? Is this how Europeans behave? Give me a break!' He snorts dismissively.

His wife has dyed short hair and a plunging neckline.

'We voted for him, hare-brains that we were!' she joins in. 'Do you know what his favourite phrase is? I'll tell you when the time comes. A woman asks him the time, and he goes "I'll tell you when the time comes..."'

A thirty-something couple in the corner laugh. They hold hands the entire time and look very happy with life in general and their suntans in particular. She has bleached hair, and her horsey but handsome boyfriend looks like a Gypsy who's going places.

'He had the so-called 800 days plan,' the old man continues, while fashioning a cone-hat out of the newspaper. 'To improve the standard of living. It's now been over 800 days and, guess what, he's improved his own standard of living by reclaiming all the royal estates.'

'Well, you know what they say: every people deserve their king,' the middle-aged woman from the corner sums up grimly.

She has a heavy Tartar face and thick ankles, and embarks on telling us in monstrous detail about her health problems, son problems, money problems, native town (Pavlikeni), and how other people are wrong about everything, starting with Simeon II and ending with her husband who voted for him. 'Me, I always vote for the Socialists, at least I know who I'm dealing with,' she concludes, and makes herself even more unpopular.

The old man, now wearing his paper hat, whips out a pack of cards. Lulled by the rocking of the train and the music of a language he is tired of trying to decipher, Michael falls asleep. Nobody has spoken to him, but as soon as he nods off, the young couple strain to look at the cover of his language book lying open on his lap.

'Teach yourself Bulgarian for Germans,' the horsey man whispers to his girlfriend.

'He's not German,' I say. 'It's just the book.'

'Where is he from?' The old woman peeks from behind her cards.

'New Zealand.'

'He's very nice.' She wobbles her head approvingly.

'Ah, New Zealand,' the old man says competently and puts his cards down. 'Lamb is very cheap there.'

'That's right,' I agree quickly.

'Is it true that they drive on the other side of the road there?' the horsey man asks.

I confirm that it's true.

'I thought so.' He grins, satisfied. 'It's because it's an island. All islands drive on the other side of the road.'

'That's interesting,' I lie.

'Yes, that's what I've heard.'

'They drive on the other side in Britain as well,' I say tentatively.

'Well, that's because Britain is an island too,' he explains, and his girlfriend looks at him admiringly. You can't argue with that.

'What is New Zealand like?' the old woman enquires.

'It's nice. Beautiful country, civilized people.' Then, seeing the wistful faces, I hasten to add, 'They have their problems, of course.'

'Well, every country has its problems,' the old man says, 'but theirs are problems of a different order. A rich country's problems.'

I must protect Michael from the accusation of wealth.

'Well, not that rich. There are richer countries. But the main wealth of New Zealand is its natural beauty. And its farmland…'

'That's right,' the old woman interjects, 'they know how to exploit their farmland. What did we do with ours? Turned it into a giant factory. Crushed the agriculture. Industrialized it. Now it'll take decades to sort out the mess.'

Everyone agrees sullenly. The Tartar-faced woman starts extracting sandwiches from a bag, biting into them with determination. Everybody else follows suit. The old couple produce a bottle of warm beer and a huge salami. They cut slices and offer them around on the tip of a knife. 'Bavarian,' they announce proudly. The happy couple produce some home-made pastries which they offer around too.

'It's good that he's asleep and can't see us with our salami and stuffed pastries.' The bleached woman smiles sheepishly.

'Oh, on the contrary, he loves that sort of thing,' I say. But she doesn't believe me.

The old man goes to the toilet and returns at once, scandalized.

'Have you seen the toilet?' he cries out in anguish. 'It has to be seen to be believed. No toilet seat, all rusty, stuff all over, words fail me… How are we going to get into Europe with this toilet? Tell me, how!'

It's a rhetorical question, so everybody shakes their head indignantly. Even the munching Tartar woman is speechless.

'Don't translate this for your husband.' The bleached woman turns to me. 'It's too embarrassing.'

'One way or another, he'll see for himself,' the old man concludes and takes off his paper hat, defeated.

'It's OK, really.' I smile reassuringly. 'He's seen much worse in his travels.'

When Michael wakes up and goes to the very same abominable toilet, an anxious silence descends on our compartment.

'I told you,' the old man frets, 'sooner or later, he'll see.'

The train stops and a sweaty woman with stuffed bags bursts into our compartment, heading for Michael's empty seat. But she doesn't stand a chance.

'It's taken!' everybody cries in a chorus of solidarity. The old woman puts a protective hand on the empty seat and gives the new arrival a dirty look.

When Michael returns from his toilet ordeal, all eyes are on him.

'So?' the old man enquires. He's the compartment's spokesperson.

'How was the toilet?' I ask Michael.

'Horrendous.' He grins cheerfully. 'Straight out of *Trainspotting*.'

'What did he say?' The compartment leans forwards expectantly, all ears.

'He said he's seen much, much worse in other countries,' I translate. There is a collective sigh of relief.

'A very nice young man.' The old woman wobbles her head affectionately and pats Michael's thigh. The mood picks up.

When we arrive in Sofia, a lifetime and a bursting bladder later — for I too attempted visiting the toilet, and *Trainspotting* has a long way to go — the old couple push the remaining half of the salami into my hands. I protest. I know how much a salami like this costs: about five per cent of their combined pensions.

'No, take it, for your boyfriend to see for himself what outstanding deli foods we produce in Bulgaria,' the old man insists. 'To have some nice memories from here.'

'I thought it was Bavarian,' I say, and accept the salami. It would be rude not to.

'It's after a Bavarian recipe,' the old woman explains. 'But it's made in Bulgaria. Look.' And she points at the label which is indeed local.

'We make very good deli foods these days,' the Tartar woman confirms authoritatively.

Then everybody in the compartment shakes hands with Michael, as if sealing an important trade deal between Bulgaria and New Zealand.

Today, the bus from Burgas isn't half as much fun as the train that summer. There's no salami, no newspaper gossip, and the few passengers stare out of the window or talk on their mobiles. Except the red-haired man in the aisle next to me, who has been looking intently at my *Lonely Planet*.

'You read in English?' he finally ventures in an Irish accent. I give him the short version.

'And are you going to Nessebur to see the sights?' I ask.

'No, I don't have time to see any sights. I'm an investor. I'm having a look at some new apartments in Sunny Beach and Elenite. I've already got some apartments in Golden Sands. There's a lot of building here, it's an exciting time for investors.'

'Do you like the sea, then?' I glance at his cadaverous skin.

'No, not really.'

He's from Dublin, he owns a car export company, or something to that effect, and when we arrive in Nessebur, he informs me stiffly that he's staying in the five-star Hotel Bulgaria in Burgas, under this name and room number, and I should feel free to give him a call if I'm at a loose end tonight. No end could be loose enough, I think as we exchange pleasantries and shuffle off in opposite directions.

Walking the length of the isthmus that connects ancient Nessebur to the mainland, I have a panoramic view of what's on the opposite side of the bay: high-rise resort ghettos where our investor is inspecting properties right now.

Little Nessebur is an oasis in the wasteland of quick glitz and concrete that the Black Sea coast has become. The Russian and Bulgarian mafias enjoy some fruitful deals along here, and Turkish and Greek businessmen have bought up the odd hotel complex or five, or fifty.

The latest gangster crime along the coast took the shape of a seaside resort complex in Strandja National Park. It was the brainchild of the brilliantly named Crash Construction Company, and it promised to deflower the last stretch of unspoilt beaches and coastal woodlands. But just as the Eco-Glasnost movement of broad-spectrum intellectuals in the 1980s heralded the birth of democracy, so the successful eco-protesters of 2007 heralded the birth of civil society and interrupted the construction. Just how democracy existed for seventeen years without civil society is another question.

Back to Nessebur, which in the high season is overrun by bus loads of lobster-red Britons and Germans, and smug new-rich Bulgarians and Russians. But now it's late summer, the trees are heavy, and the wood-panelled upper storeys of old houses lean over the streets with their window shutters open like the arms of gossiping women. The pink-white city walls and semi-ruined medieval churches are disdainfully beyond human reach. If left alone, Nessebur would happily live in a parallel time of its own. It's been a long time in the making – since the Dorian Greeks arrived in the sixth century BC, built the city walls, and called the town Messambria.

Nessebur's beauty rival is Sozopol. They sit symmetrically on each side of the huge Burgas Gulf, and stare each other down. But there are two differences between them. First, unlike Nessebur, which is an open-air museum, Sozopol lives in its own present tense. Second, Sozopol was a place where my parents felt relaxed, once a year, for two weeks. It has always been a hang-out for painters and, on contact with Sozopol, even a scientist with a head full of neural networks like my father instantly turned artist.

I sit on the steps leading down to the small Town Beach, trying to come to terms with what I see. What I see is a humble strip of sand. The Town Beach was once a vast *terra incognita* of bodies and umbrellas where I undertook exploratory missions, armed with a plastic sand bucket. Is it because we were the size of our mother's leg that the world seemed so big? Or does the magical prism of memory magnify everything when we look through it?

Either way, I see a tomboyish ten-year-old sitting under a beach umbrella with *Lorna Doone*, and stealing glances at a blond German boy. I see my father with his oils and canvases, sketching a naïve picture of this beach. So naïve that twenty years later my mother declined to hang it in the living-room of their house in Auckland. We have the entire Pacific outside our door, she said, we don't need this any more. Sozopol is different, my father insisted. But he didn't insist much and, gradually, his old paintings were demoted to the damp oblivion of the rumpus room. This isn't art snobbery on my mother's part. The rumpus room (out of sight, out of memory) is her only remaining defence against a rising tide of loss.

But as you sit in the tiny fishing harbour at dusk, crunching in your mouth those tiny salted fried fishes appropriately called tsa-tsa, you feel nostalgic even without memories. Sozopol gives you its own memories. It's that kind of sea town. The fishing boats are all named after women of vague eras and nationalities: Victoria, Susana, Tetis.

Old women sell fig jam and lace on small tables along cobbled streets, and the seagulls cry out with human voices.

The marketplace behind the beach was already happening 3,000 years ago, when merchants traded olives, textiles, wine, and honey with the rest of the known world. In medieval times, the bodies of dead sailors were displayed before burial in the small kiosk by the Town's Beach. As a child, I thought it was a public toilet because it was always locked. It's, in fact, the medieval Chapel St Spas, named after the protector – clearly ineffectual – of all seamen.

But right now, in the marketplace I stop at the stall of a soft-bodied man in sandals that have seen happier summers. He is selling fake Gucci glasses, leather wallets from a 'Collection' without a name, and bright seashell necklaces of dubious provenance. Is this coral I see?

'From Thailand.' The seller shrugs his big, defeated shoulders. He has a soft accent. 'I just take what they send me. I don't even know what it is. Might be coral, might be plastic…'

It's no wonder he doesn't know coral from plastic: he's a mechanical engineer. He and his wife emigrated here from Armenia fifteen years ago. Bulgaria wasn't doing great, but Armenia was much worse. He got a job, but then the factory closed and he found himself unemployed. 'I never imagined I'd be a trinket seller. But what else is there?'

Go back to Armenia? He nods a Bulgarian no.

'Armenia is still worse off than Bulgaria. True, they make it hard for immigrants here. We still don't have passports, after fifteen years. And every year we have to pay huge amounts to have our visas renewed. Crazy. But what can you do?'

The only thing I can do is buy a wallet from the nameless Collection, and a coral-plastic necklace. The engineer is thrilled to have a paying customer. All this activity has attracted other women so

I bid him goodbye and he shakes my hand with an optimistic smile.

Armenian migrants like him don't enjoy the concessions their ancestors did. In Burgas, at the feet of the Balkantourist sphinx that is Hotel Bulgaria, stands a wizened Armenian dwarf of a church called St Hach. In the small church courtyard, a stone memorial to the victims of the Armenian genocide is livened up by a plastic half-bottle of garden flowers.

St Hach must have been particularly crowded in the first half of the twentieth century when the survivors of the genocide poured in their tens of thousands into Bulgaria via the port of Burgas. They were followed by the elite of Armenian society in the wake of the collapsed Armenian Republic. Then arrived the Armenian refugees from the 1922 Asia Minor Catastrophe in Turkey and Greece.

In fact, it seems that the only kindness the Armenians enjoyed in the twentieth century was to be granted instant citizenship by little Bulgaria. Like the Jews, the Armenians were seen here as fellow sufferers from the Judeo-Christian world. Indeed, the numerous Armenians have been to Bulgaria what the numerous Jews were to other European nations – artistically gifted, financially smart, socially mobile, generally enterprising, and slightly exotic, a bonus of a minority. Fortunately, Bulgaria has been wise enough to realize this and embrace the Armenians instead of throttle them. Even if the engineer-turned-trinket seller doesn't have a passport yet, and the coral-plastic necklace crumbles in my hands the next day.

But, more importantly, the Apollonia Art Festival is in town. Actors, musicians, and literary types sashay along cobbled streets on their way to some last play premiere or jazz quartet. New-agers can be traced by the notices posted around the old town, the writing blurry like the content:

To all participants in Apolonia. Tomorrow, at dawn, there will be a general good vibe gathering at the rocks. All welcome to charge up with the mystic energy of the sea.

I charge up with the mystic energy of the sea by booking myself into a light-filled room in a wooden house right on the sea promenade of the old town. The house only looks old: it is, in fact, a brand-new hotel. So new that it has no name. After the nameless hotel in Plovdiv, I begin to see a theme here. The only entrance is via an abandoned construction site next door, whose cement base is studded with random iron rods like a giant bed of nails. I picture drunk hotel guests stumbling home at night and ending up decorating the site with their impaled bodies. To access the promenade down below, the hotel guest (me) must climb down the old fortification wall, which is only slightly less hazardous than the nail bed. Oh, and they don't have towels yet.

'Towels and TVs are for next year.' The sun-wilted manageress who camps in the room next door smiles apologetically. 'When we have more money.' She gives me a fluffy towel out of the goodness of her heart, but soon it transpires that I won't be needing it, not all of it anyway: the sparkling new shower tube instantly splits at the base, and I get a face full of hot water.

But the room is cheap and clean, and underneath my romantic balcony is the blue sea and a ripe fig tree which I must remember to raid first thing in the morning, instead of buying those plastic cups of figs at 2 lev a pop. Of course I don't. I end up buying a plastic cup of figs for 3 lev from an old woman in black. It's my penitence for not paying to examine those agricultural tools in Brushlyan.

In the evening there is a big concert. The world music star Ivo Papasov and his Wedding Orchestra are in town, and that's an event I don't want to miss, mostly because Ivo Papasov is a legend, but also because I need to check whether his belly really is as pregnant as it looks on photographs.

It is – about eight months gone – but the heavenly sounds he produces with his clarinet balance out the extreme gravity of his earthly form. All the virtuosos in the band are of Gypsy or Turkish origin or, like Ivo himself, both. Fidgeting in front of me are a Gypsy man and his teenage son. They're friends or relatives of the virtuoso kaval-player in the band, and so excited to see him on stage, they wave the entire time, hoping he'll notice them and wave back. But he can't – his hands are busy holding the kaval. At one point, the father walks onto the stage to shake hands with the musician. His teenage son looks as embarrassed as the musician, who is just then in the middle of a tricky solo piece.

The open-air amphitheatre of Sozopol is packed, and when Ivo and his people strike up a juicy Thracian horo, people get up to weave some complicated steps. Soon the wooden stage darkens with thick coils of dancers jumping up and down.

'That's it, that's it,' Ivo coughs into the microphone. 'Now the TV cameras are gone, we can all relax, like at home. And now we'd like to finish with a real Gypsy number. And happy anniversary, of course! That's right, for me it's still an anniversary. I like to celebrate all anniversaries, 'cause you never know these days. But let's not get started on politics, 'cause it'll get ugly…'

The audience cheer. Music must be the only occasion when an audience cheers a band of Gypsies.

'What's the date today?' I ask the Gypsy teenager in front of me. 'The ninth of September,' he says blankly. Of course! The ninth of September (1944), the day when the Soviet army liberated us from ourselves. And the day on which three generations of little Chavdars and Pioneers marched every year and waved red flags at the comrades under black umbrellas. But to the teenager here, it's just a meaningless date.

Most people go back to their seats for the 'Gypsy number', but a few of us, young enough not to be threatened by oriental vibes, remain on stage to celebrate the Soviet army – both its arrival and its departure – with a good old belly-shaking Gypsy *kuchek*.

Later that night, I sit on my romantic balcony with a throbbing head, hoping for a bit of soothing sea silence. Tough luck: the open-air café-bar under the fig tree is celebrating too. The nerd at the bar has downloaded the golden hits of Soviet pop music from the 1980s and is gleefully playing them at full blast.

A table of his thirty-something friends are knocking back vodkas like there's no tomorrow (perhaps there isn't – look what happened to yesterday) and singing along ironically to the melodies of their childhood.

To crown the evening, the nerd treats us to none other but Alla Pugacheva and her 'Million Scarlet Roses'. I now know that the song which moved my childish imagination into learning the genitive case was written by the poet Andrei Voznesensky. The story behind it is real, and slightly different from the poem.

When the primitivist Georgian painter Niko Pirosmani fell in love with a flower-loving French dancer visiting Tbilisi, he sold everything he owned. It wasn't much, but it was enough to cover the square in front of her hotel with roses. But they didn't marry and live happily ever after because he was now a pauper and she wanted a millionaire. She left and he drank himself to death before anybody noticed his talent. 'But in his life,' the song goes, 'remained that square full of roses.' Millions, millions, millions of scarlet roses.

The geek conducts with his pudgy fingers, the computer screen lighting up his bespectacled face like a halo. At the refrain, I join the drunk choir from my balcony, '*Milion, milion, milion alyuh roz...*'

We are singing an ironic but secretly nostalgic serenade to our communal lost youth of red armies, red scarves, red boots, red flags, and red stars. Here, a shot of vodka and a bouquet of a million radioactive red roses!

*

The year of 'Million Scarlet Roses' was when my grandmother Anastassia became very ill and our summers in Balchik ended. But Balchik is miraculously preserved in the pickle of memory. Which is just as well, because it turns out that it isn't preserved anywhere else.

It has now been twenty years, and if, back then, Balchik had one foot in the sea, the evil twins of time and erosion have ensured that it is now splashing in it.

After paying a hefty entrance fee to the Queen's Gardens, I discover that the waterfalls are rather thin, and the Queen's palace is a very non-palatial house with a bizarre minaret. I go to peer inside the giant amphorae and check if my childhood promise 'Bye-bye, I'll be back' is still there, but a group of Germans with well-cooked skins are in my way. They are tossing up whether to hit the beach or not. The beach?

I look down. Yes, where the jetty with my broken penguin stood before, lashed by algae-thick water, now there is a beach. A sprawling beach with umbrellas and people. The slimy green wall that stopped the sea from invading the gardens has collapsed, like a dam against time that could no longer hold out. Only the giant, furry cacti loyally stand up for the past.

And this is just the beginning of the horror-tour. I look up to the limestone cliffs, searching for the hillside villas of Dobrich. But there are only cheap, ugly new hotels and wild overgrowth. I ask the sellers at the souvenir stalls outside the gardens, but they nod no, they've never heard of the villas of Dobrich. I search their sunburnt faces and feel a strange void. We share nothing except a language. My Balchik is not their Balchik. I'm a ghost from the past, but it isn't their past.

Finally, I try a driveway leading up the hill and, sure enough, I recognize the warden's kiosk. An old man in tatty clothes is sleeping outside on a shady bench.

Where are the villas? They're still here but I can't see them for the jungle that has grown around them. The whole complex has slipped downhill, just as people predicted twenty years ago. The whitewashed houses are cracked like sandcastles dried in the sun. The alleyways along which I tested my new sandals have split open and vicious bramble bushes grow from the crevices and scratch my legs. I stubbornly beat my way through this desolate jungle, determined to find the house of my childhood. It's a bit like pushing your way back into the birth canal. It's a painful business.

I find 'our' house, or at least something that looks like it. It's unlocked, and when I step inside I see that everything has been gutted. The mattresses from the beds, the light bulbs from the ceiling, the door frames from the walls, even the sinks have been ripped out. The three empty iron bed frames – me, my grandmother and my grandfather – stare at me like eyeless sockets. How could anyone have been happy here?

But we were. We played dominoes on the veranda and turned red in the sun. We blew up rubber balls and washed the sand off with water hoses. I watched sunsets and wrote mystical poems about moonlight and eternity, so mystical that even I didn't know what they meant. We got bitten by mosquitoes and applied lavender spirit.

The playground is overgrown and strewn with garbage. I sit on a low, rusty swing and feel as if I'm about to be sucked into a plug hole. I struggle to remember other places, other people, other happinesses, but it's no use. Right now, my whole life amounts to this cemetery of childhood slipping into the drain of the sea.

'Hey, what are you doing here?'

The old man outside the kiosk has woken up and is calling out to me while tucking in his short-sleeved shirt. He smells of old age.

'I used to spend my summers here,' I croak dustily, 'with my grandparents. My grandfather worked for Dobrich.'

'Ah, of course! I remember those days.' He waves vaguely. He is glad to have company.

'Perhaps you remember him. Atanasov was his name.'

'Atanasov... You know, so many people passed through. And I wasn't working here at the time, I'm just watching it now, to make sure there's no vandals...'

What, to take the slates from the roofs? The berries from the bushes?

'What's going to happen to it?'

'A foreigner, an Englishman, I think, bought it. He's going to convert it, pull down the bungalows, build a new hotel...'

I already hate that Englishman.

'How long has it been like this?'

'Oh, years. It's been bush and snakes for years. It's the erosion. Watch where you step.'

No, it's not the Englishman's fault, it's not his fault at all. He's just an investor. It's everything else. The dismal Socialist construction, cancer, erosion, and just dumb old time passing. I shouldn't have come here at all. Alice must never go back to Wonderland once she grows up. I hate being grown up.

The old man takes pity on me, and says softly, 'Pass the camera, I'll take a picture of you before they tear it all down.'

Snap. He hands me the camera back. His hand is rough with calluses. I want to ask him what his life is like, what it used to be like, I want to hang around here and chat, and pretend everything's fine. But he understands the nature of my visit and wisely wants to stay out of it. He waves me away with 'Go well, girl', and returns to his shady bench.

Along the main road, the erosion bumps are as big as that molehill in the bedroom of Peach Street. I weave my way around them to the open-air cinema where I'd had that first clueless glimpse into my Kiwi future.

The whitewashed cinema façade is standing defiantly, and, behind it, a pile of rubble. There is an evil stench. A Gypsy couple crawl out of the ruins with post-coital flushes – or have they been… no, I don't want to know. They adjust their belts, and greet me sheepishly with 'Good afternoon'.

'What happened to the cinema?' I ask. Not the smartest of questions, and I get the answer I deserve.

'Oh, it's all ruined now,' the woman says. 'It's just used as a toilet.'

And they scurry off down the road, getting smaller and smaller and disappearing into the cracked asphalt like something out of a David Lynch nightmare.

Across the road there is a tennis court, and in the middle a topless man with a toasted belly sits on a plastic chair, watering the sandy ground with a hose. Watering the ground. I think I'm losing my mind.

I walk in a stupor by the sea, to the old town at the far end of the cracked road. But what is this? The shore is lined with fish restaurants and brightly painted new hotels with cheerful names like Helios, Jupiter, Sunshine Pearl, Holiday Beach. I don't remember any of it, and for a good reason: none of it was here.

But the grubby, old, poor Balchik is still here, like an ancient ant heap, and I climb the steep streets to the old town. Village houses and courtyards hung with washing, pot plants and miniature gardens, open rubbish tips, dirt roads winding into nothingness. Kids pedal on rickety bicycles, dogs bark in the distance, chickens peck at the remains of the afternoon, and the limestone cliffs peer down at us, slipping invisibly. Another twenty years and...

A fine warm rain begins to fall, and a bearded goat that looks like a Biblical old man, possibly Moses, is watching me critically from a small rubbish mound. I'm not feeling that good, I say to the goat, and dust comes out of my mouth. If the goat weren't busy chewing something, I'm sure it would say, 'It wasn't that smart to come here in the first place. Now you're going to miss your bus, and then you'll be sorry.'

I bid the goat goodbye and crack on to the top of town, to the bus station. The bus station consists of a vast, empty parking space with a big puddle in the middle and a vast, empty building entirely made of rust. It looks like the last time a bus passed through here, by mistake, was in 1965, and even then it didn't stop. Five other lost souls are sitting on the broken bench, waiting. We are all amazed when the bus appears thirty minutes later. It seems to be the one from 1965.

I try to catch one last glimpse of Balchik. But the bus windows are so grimy that all I see is a kind of milky mist where the sea, the houses, and the limestone cliffs are all blurred.

So it turns out that the past isn't just another country. It is another country where someone like us, but not us, lives, a queen of a distant domain. It turns out we must pay dearly when we try to enter the enchanted garden, greedy for magic, yearning to make contact with its resident ghosts who hide behind the giant cacti, at the bottom of the amphorae, down the plug hole.

I am going now, and I know never to disturb the natural laws of that country where the people we used to be stroll along the fault lines of a white-cliffed town, eating vanilla ice cream in the slightly odd, slightly otherworldly September light.

14 Danube Terminus

Just a tourist

It's just as well that I come to the Danube last, because – blissful relief – I have no memories here. Along the Danube, I tell myself, I can be just a tourist.

Danubian Bulgaria is a Sleeping Beauty: cursed, unloved, waiting for a miracle to happen.

And flooded. In the last two weeks, the Danube has risen by a spectacular eight metres. I'm standing on a narrow promontory, water lapping at my feet. On that side of the brown, swollen Danube is

Romania's coast. On this side, bunches of men and boys are fishing. Hundreds of startled little fish jiggle at the end of lines and slap onto the concrete to agonize before their last breath.

It's hard to imagine that Silistra was the Roman Empire's easternmost town in Europe, and that it flourished under Marcus Aurelius in the second century. The Romans went to town in their usual way: opulent public baths; mansions; and basilicas.

Today, united under the water lie former enemies: a Roman fortress wall; a tenth-century Orthodox patriarchal residence turned Episcopal basilica under the Byzantines; and the more 'recent' Ottoman quay wall.

At just about every point in its history, Silistra was a more happening place than today. Under the tiled central square and wide pedestrian avenues leading towards the Danube lurk the stony vias of Durostrum. The ruins in the lush ground were the foundations of the city walls. If I look at them long enough, I begin to see the ghostly outlines of Roman villas and baths. I see the patricians in their togas and sandals, sailing along in the warm river breeze, plump with all the time and slaves in the world.

And behind the brightly painted *belle époque* buildings, I see the stately houses of Danubian aristocracy of the 1920s and '30s.

Down the streets pass gaggles of bored youths munching popcorn. The women selling it stare into the still mid-afternoon while their corn pops. Time has stopped in Silistra, and everyone moves slowly, carefully, as if in a spell they are afraid to break.

Outside the museum, kids play on top of medieval tombs, using them as stepping stones for a skipping game. The well-groomed girls smile and hug each other for a photo. The boy, snotty-nosed and hostile, wants to be photographed by himself and stands with legs planted apart, staring point blank at the camera. Clearly, he is destined for great things.

There is a Roman tomb around here, with stunning murals. How can I see it? The depressed history graduate who acts as a museum guide shakes his head.

'The director is away. You could call him next week.'

He shuffles ahead of me and the other two visitors, switching on the lights and unlocking the treasury, then observing us with a mournful expression. Like many other provincial museums stuffed with riches, they can't afford to keep the lights on all day.

'But it'll be no use anyway,' he continues with the same mournful tone. 'The tomb is only opened for official visits or large groups. For conservation reasons. Otherwise the murals get damaged. I'm sorry.'

He looks as if he's about to cry, and I feel like telling him to get the hell out of here, go to Sofia, but then he's one of the few young people I've seen in town. What good would it do little Silistra if he too deserted?

'We've always been forgotten by the world up here in the corner,' complains a taxi-driver with a large gold crucifix on his hairy chest. 'Always fallen by the wayside somehow. There's eighty per cent unemployment here. All the young people have gone, abroad or to bigger towns. You know, this was Romania between the world wars. It'd be good if Romania took us back, they want us anyway. As a Bulgarian town, it couldn't get any worse, I tell you.'

'I think it's a lovely town,' I say lamely. It's a lovely town but I'd rather lie at the bottom of the Danube with a millstone around my neck than live here.

Back at the flooded promontory, two fishermen hand me a plastic bag of fresh fish.

'Thanks, but I don't have a kitchen to cook it.' I shrug.

'Are you visiting? Have you come to see our Danube rising up to swallow us?'

It's the younger man speaking, with a not entirely sane smile on his introverted face. The older man has a resigned air and a yellowish hepatic tinge.

'You know that this flood was predicted, everything has been predicted,' the hepatitis patient says. 'It's the Last Judgement coming, and you must save yourself now, while you still can.'

'I'd love to,' I say brightly. 'How do I do that?'

'You need to put your fate into God's hands. That's what we've done, and we feel the difference. But you need to act fast.'

'You know, I think it's too late for me.' I beat a careful retreat, trying not to fall into the stagnant flood waters which have already swallowed an entire basilica. On my stroll back through the mellow river park, golden with sunset, a teenager crouching by the ruins offers me yet another bag of fish.

'The nets on the Romanian side have broken.' He grins. 'We got tons.'

I wish he'd invite me round to his family's place for grilled fish and baklava, but this is no Devil's Bridge. In fact, the closest bridge is downstream in Ruse. It was built in 1954 with Soviet funds, and like most things made of steel and concrete back then it's called the Bridge of Friendship.

Such is the friendship between Romania and Bulgaria that along a 470-kilometre-long border, this is the only bridge. Although the dictator Jivkov had a special wing in his residence for the Ceaușescus, the friendliness traditionally consists of peering over the Danube to make sure the other is doing worse — which they often are. Both countries squirmed when they were bundled together on the late steamboat to EU membership. But they were wrong to squirm. Now, after years of sulking about it, the two countries have started building a second bridge, in Vidin and Calafat, some 260 kilometres upstream from Friendship. I just hope they don't call it Youth.

Everyone has now gone from the riverside, which is when I notice the swanky new Hotel Drustur. Its gilded faux baroque lobby shines implacably, and snooty young staff in stiff uniforms stand around like mannequins. I can't see any visitors in this futuristic temple to tourism. I'm tempted to book a room, but Hotel Drustur costs lots of euros, so I brace myself for the return to the Socialist-era Golden Dobrudzha Hotel.

The name refers to the fertile Dobrudzha plains in the northeast, known as the granary of Bulgaria, but there is nothing fertile about the hotel. It's cheap and nasty. Part of it has been renovated, but I'm staying in the other part because it's cheaper. Everything in my single room is excrement-brown and comes straight from the sixties. The reception desk is huge and unloved like a demilitarized zone, and the receptionist informs me that if I want information about boat cruises I must speak to the director, who is on the second floor and can be found tomorrow between 9 and 12.30, and between... This sounds familiar. I'm sure I've heard about the absent director before.

Then the bad news comes: the closest place to eat is the hotel's restaurant, also fully decorated in brown, except for the table-cloths which are a uniform navy blue. I sit at an oversized table by myself, and with fake cheer order cabbage and carrot salad and a *kavarma*. You can't go wrong with a baked casserole dish and fresh veg, I think. How wrong I am. The salad is so wilted it's almost pickled, and the tough meat and glum potatoes slump in an impersonal sauce. I complain, friendly to the point of obsequiousness, and the equally wilted waitress with blue eye-shadow whisks it off with an accusatory hand.

And if there was any doubt that I have stepped into a time-loop, a plump chanteuse with greasy lipstick, and a keyboard player with glasses bigger than his face bounce onto the musical platform. And with no warning or anaesthetic, they catapult me straight into the eighties with the song 'We'll meet again in twenty years'.

I'm made of strong stuff, but I have no resistance against 1980s pop ballads about small towns where there's nothing to do except fall in love, about the impermanence of first snow, about last summer's sandcastles, about 'telephone love'. A lump gathers at the back of my throat, and it's not the pork. Dams the size of Koprinka – with Seuthopolis submerged at the bottom – threaten to burst out.

No, I resolve, not here, where Politburo commissars have sung drunkenly, slammed their meaty palms on greasy tablecloths, pinched waitresses' bottoms, and toasted the Party. No way is this canteen going to break me.

To distract myself, I look at my neighbours. A fat-necked man in a short-sleeved shirt is knocking back small Fanta bottles like vodkas. A group of musty men in half-undone ties and polyester suits smoke around a table, stab at the tired salad, and talk business: yesterday's Politburo commissars, today's businessmen. Nobody makes eye contact. Cigarette smoke descends on the room like smog from the past, blurring all reason. I look at my watch but it's no use. What year is it?

Between Hotel Drustur and the Golden Dobrudzha, I have walked exactly five minutes and twenty-five years.

And let's face it: since arriving a few weeks ago, I haven't been myself. A few weeks alone in the country of your childhood wreaks havoc on your imported adult personality.

Every morning, I wake up alarmed. Where is my passport? Can I leave the country? Where is everyone? And who is everyone? I'm sure there's a word in psychiatry to name this state. I don't know the word, but I know how it feels: like psychic jet lag.

My mental furniture is not in its usual place. The walls have gone, all defences have broken down, wild growth creeps in. The door is the window. The window is showing weird fragments, like in a Dali painting. My head is screwed on the wrong way.

I flee from the treacherous restaurant, leaving behind my favourite New Zealand scarf in the rush, the only beautiful item in my pragmatic luggage. I lie in the mean single bed under a mean single blanket and inhale the cocktail of fragrances: the stale ash smell of the brown Balkantourist carpet; the mouldy, sewagey stink of the Balkantourist bathroom.

How wrong I was about being just a tourist, about putting myself back together. How naïve not to understand the basic mechanics of time-travel. Because it turns out that's what travel is, in Bulgaria. You may consult the latest bilingual map all you like, but one way or another, you always end up somewhere else. Somewhere like here.

I fear that I'll never emerge from this bed. That I'll be stuck in the expired Golden Dobrudzha for ever, an oversized grown-up squeezed into a twilight world of vinegary salads and slightly off-key Ionica keyboards. A guest from the future petrified in the amber-brown time of a Balkantourist holiday.

The bathroom tap drips. It's as if the whole building, the whole flooded town, is weeping rusty tears.

*

Things dramatically improve in Ruse, when I sit down to a crisp tomato salad and a lentil soup in a courtyard mehana. Above the courtyard, I've rented a spotless room with a polished floor. The new bathroom sparkles furiously and hurts my eyes.

I'm overjoyed to have made it here, after scare reports of the road between Silistra and Ruse going under the ever-swelling Danube. The Danube withdrew politely just on time for our bus, and I am now sitting beside a rumbling courtyard fountain, opposite a middle-aged German with the intriguing leathery look of an arms dealer. We agree to speak French.

'*La soupe est bonne*?' He has pushed aside his steak. 'I'm too tired for meat. I feel just like what you're having, comfort food.'

He orders a soup from the German-speaking waiter and tells me about his clothes business with shops all over the Balkans. That's why he's often on the road. I try not to show my disappointment.

'Sorry to disappoint you.' He smiles. 'Clothes, that's my trade. I always rent the same rooms in Sofia, Istanbul, Thessaloniki. It's like coming home. I like it.'

I ask about doing business in Bulgaria.

'The Bulgarians are very nice people, civilized, gentle. They really are the Prussians of the East as they say, hard-working, unfussy. But they're fatalistic, resigned. They always shrug their shoulders philosophically, as if things are foretold. The Greeks are quite different. Also nice, but more arrogant. They can really say no. And you know how they say "never do business with Greeks"? It's true!' He laughs. 'I mainly deal with Armenians in Greece, they're more trustworthy. The Turks... nice people on the whole, but too nationalistic. Look what they did to the Armenians, and they still refuse to admit it.'

His French is faultlessly melodious.

'I can't stand nationalism, it's ugly,' he continues, on a roll. 'Turkey shouldn't be let into the EU. Not in the next fifty, hundred years. Islam is a big problem, the way they treat women. Bulgaria, Romania, they've always been part of Europe. It's the Turks that prevented them for so many centuries, pulled them to the East, and then of course the barbarism of Communism... There's no question that right now we're in Europe. But Turkey is another story.'

He looks at me, it's my turn to express an opinion.

'That's right,' I say quickly. It *is* another story. But the truth is, I don't know whether I support Turkey in the EU or not. It's a question so vast it swallows me up as soon as I think about it. We slurp our lukewarm lentil soup, and he lights a cigarette.

'Food is never piping hot in Bulgaria, have you noticed?' I say apologetically. Am I fatalistic and resigned, a typical Bulgarian? And what exactly am I doing now – apologizing to the foreigner as a Bulgarian, or complaining under the false guise of a foreigner? How tiring, this business of national self-consciousness.

'I've noticed,' he says. 'But I don't mind because it's always good.'

I like him so much I invite him to the symphony concert I'm running late for. But he's tired and I go alone. The concert is top-notch, but the audience is so sparse I pray that the musicians are all short-sighted so they can't see how few of us there are. Next to me sit an Englishman in Jesus sandals and a small Bulgarian boy who speaks accented English. They look like uncle and nephew: close, but not quite father and son. Ruse is the kind of city where such cosmopolitan anomalies don't seem as strange as elsewhere in Bulgaria.

This spirit of refinement vanishes later that night when the mehana downstairs turns into a thumping *chalga* club. The entire nation has come to party, with their children. The grossest of 'retro' *chalgas*, meaning from the nineties, is pumping through mega-speakers. It's called '100 Mercedeses', and it's sung by a fully lobotomized fake blonde called Tzvetelina who wants 100 Mercedeses and 100 men – though presumably in the reverse order, or else how will she get the Mercedeses? I lie in the dark and think misanthropic thoughts.

In the morning, I come out to find that Ruse's plump, cake-shaped buildings are gripped by a fairy-tale whirlwind of white pollen. The streets are carpeted with fluff and people paw across the sleepy weekend, from shop to café to park bench.

Amazingly, many buildings are renovated. The city fathers sit stonily atop banks, and grotesque faces leer from baroque façades. New-Romanticism, Secession and Art Nouveau chatter to each other over the heads of passing townsfolk. You could be in a tiny Vienna or Paris, which was precisely the idea.

The energetic crudeness of Communist town planning didn't manage to mar Ruse's elegant past. Its stately centre of squares and cupolas live in a parallel world of *fin-de-siècle* Europe. What eventually dragged this princess city into the mire of the late twentieth century was the mega-pollution wafting in from the sodium and chlorine plant across the river in friendly Romania. It became so bad that people walked around with masks, despite which they developed strange respiratory diseases.

My one and only visit as a child took place before the plant started leaking. My parents were witnesses at some relative's wedding. My sister and I wore bridesmaid dresses made by our mother from medical gauze bought in a pharmacy, the closest she could find to tulle. The bride and groom looked grotesquely old to me, he with his receding hair, she with her thick waist. In fact, they were only in their twenties.

The wedding cake was five-layered, a thing of wonder, and we danced into the small hours to a live band playing top of the pops like 'Yes, that's how it is in the small town' and 'We'll meet again in twenty years'.

Out of four town clocks, the one in the main square is showing the current time. Its inaudible ticking is reassuring. Danubian time hasn't stopped completely.

Ruse may not be the most exciting place to be now, but it used to be. In the nineteenth and early twentieth centuries, while Sofia was still a muddy Turkish vilayet, Ruse-Rustchuk grew fat on international trade and looked to Vienna for ideas. Bulgaria wasn't on the map of Europe yet, but at least Ruse put together the first map of the country and the first newspaper. The paper was initially printed in Strasbourg because Ruse didn't have its own press. Soon it did, and the press was followed by the first bank, the first chamber of commerce, the first meteorological station, the first Navy School, the first pharmacy, the first professional theatre, the first film screening, the first railway... You get the idea. Ruse left the rest of the country practically nothing to pioneer.

And, since I'm walking past the mute Catholic Church of St Paul the Crucified, here is the country's first church organ. The 700-pipe beast is apparently still played on Sundays, but either I've missed the moment or the Catholics of Ruse have lapsed. Or, quite possible in my current unreliable state of mind, it isn't actually Sunday.

In another first, Ruse built and lavishly inhabited the first urban houses in Mitteleuropean style. The town planning was revolutionized by giving streets names and houses numbers. It might seem a tiny revolution, but it was a step away from the feudal lifestyle of the Ottoman provinces and a step towards Europe. The credit for this goes, ironically, to the local Turkish governor Mithad Pasha. The Pasha was a cosmopolitan reformer and, like many of Ruse's elite, a Mason to boot. He did everything in style, even his affairs: he fancied the Prussian consul's wife, the mellifluously named Kaliopa, so much that in 1865 he gave her a house on the river bank.

This is where I'm standing now, in the cream-coloured, wood-panelled, Levantine-style House of Kaliopa. I touch the exquisite draperies, the furniture, the porcelain. I lean to examine a hairbrush. Is that a blonde hair I see? Beside the grand Viennese piano (Bulgaria's first, of course), I smell the faded face powder of society balls. I hear the murmurings of city intrigues and shady deals between merchants, canny consuls making a buck on the side, and slick-haired, eagle-eyed international opportunists whose names read like a roll call of the Foreign Legion. I brush up against the starched consuls and their crinolined wives, the groomed officers of the Lloyd Triestino Line eyeing up the ladies on the evening promenade. The studio Photographie Parisienne receives a family in Sunday-best clothes from the 'Spanioli' district of the Sephardic Jews, where the Nobel Prize-winning author Elias Canetti was born. The girls at the French school are chatting in a shady courtyard, and the pastry chef at the oriental patisserie is waxing the end of his moustache. I spy the bearded Mithad Pasha in his fez, glancing coldly across a ballroom at the Russian consul. In only a few years, Russia and Turkey would be at war. Ruse would be free, Bulgaria's richest city for decades to come. Such wealth doesn't go away overnight. Ruse was the kind of city where fortunes and mansions were gambled away in a night's game of poker.

Next door to Kaliopa's House is the House of Baba Tonka, the symbolic mother-fighter of unfree Bulgaria. It makes perfect sense that the houses are so close together. Because while Kaliopa's House echoed with waltzes and chiming crystals, next door a revolution was fomenting.

Baba Tonka's four sons and one daughter were all involved in revolutionary committees in Bulgaria and Romania, and the Ruse cell operated out of her house. In the bloody wake of the April Uprising, Tonka's children were all killed or exiled to Asia Minor. Her son Nikola was paraded around Ruse by Mehmet Pasha's government, with his sentence – jail for life – around his neck. But he was lucky. Two years later came independence, and a jubilant Nikola returned to his home town to rebuild free Bulgaria. He lived to the age of ninety, and died just in time not to see what happened to his only daughter.

Her name was Tonka, after her illustrious grandmother. In 1944, less than a century after Baba Tonka's struggle for a free Bulgaria, Tonka Junior and her husband were branded 'enemies of the people'. The reason: her husband, director of Ruse's Boys Gymnasium, had reprimanded a teacher for boasting to his students about visiting brothels. The teacher, who knew the right organs of power as well as the right organs of brothels, wrote a little 'report'. It took as little as that in the murderous 1940s. The organs worked fast and without trial, and the director was executed together with his wife Tonka.

One of their daughters died soon after, and the other one, Liliana, became lifelong muse to one of the country's great post-war artists, Nenko Balkanski. Despite his dark, individualist style, Balkanski somehow gained the double title of People's Artist and Hero of Socialist Labour – whether he wanted it or not. Nenko and Liliana's grandson, called Nenko after his illustrious grandfather, is about my age and paints churches. The story of modern Bulgaria in a nutshell.

And here, across from Kaliopa's House and Baba Tonka's House, is the monumentally ugly high-rise of the Hotel Riga. It's been refurbished, and every room looks over the Danube. But this is beside the point.

The point is that Kaliopa's House was Bulgaria's gateway to Europe, Baba Tonka's House was Bulgaria's gateway to the nation-state, and Hotel Riga is the back door of both. You wonder who will come through that door.

'Let's hit the town, guys! Have you got the map?' A group of chirpy young Brits with narrow blond faces emerge from the Hotel Riga and head uptown.

A historical turnaround has occurred here, and to reverse it would involve acrobatics too complex and too tied up with money for us to ponder now. Elias Canetti became one of the cultural barometers of twentieth-century Europe, and he first took Europe's temperature here. But he left Ruse-Rustchuk, and only remembered the town of his childhood in the portentous autobiographical sentence: 'Everything I lived through later had already happened some time in Rustchuk.'

And after everything Ruse has lived through, I want to believe that while the best is probably over, so is the worst.

The bus from Sofia to Vidin treats the unfortunate passengers to a scenic, bowel-rearranging drive along roads forgotten by the transport ministry. Vertical cliff faces peer down at us.

We pass Vratsa, the mini-Siberia of our family. This is where in the mid-seventies my father wore a brown uniform and crawled in the mud for two years that felt like two hundred. But I can't see how the military Vratsa of family lore is the same place as this little mountain town pressed against the Vrachanski Balkán ranges and choked with greenery and oblivion. Oblivion is the keyword. Let Vratsa sleep here, in this impenetrable mountain. It's an ideal place for the past.

Vidin sits in a bend of the river at the very western end of Danubian Bulgaria, on the bare bones of its arse. It makes Silistra look plump with wealth. Ruse is practically Vienna. Vidin's past and present, on the other hand, have endured a divorce so bitter that it's hard to believe they were ever married.

For a thousand years, Vidin was one of the Danube's biggest ports and the medieval hub of the whole region. Over the centuries, Vidin was broken off from the rest of Bulgaria by a succession of energetic brutes. The most interesting of those was an eighteenth-century janissary by the name of Osman Pazvantoğlu. Osman carved out a name and a fortune for himself after seceding from the Sultan's administration and declaring Vidin and the north his own district. To ward off the Sultan's army, he gathered a motley crew of cut-throats: rag-tag mercenaries, fellow janissaries, and the dreaded marauders known as *kirçali*. *Kirçali* meant literally field brigands, and their reign over large swathes of land meant figuratively that the Sultan's empire was in a bad way.

This chapter in Bulgaria's history became known as the time of the *kirçali*. From Pazvantoğlu's base in Vidin, his army from hell terrorized the Bulgarians on this side of the Danube and the Wallachian Romanians on the other. 'Who needs leprosy,' the Romanian philosopher Cioran wrote, 'when the fate that roused you to life also placed you in Wallachia?' During the time of the *kirçali*, and on many more occasions thereafter, Bulgarians shared that leprous fate with their neighbours across the ditch.

Though I wouldn't volunteer to live in Vidin at the turn of the nineteenth century, at least it wasn't dull. Today, a broken fountain made of three plaster graces receives the cigarette butts of three Gypsy brothers in identical shirts and with blond highlights in their hair. Drowsy locals sip coffees in plastic chairs and fiddle with their mobiles. The pedestrian mall is lined with pretty turn-of-the-century façades, and trodden by locals who move in a kind of slow motion trance, like denizens in the kingdom of Sleeping Beauty after the evil fairy's spell has taken effect.

In the main square, the Turkish fourteenth-century Stambul Kapiya gate stands in a permanent face-off with the monolithic Communist Party building on the other side of the square. I take a walk through the green, tranquil riverside park. It's empty save for a giant stone monument to the Russian army generously defaced with a huge splash of red paint.

A beautiful, derelict Sephardic synagogue stands in a deserted street beside the park. Its chewed cupolas circled by black crows remind me of abandoned maharaja palaces and resident vultures. The blue sky peers through the missing roof, and I stand on the chipped floor mosaic, looking up, for a minute or an hour, caught in the spell.

The synagogue is at the heart of Kaleto district, and Kaleto was the heart of the old fortified town. At the turn of the twentieth century, many Jews populated Kaleto with their trades, European-designed houses, and names that fluttered with exotic plumage, like birds that brought glad news of the world. Here were the houses of printer Finto Alhalel, trader Moreno Pinkas, architect Mayer Aladjemov, the philanthropists brothers Haim and Chelebi Pisanti. Even the cobbler's shop was called Paris, and the tailor's Milan. The Communist regime, like its Fascist cousin, found cosmopolitanism deeply suspect. In the 1950s the Jews left en masse. Israel was a construction site, but a construction site was better than a back yard, which was what Vidin had become. As the old-time residents moved out, the Politburo comrades moved in.

I step out of the synagogue, and continue through the river park to Vidin's famous landmark: the Baba Vida Fortress. Legend has it that the fort was built by Vida, one of the three daughters of a medieval Bulgarian boyar, or nobleman. Her two sisters Kula and Gumza married unwisely and squandered their father's fortunes. But Vida defended her land, and the locals named the fort Grandma Vida in her honour. Except Vida was nobody's grandma, because she remained celibate.

Sandbags are piled around the mighty walls to stop the river. An old man in a sleeveless cardigan emerges from the ticket-house at the entrance, blinking in the bright sun, startled by the lone visitor.

'You're lucky.' He points at the water forming a thin film over the access bridge. 'See the moat bridge? Until yesterday, it was all under water, you couldn't go in.'

I browse the shop's stock of cards and brochures. They're all from the seventies, faded buildings in faded light, faded people in bell-bottomed trousers. The kind man spots my disappointment.

'They're old. We need new ones, but with what money?'

I go inside and for an hour I spook myself thoroughly. I imagine crowds of ghostly barracks men – Roman, Bulgarian, Turkish, Romanian – in various states of wretchedness, drunkenness, and cheer, rushing through the empty courtyards. In a dark cell I see a hunched human, and scream. On closer inspection, it's a waxy blacksmith and this is the armoury. There's no one to hear me anyway, except the guard who can hardly move.

From the top of a watchtower reached by a wooden ladder in the last stages of rot, successive rulers surveyed their domain. Stratzimir became despot of the city-state Bdin and, like Pazvantoğlu four centuries later, minted his own coins. But the Bdin city-state only lasted for thirty-two years until the Ottomans arrived. Before they did so, from up here Stratzimir saw a busy trade crossroads, caravans and ships coming and going from Dubrovnik and Ungro-Wallachia.

Pasha Pazvantoğlu saw a skyline pierced by ship-masts and minarets. What do I see, before I fall through the rotten floorboards and give the nice ticket-man downstairs a heart attack? I see a town that desperately wants to belong to the rest of a country and a river that has forgotten its existence. The Danube lies inert and swollen, and Romania's cargo ships in Calafat look just a short swim away. In a few years' time, they'll be just a short stroll down the new bridge, if the two countries don't fall out in the meantime.

The wooden planks through which I can see the next landing down are covered in the inscriptions of students brought here on educational school trips. 'YANKO from class 10C, 29.VIII.69' was here, and so was, at an unknown time, BOJKO MAKARONA. Someone else shouts in thick felt pen: 'Me too! I too was here.'

On the pebble strip that passes for a beach, two teenage lovers are lying atop each other in the sun in the form of a cross. I have clearly reached the end of something, an eerie blind alley. It feels as if I've reached not just the far end of Bulgaria, but also of history itself.

Perhaps, as with Silistra's flooded ruins, what I've reached is also the beginning of history. A whirlpool where the river bends around a sharp corner, and anything could happen.

On the empty train south, I have company in the compartment: a woman in her fifties with a handsome face and eyes blue and pure as mineral. She starts eating a banana. I look at her hungrily.

'Would you like some?' she offers.

'No, thanks,' I lie.

'I'm a diabetic. I have to eat complex carbohydrates every two hours to keep my blood sugar up.'

Ill health: the older Bulgarian's second-favourite topic of casual conversation after money problems.

'It must be difficult,' I say.

She shrugs, and delicately lays the banana skin on the torn seat beside her. 'It's the least of my problems.' Then she adds, 'It's all from the camps.'

'Which camps?'

'Skravena, mainly.'

In the annals of Communist labour camps, Skravena is second only to Belene on the Danube. My grandparents had a friend called Mats who'd done time in Belene. When Mats laughed, his face looked strangely lopsided. Years later I learned that they'd broken his jaw in Belene.

'When were you in Skravena?' I ask.

'My first ten years,' the woman says breezily. 'I was one of the 1,643 babies and children in labour camps at the time.' She sounds almost proud. 'Did you think they only interned adults?'

'Well, I... didn't know. Why were you there?'

'I was there with my mother and my grandparents. And they were there because of my father. My father was the one supposed to be deported, but he did a runner on the eve of our arrest. Went across the border into Yugoslavia, and then to Germany.'

'And they deported you instead?'

'The whole family went on the trains,' she says with grim relish.

'Actually, I'm lucky to be alive. Because at the train station, on the way to the camp, some commissar picked me up from my mother, I was a year old, and tossed me into a barrel of dirty water on the platform. Kids were a nuisance at the camps. My mother begged them, but they bundled her onto the train, and she thought that was it. But another commissar picked me out of the water, he had a bit of humanity in him. And he made sure I was sent onto Skravena.'

We trundle past a giant disused factory with broken windows, crouching in the empty field like a dying dinosaur at the end of the cretaceous period.

'What was it like living there?'

'Have you seen films about the Nazi concentration camps? Like that, more or less. I saw a man eaten alive by pigs. They tied him up. I remember one night, I must have been six or seven, finding myself outside among lots of stripped bodies. My mother was there too. I thought she was dead. They had left us for dead, you see. And the dogs were eating the fingers of the dead. Crunch, crunch, I can still hear it. That's why I can't stand bones in meat, and dogs. Whenever I see a dog, I hear that awful sound, crunch, crunch. But my mother was alive. And there were good moments too. Kids' birthdays for example, mothers tried to organize cakes. It wasn't like a normal party, obviously, because we had rations…'

'What happened to your father? Did you ever see him?'

'He settled in Frankfurt. In the sixties I was barred from university here, as the daughter of an enemy of the people, but I was given special permission to visit him in Germany. They didn't mind if enemies of the people left the country for good. So I went to university there, my father paid for me.'

'Why didn't you stay there?'

'Well, I stayed for a while. Then I came back. I've been trying to get compensation for the last fifteen years, since they opened up the secret files. Still haven't got it, but I'm determined. I went to court and you know what they said? There's no compensation for minors, because we were too young to experience the effects of the repression. Too young! But I'm not letting this pass. We have an organization, Children of the Camps, and we'll get our way. Justice is on our side.'

'You know,' she says suddenly, 'I mentioned the Nazi camps just to give you an idea. But, of course, the whole thing with the Jews is exaggerated.'

'How do you mean?'

'They didn't kill six million or whatever they claim, it's exaggerated. They killed some, but the whole thing is blown out of proportion. The Holocaust is a Zionist conspiracy...'

I stare at her for an incredulous moment. She's been shopping from that 'Buddhist' bookseller in Sofia. The inevitable vile argument follows. I accuse her of being brainwashed by neo-Nazi propaganda, and she hits back with, 'And what did Communism teach you, huh? You and your whole pathetic generation who were brainwashed by it, huh?'

The argument ends when she offers me one last chance. 'Why are you so worried about the Jews anyway? I don't understand. Are you Jewish or something?'

I try to convince myself that her traumatic childhood stunted her emotionally, made her unable to empathize with anybody other than herself and her kind, the 1,643 Children of the Camps. Or perhaps her father was a Nazi.

Or perhaps, after an extraordinary childhood, she is now an

ordinary woman, ignorant and keen to swallow any piece of information banged out loudly enough – and the voices of revisionists are loud. Am I sitting here with Mrs Middle Bulgaria: damaged, self-obsessed, provincial, hardened, handsome of face, blinkered of thought, selective of memory?

No, this is not my country. I won't allow it. Someone please hand me a gun, I'll shoot myself. But first I'll shoot the Woman of the Camps.

Maybe I just need a cup of tea and a lie down. This has been a long journey.

We sit in squalid silence for a while, then I get up and move to another compartment.

A swarthy middle-aged woman is already sitting there with two stuffed bags. Unfortunately, she has some emotional baggage too. Without any preamble, she pounces on me with a litany of woes.

'Twenty-five years in the Kremikovtsi Factory, in the dirtiest department, that's me. Twenty-five years, and an accident. Look at my hand. A work hazard, they said. But I went on working. When they closed Kremikovtsi, they kicked us out, and didn't offer anything. That was it, and do you know how much my pension is? Eighty leva, minimal pension. I can buy a loaf of bread after I've paid for heating, water and medication. And my son? Unemployed. Can't find work. So I have to help him and his family too. With 80 leva.'

Her voice clatters along with the train and rattles inside the cold compartment like broken furniture. After the Woman of the Camps, I have exhausted my daily quota of empathy. Nobody asks me about my problems!

'Why are you telling *me*?' I say plaintively. 'Do you think I can help?'

'I'm telling you so that if you work for a newspaper you can write about it, about people like me who gave twenty-five years to this State, working in heavy conditions and poisonous fumes, only to be living (on 80 leva a month) on the minimal pension. My daughter went to Italy to work, she earned euros. But she came back, she was homesick, she suffered there. Why should our children be made to suffer abroad, feel like second-class citizens, when they want to be here with their families? Tell me, why?'

She is gesturing with her maimed hand, on the verge of angry tears.

I too am on the verge of something angry or tearful. Kremikovtsi was always there, in the sky, when you looked up. And when you looked down from the pristine top of Vitosha Mountain, Sofia was hidden behind a thick layer of smog. If you felt unwell in Vitosha's clean air, they said, you should be placed under the nearest exhaust pipe to recover. I think of all the cancerous factory people I knew: Auntie Petrana's husband; Auntie Petrana; Malina's father in Pavlikeni; Malina's brother Ivo. Especially Ivo.

'I don't work for a newspaper,' I say. 'We're in the EU now, things will change. Pensions and employment will rise.'

'Let's hope so.' The woman wipes her eyes with her mangled hand. 'We have to live with hope, don't we?'

We do. I live with hope that I won't meet anybody else today with a ghastly story to tell.

At Oreshets station, the three of us get off. Cargo trains rust in the drizzle. We must wait for the mini-bus that will take us to Belogradchik, my last destination.

Three young Gypsy men drink espressos in plastic cups in the platform café. In the café I buy a plastic cup of herbal tea, which in my distress I spill on a couch and on myself. The smoking men timidly offer a paper napkin, without a word. The old man at the counter pours me another tea, also without a word, and waves my proffered money away.

And we sit in a cloud of cheap tobacco smoke and silence. The resigned old man in an ancient ski-jacket, the three young Gypsies with battered shoes and faces, me with tea-wet trousers and ears ringing with voices. Outside, two figures stand on the platform. They are blurry around the edges like ghosts, but I know who they are: the Woman of the Camps and the Factory Woman.

And we wait for someone to remember us, the last passengers of Danube Terminus.

*

Belogradchik, literally the 'little white town', is both little and white, and dwarfed by a petrified landscape of giant, reddish rock formations thirty kilometres long. Sedimentary rock and red sandstone mingled and eroded to form a fantastical landscape of shapes where you can imagine all sorts of life forms, depending on your mood and your drug-taking habits.

Two hundred million years ago this was the bottom of a sea. And as far as the tourist industry is concerned, it still is.

In the town's main and only square, a festival is on. White-and-red-costumed girls are dancing on a podium under the national tricolour. A brass band of men in poppy-red shirts blow into shiny trombones. Families mill about with popcorn and soft drinks. I ask a bent-over old woman if this is some local festival.

'It's the ninth of May!' She is incredulous at my ignorance. 'Europe Day.'

So it is. I'm incredulous at my own ignorance. Europe Day is the opposite of a local festival. It's a national dream. Dancing and blowing shiny trumpets on our way to Europe — finally, finally. A group of middle-aged men at an outdoor table overhear this exchange, and raise their beer glasses.

'To Europe!' they shout. 'Take some.' They point to the huge bag of popcorn in the middle of their table. I reach to take some popcorn, but they collectively gather it up and hand me the whole bag. 'Be our guest,' says a white-haired man with round John Lennon sunglasses. 'You're from Sofia, aren't you? We like to have visitors from afar. Even journalists.'

It's hard to protest convincingly when your mouth is full of popcorn, so I just accept the now familiar well-meaning insult. In the valley behind the dancing girls and men with trombones, the petrified rock sea begins. I try to make out the best known rock formations: the Schoolgirl; Adam and Eve; the Bear; the Dervish. It's a surreal landscape in the declining light of late afternoon.

More surreal yet is the derelict, chipped Balkantourist hotel on the side of a road that plunges into a green valley. And suddenly I recall a musty, threadbare-carpeted room I once stayed in there.

It was the year of waiting for British visas. My parents brought us here one weekend. I can see us, wandering among the rocky creatures: a tiny family in shorts, holding onto each other in the freefall of post-Communism. The miniature figures are climbing and descending, climbing and descending. They look at the rock formations and they see the Schoolgirl, Adam and Eve, the Bear, the Dervish, the Passport Official, the supplicant Migrant, the British Home Office Clerk...

Who could have thought, in those bare-bone survival years, that little Belogradchik would blow trumpets on the way to Europe? The Balkantourist hotel had sweeping views over the rocks, but all I saw from the window was the terraced brick houses and lasciviously bulging shops of England. That's where I wanted to be, not at the bottom of a petrified ocean.

Despite the stupefying rocks and the festival, there are no other obvious tourists in town and only one place to stay: the Madonna Hotel. Climbing up a steep street, I catch up with a young couple pushing a toddler in a buggy. I ask them about the abandoned Balkantourist Hotel. The guy shrugs.

'Who knows? It's been sitting there for ages. Somebody bought it two years ago, some work started on it, then stopped...'

He probably wouldn't mind terribly if the Balkantourist hotel never reopens, because, as it turns out, he owns the Madonna Hotel.

It is the family house, and the entire family is involved in running it. The mother is the homebody, the son is the business brain. The daughter, a slow-moving, thick-waisted girl of few words and few facial expressions, is the decoration. She waits monosyllabically on a pack of unwashed, wolf-hungry German rock climbers who occupy a table with a sweeping view down to the rocks.

They are staring at the English language menu, which is hopelessly lost in culinary translation. I spot *drusan kebab*: jogged, highly seasoned stewed meat, *kachamak*: puree of a flour of a grain of maize, *kavarma*: meet with an onion. The worried-looking Germans settle for grilled meat and salad.

The redundant father sits eating spinach soup by himself, served by mother and daughter like the patriarch he is supposed to be. But he isn't any more. He is a slow-chewing peasant lagging behind in the shadow of this brisk little capitalist enterprise.

'A million-dollar view,' he says. We look out to the rocks drenched in golden light. 'I wouldn't change it for anything in the world.'

And this exhausts our topics of conversation. Back inside, the energetic hostess advises me to go and see the mosque.

'The mosque has a tragic story. Now, the local ruler, Hadji Hussein, commissioned a Bulgarian master-carver to decorate the ceiling of the new mosque. It was going well until, one day, the carver saw the daughter of the Hadj, and they fell in love. He asked for her hand, but the father would only concede if he converted to Islam. The carver refused, and the Hadj had him murdered. As proof of the murder, the killer brought the Hadj a medallion from the young man's neck. Seeing it, the Hadj fell to the floor. You see, he had the same medallion around *his* neck. As a child he'd been taken from his family as a janissary and forgotten his Bulgarian roots. He and the young man were, in fact, family. The Hadj then committed suicide.'

'No, his daughter committed suicide when she learned that her lover was dead,' the son pipes in. He's busy doing accounts on a laptop.

'Well, there are different versions,' the mother concedes. 'People's imaginations have embroidered the story. Some say when the carver first saw the daughter, she carried a rose, and that's why he carved a rose on the ceiling.'

'It's not a rose, it's a crown,' the son butts in again. The mother throws up her arms in exasperation and goes to dish out some more spinach soup.

The next day, in the fine spring drizzle, I walk the two kilometres across town up to the Belogradchik Fortress. On the way, I find the mysterious mosque from 1751. It is derelict, bars on the glassless windows, and on the exquisitely decorated flowery doorway is a solid padlock made to last for centuries. Through the iron bars, in the gloom inside, I glimpse fragments of wall decoration and carvings, but mostly I glimpse rubbish.

This is the heart of what was once the Ottoman quarter. The Christian Bulgarians lived further below, in houses so dazzlingly whitewashed that the Turks kept the original name of the little white town. The Ottomans are gone, and so, clearly, are the Turks.

I reach the top of the hill and the end of the road. The spectacular Belogradchik Fortress begins here, snakes over the hill, and ends somewhere out of sight. Inside the stone gate, two workers in overalls are having a smoke away from the drizzle.

'Terrible weather, isn't it,' I greet them.

'Fate, that's what it is.' One of them smiles under a heroic moustache. I can't help having a private chuckle at this classic Bulgarian comment, in a classic Bulgarian spot.

It's classic because it follows a typical timeline. It was built by the Romans along the road linking the Danube with Rome and the Near East. The Byzantines and medieval Bulgarians improved on it, especially the energetic Despot Stratzimir up the road in Vidin, keen to fortify his fiefdom. The Turks too used it from the fourteenth century onwards as a garrison and defence post. And now it's a popular location for historic Euro film sets, one of which is being built right now.

'Careful out there on the rocks, they're slippery. Call us if you need a hand,' shouts a young carpenter working on the film set, and his mates whistle.

I could do with a hand or two. I slide and scramble up the wet rocky steps. At the top, I stop to catch my breath, but it's hard, because what I see takes my breath away again.

In the rocky sea below, geology displays her patient artwork of folding matter. If eternity could appear to us in material guise, this is how it would look. My ears start ringing. The French traveller Gérome-Adolphe Blanqui, who passed through here in 1841, must have been equally stricken. 'The Alps, the Pyrénées, the most breathtaking of Tyrolean mountains and Switzerland cannot offer such a sight,' he wrote, '...all this would impress even the most hardened of souls.'

My hardened soul is impressed, and I wonder whether on starry nights Roman legionnaires sat here on this polished rock, playing dice. Did the Turkish soldiers smoke hashish up here while contemplating the brevity of their lives?

On my way out through the gates, a different pair of men in overalls are smoking. One has enormous forearms tattooed with mermaids, the other is lost in his roomy overalls. True to my Anglo-Saxon reflexes of small talk, once again I resort to the weather. 'Yesterday was so warm and sunny, and look at today!'

'Yesterday we were also a day younger.' The sturdy one gifts me with a tobaccoey smile and unfolds the mermaids of his arms.

'Yesterday was altogether a different story.' The weedy one waves a small cigarette stub.

We nod succinct goodbyes and they continue to puff on their stubs, gazing into the misty drizzle of yesterday.

And tomorrow? Tomorrow the Italian film crew arrive. Tomorrow we join Europe with shiny trombones. Tomorrow the spell of the evil fairy might be broken. Anything is possible tomorrow.

A journey through Bulgaria, Felix Kanitz wrote in the nineteenth century – though he could be writing it now – is marked at each turn by the catacombs of disappeared peoples and eras.

I have seen those catacombs. They are everywhere, they have open lids, and often they take the shape of entire towns. But for as long as they see the sun and breathe the bitter-sweet seasons of sea, river, mountain, and hope, they will always have a stubborn, sprouting life inside. A stubborn, sprouting future.

EPILOGUE

Back in the Peach Street flat, I lift the bedroom carpet. I don't know what I expect to see, but it's not this. The bump has gone. The under-floor moles have cleared out. The broken and cracked tiles are the only proof that I haven't gone insane and imagined it all.

The gangsters have cleared out too, for now anyway. I look up the latest news on the shooting, and find out that most of the flats in our building had been rented by citizens with Serbian and Macedonian passports. Stolen or forged passports, that is. One of the wounded, a

Serb wanted by Interpol for trafficking, has just died in hospital of his wounds. The father of the baby is alive and also wanted by Interpol. He is probably no longer wanted by his girlfriend who is in hospital, beating him, I imagine, with a crutch. The baby is fine. At least it'll have a story to tell. Having a drug-dealer father could happen to anyone, but not everyone gets to be shot, aged six months, by men in balaclavas.

I call my parents about the floor. Well, my mother offers on the line from New Zealand, it's a new building. New buildings take a while to settle. Besides, the construction site next door could be impacting on us. Nothing to worry about, the floor is just breathing. Breathing!

Anyway, I have one last visit to make: to my native Youth 3. I haven't dared return since we left in 1992 with crumbs in our pockets. Such things take courage. It's not that I'm feeling especially courageous today, but all important journeys are supposed to be circular, and I must close this circle.

Youth 3 has grown up almost beyond recognition. Rows of trees, green fields, pizzerias, shopping malls and children's playgrounds have covered up the stark childscape of mud and concrete. It's a leafy neighbourhood now. Our street has a name. It's now called Transfiguration Street. Just a fraction of all this would have made a difference to us, the Cold War Youths – just one tree, one playground, one full shop, one pizza. But no.

The Unitary Secondary Polytechnic School 81 Vi_tor Hugo is missing a 'c', and celebrating its twenty-fifth anniversary year with a disconsolate white banner, like a flag for help. It is, I realize with a jolt, exactly that long since the Russian teacher broke her ruler because of Number Sixteen's abject failure with the genitive case.

The beginning of the new school year is a few days away and the iron-and-glass door is still locked. In the school yard where we convened with our bundles of *The Workers' Deed* on Recycled Paper Day, stood listening to 'Rise, oh Mighty Country', and did morning gymnastics, young parents sit on benches while their toddlers waddle around. I glance at the faces, afraid I'll see the grown-ups from Class E. And hoping I will. As with the broken tiles, I need forensic evidence. But I lose my nerve, as if recognizing someone would turn me to stone, like looking straight at the Gorgon's face. I walk across the school yard to Block 328, searching for the familiar fourth-floor balcony. But it's hidden by the trees. I don't know who is living in our flat.

Neighbours sit on a bench outside the entrance door. There is something familiar about one of them: the vague woman with the sweet smell of laundry emanating from her. 'Hope?' I say tentatively.

Beside her is a boy of about ten, built like Thomas the Tank Engine.

'Kapka, is that you?' Hope smiles shyly and gets up.

'What's your name?' I turn to the boy.

'Alexander,' he growls.

'Alexander-James,' his mother corrects him, and explains proudly, 'His father is Irish.'

Alexander-James is handed over to Hope's mother, who lives with them, and the two of us take a stroll around the block. The first thing Hope tells me is that her Irish ex-husband is a property investor. The redheaded man on the bus from Burgas perhaps. He travels all over Europe, Hope says. And you, she asks, have you made a child? I confess that I haven't even made, or unmade, a marriage.

I don't know what it is – the thick shadows of the trees, the missing 'c' in Victor Hugo, the twenty-five years SOS flag, Hope's hyphenated offspring, Hope looking like her mother, or just being in Youth 3 after so many years – but I have an urge to go and never come back. I say goodbye to Hope.

My punitive journey ends with a visit to the Bells complex across the motorway. I find a wilderness of naked concrete and burnt grass. Many of the bells are missing: they've been wrenched from the concrete wall and sold as scrap. Those that are still in place are without tongues, like mute witnesses. Only the plaques remain, a cemetery of urns marking the names of the deceased. They were too worthless to steal: From the Children of Morocco, Nicaragua, Campuchia, The Republic of China. This is the graveyard of Socialism's best dream.

And like a living denouement of that dream, a young family: a white woman, a dark-skinned man, and their child who is trying to reach up to some impossibly large bell, too big for the thieves to carry.

So the many-coloured children of the Flag of Peace that were promised to us have finally arrived. It's a pity there is no one to greet them with a brisk Pioneer salute: Always Ready!

Back on the hazy motorway that separates the Assembly from the Youths, two prostitutes stand on stilettos, shoulders hunched, mouths chewing gum. In a black Mercedes nearby sits their big-necked pimp who gives me a broad-spectrum filthy look. An articulated lorry is parked up, and three greasy men are scratching their bellies, trying to decide who goes first, second, and third.

I run across the motorway in a daze, looking for a taxi, looking for the quickest way to get the hell out of here.

Closing the circle of your journey is fine. Until you strangle yourself in the noose.

I call Rado and he comes to the rescue in his father's old Renault.

We drive to Boyana district, a pleasant village on the outskirts of

Sofia. It used to be Politburo-ville. Party officials had villas here, and Todor Jivkov lived in the 'Boyana' Residence.

Now, the gated luxury villas belong to the new elite: the 'businessmen' of new Bulgaria, those with vague fortunes and accounts in Madagascar and Bermuda, those who bought state industries for five dollars. Over time, Boyana has gone from Politburo-ghetto to *mutra*-heaven.

These are the people who ruled Bulgaria when Rado and I left in the nineties along with a million others. And they are the people who still rule, while gradually washing their dirty money. Yesterday's gangsters become today's businessmen, and tomorrow the capital inherited by their children will be clean. Almost clean. This is how capitalism works in the Wild West. They did warn us at school.

And over time all this will become the stuff of films, the *Fistful of Dollars* story of the post-Communist world. Just as the story of our Wild East is now the stuff of bitter-sweet films like *Goodbye Lenin*.

We're climbing a quiet old street in Boyana village.

'You know, my company has offered me a job in Sofia,' Rado says suddenly. 'They want to branch out here, with the EU and all.'

'Will you accept?'

'I don't know. It's taken me by surprise. I've been in France for so long, the idea of coming back hadn't occurred to me. I don't know if I could live here. The chalga, the mutri, I don't know if I could live with it. Could you?'

'I don't know,' I say.

'I know. You already couldn't live with it before. I remember when you stopped eating.'

We walk around the vast gated park that surrounds Jivkov's former 'Boyana' Residence. Now it's the grounds of the National Museum of

History. The fence that once looked impregnable around this property of the Communist State is now rusty and overgrown with shrubs. Paths run from one end of the park to the other, but we are told they are full of snakes, and there are no openings in the fence. Instead of a nice walk in the park, we end up walking around it, inhaling the traffic fumes of the open road.

Half-finished buildings and cranes dot the horizon. The dreamy blue bulk of Vitosha Mountain rises above us. Dust in the mouth, warm clouds overhead, and our farewell tonight. Rado is in a strange mood.

'And yet. All this.' He points at the building sites. 'All this means so much more to me than France. All that's happened here, all the emotions this place contains. First love that never dies. First dreams. First car. First car-crash. First shag. First job. Not in that order. All of me is contained here, in these panels, in this mountain. I'm not a poet, poetry is your thing. But you know what I mean…'

'Yes,' I say.

Yes, here we are, the top crop export of Socialism. With several passports, foreign spouses and ex-spouses, dynamic careers, borrowed identities. And fractured psyches. Here we are, trying to heal ourselves.

For our farewell dinner, I take Rado to a pizzeria which is also a satirical museum to Socialism with a Human Face. Public signs and warnings decorate the walls.

THE HERO IS ALWAYS PRESENT!

LET US FULFIL OUR FIVE YEAR PLAN IN TWO YEARS!

DANGER: BEWARE OF FALLING BODIES!

WE ARE FIGHTING FOR AN EXEMPLARY WORKPLACE!

DO NOT WALK ON THE GRASS BECAUSE IT IS YOURS!

Rado jots these gems down on a paper napkin for me.

'I'll remember them,' I reassure him.

'You won't. You forget everything. You're so focused on the present, on your itinerary, on tomorrow. And you're right.' He crumples the napkin in his fist. 'Maybe I just can't let go. I hold onto these things like a drowning man.'

It's true: while I have partial amnesia about the eighties, Rado remembers every incident from the Lycée, every schoolmate, everything we said. I couldn't bear to remember that much.

We stand outside the building in Peach Street, a puddle between us.

'You're the only person in the whole world who understands how I feel here,' Rado says. 'You realize how much this means to me.'

Me too, I want to say, me too. But I don't, the words remain lodged in my throat. We make squirming attempts at saying goodbye. We try humorous, casual, mock-sentimental, we try to predict the next time, maybe soon in Sofia for the fifteen-year reunion of the French Lycée, maybe in France. We give up. It's an impossible farewell, and, in the end, before he walks away in his trademark bear-awkward style, Rado says, 'I'll see you in five years.'

I drag the suitcase back over the potholes of Peach Street and wave goodbye to the man up in the harness, hoping that he won't break into the flat and steal the TV from 1984 while I'm gone.

The Gypsy taxi-driver tosses out a half-smoked fag and takes off with a screech. He then treats me to the second most hair-raising ride in my life, after that last one with Uncle and Auntie. He either wants to prove that he can get me there for the cheapest possible fare, or is running late for a date with death. I grope for seat belts but they have been ripped out, like most of the car's interior. The driver looks as if something has been ripped out of him too. His face is wilted with tobacco and hardship.

'I'd rather get there alive than fast,' I shout over the engine. The driver slams the brakes and my face kisses the back of his head. It's a red light, the first one he's taken notice of.

'Fifteen years,' he mutters, indignant. 'Fifteen years I drive this taxi and not a single accident!'

The patron saint of taxi-drivers must be watching over him. I try to keep my mouth shut until we reach the airport, and collect my thoughts, which is impossible at this speed, in this car, on this road. Tsarigradsko Road has been newly tar-sealed. Unfortunately, the company that did it botched it up and now the new tar-seal undulates with bumps. Dozens of bumps large and small.

'They've turned it into Tsarigradsko Sea, dimwits.' The driver spits out what could be chewing-gum or a tooth.

'The road is breathing,' I shout. 'Maybe it'll settle down.'

'Breathing, huh!' His face cracks into a smile. When we arrive with a screech at the airport, he hands me my suitcase triumphantly.

'So, you're alive,' he offers instead of a goodbye. Which is somehow fitting.

I climb the staircase of the shiny new terminal on unsteady legs.

Without realizing it, I have travelled anti-clockwise round the map, starting from Sofia and ending back here. This seems appropriate, given that travelling in the present tense has proved impossible.

One of the few things I'm now sure about is that Bulgaria is a country living simultaneously, effortlessly, casually almost, in several different time planes.

It is now 2007. From the terminus of Oreshets, I've been catapulted straight into the future. The Bulgarian nurses in Lybia have been freed, with help from our EU friends. Bulgaria may not have gifted a single rude word to the EU, but it has given it a third alphabet. You can't ask for everything.

I arrived at Terminal Hostile together with the old émigré from Amerika. I'm leaving from the brand-new terminal. Its hallways gleam and sparkle with unearthly steel like something out of *The Matrix*. There are no shops yet. Just huge empty halls full of light.

The 'Other' queue at passport control has gone. Confident people in smart clothes stroll with their tidy luggage, speak a smattering of languages, and sip expensive espressos. They are Bulgarians with European passports.

I have one too. I had it issued in the space of one afternoon in a marbled hall by a polite clerk who smiled as she handed it to me. Bureaucracy? That's a French word.

But to get my new passport, I need a photo. The woman photographer looks at the first prints and nods, 'No, it won't do. You look startled, like a rabbit caught in headlights. We'll do another one, I won't charge you extra. And this time smile!'

'But isn't it prohibited to smile on passport photos?' I protest.

She looks at me curiously. 'That was fifteen years ago, sweetheart! Where have you been? Come on, give us a nice smile.'

I blink a few times in the silver light, unsure. Then I smile.

ACKNOWLEDGEMENTS

I owe this book and my deep gratitude to Laura Barber at Portobello who conceived the idea for it, and patiently nurtured it from bumbling beginnings, through messy incontinence, to its present form.

I have been steadied along the way by the firm hand of my agent Isobel Dixon of Blake Friedmann, and for this I thank her and count my blessings.

I am grateful to my family for not being a pain and graciously pretending to trust my unreliable vision of things past and present.

In my reading on Bulgaria, I found the following books useful, inspiring, or both: *The Iron Fist* by Alexenia Dimitrova (Artnik, London, 2005), *Az jivyah socialisma* edited by Georgi Gospodinov (Janet 45 Editions, Sofia, 2006), *The Balkans 1804–1999* by Misha Glenny (Granta, London, 1999), *The Miss Stone Affair* by Teresa Carpenter (Simon & Schuster, London, 2003), *Bulgarski Rodove I and II* by Mariana Purvanova (East and West, Sofia, 2005–2006), the lyrics on p. 35 are by Naiden Valchev, *Crown of Thorns: the Reign of King Boris III of Bulgaria* by Stephane Groueff (Madison Books, Boulder, USA, 1998), *Danube* by Claudio Magris (Random House, London, 2001). And hats off to Anthony Georgieff of Bulgaria Air and Vagabond for producing and publishing intriguing investigative stories on Bulgaria old and new. They have been an inspiration.